D0794539

CALGARY PUBLIC LIBRARY

NOV / / 2006

Eastern
Philosophy

Eastern Philosophy

KEVIN BURNS

ENCHANTED LION BOOKS
New York

To Andy, Tom, Alex and Alex, who made it possible.
For advice, hard work and encouragement I would like to thank Carla and
Siobhan. I would also like to acknowledge the invaluable help and advice of
Professor Chad Hansen on classical Chinese thought, and that of Macksood
A. Aftab on the Islamic section.

First American edition published in 2006 by
Enchanted Lion Books, 45 Main Street, Suite 519,
Brooklyn, NY 11201

Copyright © 2004 & 2006 Arcturus Publishing Limited
26/27 Bickels Yard, 151–153 Bermondsey Street, London SE1 3HA

All rights reserved. No part of this publication may be reproduced, stored in a retrieval
system, or transmitted, in any form or by any means, electronic, mechanical, photocopying,
recording, or otherwise, without written permission or in accordance with the provisions of
the Copyright Act 1956 (as amended). Any person or persons who do any unauthorised act
in relation to this publication may be liable to criminal prosecution and civil claims for
damages.

For information about permission to reproduce selections from this book, write to
Permissions, Enchanted Lion Books, 45 Main Street, Suite 519, Brooklyn, NY 11201

A CIP record is on file with the Library of Congress

ISBN-13: 978-1-59270-053-0
ISBN-10: 1-59270-053-5

Printed and bound in China.

2 4 6 8 10 9 7 5 3 1

Editors: Rebecca Panayiotou and Anna Amari Parker
Text design by Chris Smith
Cover design by Alex Ingr

Picture Credits

Hulton Getty Images Ltd: pp17, 20, 31, 71, 72, 73, 78, 82, 84, 85, 89, 92, 96,113, 115, 123,
135, 137, 138, 139, 145, 160, 161, 169, 174, 177, 178, 181, 182, 185, 186

Mary Evans Picture Library: pp22, 23, 24, 39, 54, 76, 77, 102, 107, 109, 110, 120, 126, 129,
156, 163, 171, 188

Corbis: pp12, 18, 47, 81, 99, 105, 121, 175, 179, 186

Topfoto: pp25, 26, 33

AKG: pp191

Everything should be made as simple as possible, but not simpler.

ATTRIBUTED TO ALBERT EINSTEIN

CONTENTS

Part One

INDIA

INDIAN PHILOSOPHY: INTRODUCTION

*The defining characteristic
of Indian thought,
from whatever tradition,
is its spirituality.*

Brahma, Vishnu and Shiva: the main deities of Hindu tradition.

One of the oldest bodies of literature in human history is that of the Veda, dating from at least as far back as 1200 BCE.[1] For this reason alone, Indian philosophy deserves special attention. There are four Vedas: Rig Veda, Yajur Veda, Sama Veda, and Atharva Veda. The earliest and most important is the Rig Veda, while the Atharva Veda is thought to be much the latest. The Vedas were originally collections of hymns (the Mantras). At a later period when formal religion existed the religious precepts of the Brahmanas were appended. Still later, perhaps 1000–200 BCE, the philosophical discussions of the

Upanishads were also added. So each Veda now consists of these three sections. The Mantra section of the Vedas, known as *Samhita* has many affinities with the Avesta, the scripture of the Zorastrian religion of Persia (see chapter on **Zoroaster**). The two traditions share many of the same deities and seem to have been linked at some point. Until recently, it was thought that a tribe known as the Aryans had come from central Asia to both India and Persia, but much of the evidence for this has now been called into question. Present speculations now centre on the existence of a common language usually called 'Indo-European' that seems to underlie most of the languages in a wide area stretching from Iceland to India. The suggestion

THE PRINCIPAL NASTIKA
(UNORTHODOX) PHILOSOPHIES

Buddhism
Charvaka
Jainism

THE SIX ASTIKA
(ORTHODOX) PHILOSOPHIES

Nyaya
Vaisheshika

Sankhya
Yoga

Mimamsa (or Purva Mimamsa)
Vedanta (or Uttara Mimamsa)

is rather than there being a single tribe of Aryans (the word means 'noble' in Sanskrit), there may have been a much more broadly-based culture spread across the continent. Recent research has even suggested links to some Far Eastern languages, which if true, would radically alter our perception of ancient prehistory.

The traditional division in Indian philosophy is between those schools that are *astika* or orthodox and *nastika* or unorthodox. This division dates from the time of the principal challenges to the main tradition, around 600–200 BCE. The orthodox schools are those that, nominally at least, accept the Veda as revelatory. However, the question is much more complex than this. Even today it is a commonplace in India that the Vedas are divinely revealed and contain all knowledge, but this does not mean that people actually read them. 'Veda' is not a term used with any great consistency, meaning anything from the actual books of the Veda to a kind of divine and transcendent revelatory power, as expressed by a modern thinker such as **Vivekananda**.

The only school that seriously bases itself on the earlier two parts of the Veda is the Purva Mimamsa. After that, the Uttara Mimamsa or, as it is more commonly known, the Vedanta is the most orthodox: Vedanta means 'the end of the Veda', meaning that it bases itself on the Upanishads. However, even here there could not be said to be unanimity. The Upanishads represent a conscious turning away from the ritualized religion of the Brahmanas (the second part of the Veda) and, to a lesser extent, from the nature religion of the early Vedic hymns. So the Vedantin thinkers, the most prominent in India from the early part of the Christian era onwards, are not really interested in much of the Veda. Of the other four orthodox schools, Sankhya is atheistic or perhaps agnostic on the subject of God, and is mainly influenced by the Upanishads; Yoga is theistic but otherwise identical to Sankhya; Nyaya is concerned with logic; and Vaisheshika is a realist philosophy dealing with the nature of the physical world. Some of the philosophies and religions regarded as unorthodox are closer to certain orthodox systems than they are to each other. Buddhism has remarkable affinities to Vedanta despite their antagonism.

We can see from this that the traditional definition of orthodoxy is unsatisfactory. By the standards of other philosophical traditions, the Indian one is extraordinary for its flexibility and openness. In the *Bhagavad Gita*, which is one of the most significant and influential books in Indian culture, Krishna, speaking as an incarnation of God, says, 'however men approach me, even so do I welcome them, for the path men take from every side is mine'. This should be understood not as a meek ecumenism, but as central to the whole Hindu system, in which the divine is regarded as infinitely beyond any human system of understanding, form of devotion, or way of life. This leads to a broad tolerance and even encouragement of alternative approaches. As Hindu scholar K.M. Sen has said, 'Hinduism is a great storehouse of all kinds of religious experiments'. The real issue in early Indian philosophy is not the acceptance of Veda as normative, but the authority of the Brahmin[2] caste. The groups that rejected the Brahmins and the caste system are those that came to be regarded as unorthodox: notably the materialist Charvakas, the Jains and the Buddhists. From around 1000 CE certain

Ganesha, one of the most popular deities in the Hindu pantheon.

orthodox sects began to work against the caste system, allowing lower-caste Hindus to study and participate fully, but this is a much later development.

We have now started to use the word 'Hindu', which is inevitable. In many ways it is an unsatisfactory label. It derives from the name of the river Sind or Indus and was the name given to the people who lived beyond that river by their Western neighbours. 'Hindu' is therefore cognate with 'Indian'. As with many Eastern systems, it is hard to say where philosophy stops and religion begins. There are good reasons to question whether Hinduism is a religion at all: it has no founder, no fixed dogma, no consistent set of beliefs, and there is no tradition of 'conversion' to Hinduism. The Buddha may have defined himself against the tradition, but his doctrines (almost all of which are to be found in the orthodox systems) are far more clear-cut than those he rejected. It would be wrong to regard the Hindu tradition as amorphous, however: rather it is impossible to formalize because of its rich variety. We should also distinguish between the Hindu religion or religions and the earlier belief system of 'Brahmanism' that predominated until about 500 CE.

There seems no good reason to regard the classification of *astika* and *nastika* as final. The traditional narrative of India is that the unorthodox nastika systems are rebellions, breaking away from the great tradition. As we have seen, however, the tradition itself is impossible to define either positively or negatively. We speak of Hindu or Jain or Buddhist philosophy, but there is a strong case for grouping them together. India, though huge, is geographically single, being surrounded on three sides by ocean and on the fourth by the world's highest mountain ranges. Most Indian philosophy is practical, offering means to an end, usually the liberation of the spirit from the wheel of life. The defining characteristic of Indian thought, from whatever tradition, is its spirituality. No other culture is so indefatigably concerned with the human spirit and its relation to the universal.

We will consider firstly the Upanishads, and then the schools that emerged from the sixth century BCE onwards, followed by the *Bhagavad Gita*, dated to around the fourth century BCE. We will then look at the development of the two most important Indian schools in the Christian era, Buddhism and the Vedanta.

THE PRINCIPAL UPANISHADS
Various authors, 1000–200 BCE

In considering Indian thinkers, it is essential to look first of all at the Upanishads, although their authors are not known. The Upanishads are a fundamental source for all the orthodox Indian systems of philosophy except the Mimamsa, and for many of the unorthodox as well, including Buddhism. According to Radhakrishnan, 'later systems of philosophy display an almost pathetic anxiety to accommodate their doctrines to the views of the Upanishads, even if they cannot father them all on them.' If the authors of the Upanishads had been concerned to identify themselves, they would feature prominently in this book. As it stands, some comments are essential.

The word 'Upanishad' is variously derived but probably indicates, 'sitting down near to' a teacher. An Upanishad is a philosophical discussion or a collection of philosophical discussions, often framed in the form of a dialogue between a teacher and a student, or in a more dramatic form, such as a contest of sages or a dialogue between a boy and the god of death. One dialogue features a sage whose philosophy is exposed as shallow by the king he attempts to teach. Others are simple expositions without any dramatic context. There are 108 Upanishads, of which around ten to sixteen are regarded as essential. The earliest Upanishads, sometimes known as the 'Vedic Upanishads' because their authorship is thought to date from as early as the later parts of the Vedas, include the *Brihadaranyaka*

and *Chandogya* Upanishads. The 'Middle Upanishads' such as the *Isha* and *Katha* date from around the same period as the *Bhagavad Gita* (c. 500–100 BCE), while others such as the *Mandukya* have a slightly later date.

The greatest commentator on the Upanishads is undoubtedly **Shankara**. Some of his commentaries may be by later *Shankaracharyas* (Shankara Teachers), but regardless of this, the Advaita Vedanta philosophy he derived from the Upanishads, following **Badarayana** and **Gaudapada**, came to be identified with that of the Upanishadic thinkers. Others within the broader Vedanta tradition such as **Ramanuja** or **Madhva** advanced their own theories of what the Upanishads said. An impartial reading shows that the Upanishads cannot be said to 'really' teach any of these alternative views. The attempt to foist a particular consistent philosophy on the Upanishads obscures rather than illuminates what they are: a magnificent set of speculations on the most fundamental questions facing humanity. A scientific analogy would be with the theories on the nature of light: scientists have found evidence to support its being particle-like as well as wave-like. Today, science can only say that it seems to be both a particle and a wave depending on one's viewpoint, or that the nature of light is something else that has the qualities of both. Radhakrishnan's comment is telling: the Upanishads 'have the consistency of intuition rather than of logic'. Just as scientists must admit that the nature of light is not logical at the present level of understanding, so philosophers must admit that the different metaphysical theories in the Upanishads, though not entirely consistent, seem independently and

Shankara

which their philosophy grew, without necessarily respecting all of its rigid superstitions (an attitude not unlike that of **Confucius** in Chinese culture). The first six Upanishads are written in prose. Later Upanishads are written in verse and refer to the *Gita* and to the later philosophies such as Sankhya and Yoga.

The Vedas already contained in them the idea of a single reality, a divine fundamental and transcendental principle that corresponds to the Brahman or Absolute of the Upanishads. A concept that seems to be original to the Upanishads is that of the Atman or self. The Vedic background already expressed the idea of an objective God essence; the Upanishadic thinkers posited a subjective Man essence. Their reasoning is as follows: I am not the body, because the body is impermanent and subject to growth and decay; I am not the mind and its thoughts and feelings and dreams, because they too change and pass away; I am not the consciousness in deep sleep, because although there the perception is freed from duality and division, it comes to an end on waking; what I am is the witness of all that persists through all these states[3]. The Atman is therefore the eternal subject: anything that is perceived is an object, and therefore external; only that which perceives all and is not itself perceived can be the true Self, the Atman. Although negatively defined, the Atman is a positive being, enjoying all. It is not to be confused with the ego, or as the Sanskrit has it, '*ahankara*', the artificial sense of individual self.

One of the most important questions in philosophy is that of the relation of man to God, or of the world to the transcendent. The Upanishads assert that the Atman is the Brahman:

intuitively valid. They are not without their deficiencies, but are of unquestionable greatness.

Historically, the earliest Upanishads were written after the earlier parts of the Vedas. The attitude to the Vedic hymns in the early Upanishads is, on the whole, respectful; their view of the Brahmanas, the formalized sacrificial religion of the Vedas, varies from one of respectful distance to one of amused contempt. On the whole, the Upanishadic thinkers wished to preserve the culture from 'sa atmatvam tat asi'; 'That self, you [the Brahman] are that'. If all that we had left of the Upanishads was this one idea we would acclaim the culture that produced it as one of the high water-marks of human history and long to know more. The identity of the individual and the universal is one of the few truly necessary ideas to be considered and either accepted or rejected in philosophy.

The next question is of what relation the absolute reality bears to the world. The most common modern view follows Shankara in maintaining the world is an illusion or *maya* superimposed on the fundamental reality of the Brahman. This does not seem to be borne out by the Upanishads, which nowhere deny the reality of the cosmos. To say that the final reality is Brahman or Atman is not to say that the world is unreal. Illusionism or *vivarta* as a doctrine did not exist until the Madhyamika Buddhism of **Nagarjuna**, where it is called *shunyata* (emptiness). From there it was adopted by Vedantins from Gaudapada onwards. Illusionism is a possible interpretation of the Upanishads, but it could not be said to be essential to them. An alternative view is held by Ramanuja's followers, who assert that the Upanishadic view is a qualified non-dualism, Vishishta Advaita: the world has reality, but at a lower level than the Brahman. The Advaitins maintain that the ultimate reality is one and unchanging; the Vishishtadvaitins hold that the world is the expression of the ultimate. A sensible view seems to be that the Upanishadic thought contains both possibilities but sees no contradiction. A second area of controversy between these two great views of the Upanishads is as to the nature of God. To Ramanuja, the

God of the Upanishads is the Ishvara, the beloved Lord or Saguna Brahman. To Shankara it is the unqualified Nirguna Brahman, impersonal, absolute, beyond human definition, one without a second. Both schools regard the other's ultimate to be a preparatory stage for theirs. Shankara's approach is lofty, intellectual and superhuman; Ramanuja's is warm and devotional. Again, it is not necessary for those without a partial interest to choose.

This brief examination of the ideas of the Upanishads could wrongly suggest that they are dry and intellectual. Nothing could be further from the truth. The Upanishads especially the earlier prose Upanishads such as the great *Brihadaranyaka* – are playful, literary, entertaining and full of the joy of untrammelled philosophy. Many are cast as dialogues, anticipating the philosophic atmosphere hinted at in the *Analects* of Confucius and found in the Socratic dialogues. Indeed, recent research suggests that the pre-Socratic philosophers, such as Thales and Parmenides, developed their philosophies from ideas that had found their way to Greece from the Upanishadic thinkers of northwest India.

The great figures of the Upanishads are well aware that the ideas they deal with are audacious and improbable to ordinary awareness, and revel in the humour of the situation. One comes away from them with the exalted sense of an open society of passionate seekers, living in the real world but looking beyond it.

CHARVAKA

c. 600 BCE

The name of the materialist philosopher Charvaka is doubtfully derived from a word meaning 'sweet-tongued', indicating perhaps the importance of pleasure, a key doctrine. Also known as Lokayata, perhaps best translated as '[the philosophy] of the world' or 'of the people', Charvaka's philosophy seems to have enjoyed wide popularity up until its disappearance in medieval times. This may have been more due to its convenience as an explanation for pragmatic self-interest than to a genuine interest in its philosophical value, just as Epicureanism was a pretext for hedonism in the West. His doctrines are said to be embodied in the lost *Barhaspatya Sutras*. Since no work of his and few works of his followers' (known as Charvakas) are extant, much of what follows is speculative. It is often difficult to surmise what the original

'Live well,
as long as you live.
Live well even
by borrowing, for,
once cremated,
there is
no return.'

teaching of Charvaka was and what was a later addition. The only substantial systematic work of Charvaka philosophy comes from almost a millennium after Charvaka himself, the *Tattvopaplavasimha* of Jayarasi, which argues that nothing is real except the evidence of the senses and that

therefore morality is an illusion. Again, this may be a corruption of Charvaka's original doctrine. The philosophy is best known from its numerous refutations by other schools, both Hindu and Buddhist, who regarded it as the lowest form of philosophy and ethics. One aphorism of Charvaka became a well-known Hindu proverb and gives a flavour of the school: 'Live well, as long as you live. Live well even by borrowing, for, once cremated, there is no return.'

Charvaka was unorthodox in that he rejected the authority of the Veda, as well as the existence of God, an afterlife and the self. Of the three *pramanas* or means of acquiring knowledge accepted by all the orthodox schools, he rejects both inference and revelation (or verbal testimony). Charvaka accepts only sensory perception, which in some ways anticipates the modern Empiricists, notably David Hume. The Charvaka argument against inference is as follows. The classical Indian example of inference is 'Where there is smoke, there is fire. There is smoke in the mountain. Therefore there is fire in the mountain'. Charvaka says that unless we have seen all examples of smoke and fire, we cannot know that the initial premise is true. If we had seen all examples then we would have no need to infer the existence of fire in the mountain, because we had seen it. Thus inference is impossible or unnecessary. This foreshadows Western critiques of inference and inductive reasoning.

Charvaka's attack on testimony is even stronger: if someone tells me something, I must infer a fact from his or her words, such as 'I have seen fire', that I have not myself perceived. However, not only is inference invalid, the words may themselves be a lie. Thus testimony is still more unreliable. This last example

Bathers in the River Ganges during the Kumbha Mela *Festival in Varanasi (formerly Benares). The festival takes place at the confluence of the three sacred rivers (Ganges, Yamuna and the invisible Sarasvati), the holiest of Hindu sites. Bathing here is said to purify the body and the soul and leave one free from the continuous cycle of birth and death.*

illustrates a limitation in the knowledge that can be gained through such a severely positivist outlook: we are prevented from accepting inference and testimony even hypothetically ('let us assume that Kate was telling the truth when she said that the house is on fire'). Jayarasi in his *Tattvopaplavasimha* (delightfully translated as 'The Lion That Devours All Categories') takes this to its extreme. Not only are testimony and inference invalid, even sense perception is not totally reliable. Therefore we cannot conclusively know anything about the world. The Charvaka philosophy, because it makes no assumptions and appeals only to common sense, is therefore the only acceptable view.

A key problem for the Charvakas is the evident existence of consciousness.

Their solution is similar to the theory of a 'primeval soup' from which life emerged, but they use the analogy of making alcoholic liquor. None of the ingredients are alcoholic but through mixing and the fermentation process, alcohol eventually appears. Thus, consciousness (and indeed life) is the result of the right combination of elemental substances. Only matter is real and inference is invalid so we cannot prove the existence of the self, God, afterlife or anything else not perceivable by the senses. Note the similarity of Charvaka's views to those of present-day theorists of science, who face the difficulty of building an ethical system on materialist foundations. Charvaka, of course, has no such problem.

Out of all other philosophies, Charvaka's particular distaste is reserved for the Mimamsa (see **Jaimini**), which is principally concerned with the Vedic rituals and way of life. The Vedas enjoined devotees to earn the approval of the gods and ancestors through the performance of rites, and to give gifts to the Brahmin priests. For the Charvakas this system is designed self-servingly by the Brahmins for their own ends. The Mimamsa philosophy was easy meat for the devouring lions of Charvaka, but the attacks it suffered were to strengthen it in its later, more rational re-emergence, for example in the work of Kumarila.

A Brahmin priest. The Brahmins were attacked by the Charvakas as self-serving.

This is just one example of the useful effect Charvaka was to have on other philosophies, compelling them to defend and improve their ideas against his ruthless opposition. As Radhakrishnan observes in *Indian Philosophy*, 'When people begin to reflect with freedom from presuppositions and religious superstition they tend to the materialist belief, though deeper reflection takes them away from it'. The materialism of Charvaka, for all its faults, is a natural and positive step away from rigid ritualism.

Of the four traditional Hindu social values, Charvaka rejects *dharma* (duty) and *moksha* (liberation) because they are not based on the senses. Of the other two, Charvaka holds that the chief aim of life is *kama* (pleasure) and the chief means to that end is *artha* (wealth). The pleasures to be desired are eating, drinking, song and women. Any means towards these ends are acceptable so long as they are successful. The Charvaka system does attempt to rein in unfettered pleasure-seeking, because this leads rapidly to pains such as illness. As natural supporters of 'might is right', many of the Charvakas are said to have written Machiavellian handbooks for the education of rulers. An example is the *Artha Shastra* (Handbook of Profit) of Kautilya, written around 300 BCE. As chief minister to King Chandragupta, the founder of the Mauryan Dynasty, Kautilya outlines the steps a king should take to retain and strengthen his power. The *Artha Shastra* covers a number of practical topics including taxation, the appointment of ministers, warfare and, above all, how to run a secret service. Although Kautilya regards anyone and everyone as corruptible and therefore potentially an enemy, he says – rather self-servingly – that the one person in whom the king should have absolute trust is the minister who runs his kingdom. As with Machiavelli, however, it is easier to feel moral outrage with Kautilya than it is to demonstrate that his advice is not in most cases eminently practical. Other Eastern Machiavellis include the Arab **Ibn Khaldun** and the Chinese **Hanfeizi**.

VARDHAMANA
c. 540 – 467 BCE

Along with Hinduism and Buddhism, the third major religion present in Indian culture from around the fifth century BCE was Jainism. Its founder, at least for historical purposes, was Vardhamana, also known as Mahavira (the Great Hero), although Jains regard him not as its founder but as the restorer of ancient teaching. He is supposed to have been the 24th Tirthankara or 'ford-builder', but the previous 23 are legendary. He may be the successor of the tradition of Parsvanatha, said to have died in 776 BCE, and of Rishabha, supposedly the first Tirthankara and one of three Jain sages mentioned in the Yajur Veda. On this evidence the Jain religion is, in some form, at least 3,500 years old. Certainly, there are aspects of the faith that seem thoroughly archaic. Alongside these, however, are some highly refined philosophical concepts that are worthy of consideration here, notably Vardhamana's theory of knowledge.

Vardhamana lived during a period of considerable fertility for new systems of thought and belief. He is said to have realized a calling at the age of 30 and, like the **Buddha**, left a life of comfort and a wife and child behind to become an ascetic. He spent time with Gosala, the founder of the Ajivikas, another unorthodox sect that was important in its time although now extinct. He was known to early Buddhists as Nigantha Nataputta and may have been a near contemporary of the Buddha. The Buddhists record debates between the two traditions, which co-existed in friendly rivalry. They have so many similarities that some have speculated that Gautama and Vardhamana were the same person, but this theory is no longer credible.

Like the Buddha, Vardhamana rejected the revelatory status of the Veda and did not see the need to posit the existence of God. He did, however, believe in the existence of a multiplicity of souls, each tied to a body from which it must strive to liberate itself. There are parallels in this soul-body dualism with *Sankhya Yoga* philosophy but perhaps still more with the Nyaya Vaisheshika view which sees the soul as active rather than passive and, like Vardhamana, holds an atomistic theory of matter. In the Western world there are parallels with pre-Socratic philosophy and with Platonism, another contemporary though unconnected development. At the age of 42, Vardhamana is said to have achieved enlightenment, thus becoming a *jina* or 'conqueror', from which his faith takes its name. He lived for about 30 years after this, in which time he built up a considerable following. He finally starved himself to death, an important sacrifice for the Jain religion.

The ultimate Jain ideal is to achieve liberation from all bodily attachment through the most severe asceticism. This is depicted in huge Jain statues of naked men, so detached from the physical that vines have begun to climb up their bodies. As with Yoga, the soul is thought of as ascending through the physical body to the highest region of motionlessness, the head. Thus we have the paradox of liberation conceived of as a complete and endless immobility. Ethically, Vardhamana taught the principle of *ahingsa* (harmlessness),

which included strict veganism and was to greatly influence Indian society. Jainism takes this much more seriously than either Buddhism or Hinduism and not only are Jains prohibited from any activity that involves killing animals, such as farming, but they are tolerant of insects and will go to great lengths to avoid accidentally killing one by stepping on or swallowing it. Even vegetables are thought to have souls, which is perhaps linked to the practice of total starvation as death approaches.

This most severe discipline is accompanied by a philosophy both gentle and relativistic. Firstly, there is the idea of *syadvada*, perhaps

The Parasnath Jain Temple in Calcutta.

best translated as 'maybe-ism'. For Vardhamana, who must be regarded as the founder of Jain philosophy if not its religion, all viewpoints are partial. The classic story is of a group of blind men who come across an elephant. One grasps its tail and claims that an elephant is like a rope. Another takes it by the trunk and says it is like a snake. A third decides that its leg is like the trunk of a tree, and so forth. The meaning of this is that whatever our worldview, we had better appreciate that it is a partial one and precede our statements about it with a *syad*: 'maybe, this is how it is...'. Jain statements are expressed in seven logical formulae:

Maybe it is
Maybe it is not
Maybe it is and also is not
Maybe it is inexpressible
Maybe it is, and is also inexpressible
Maybe it is not, and is also
inexpressible
Maybe it is and is not, and
is also inexpressible

Of course, these formulae could function without the *syad*, but its constant presence is a useful reminder of the uncertainty of human understanding. The paradox of tentative relativism and harsh discipline is resolved when we reflect that the Jain logic assumes a fundamental, intractable and objective reality. The blind men may have grasped only part of the elephant, but there is definitely an elephant. The elephant may be grasped fully, as it were, only by the 'knowledge of the free', that understanding possessed by the perfect victor. The Jain ideal is *kevala* (liberation) or

Vardhamana

Nirvana (deliverance). The Jain view of the latter term is definitely not the extinction professed by some Buddhists, but a positive existence of freedom from the body, a dwelling in peace and blissful rest.

Jainism was for a time a serious rival to Hinduism and Buddhism, but it became a minority faith. There are two traditions in Jainism resulting from a schism in the first century CE, between the Svetambaras ('white-robed') and Digambaras ('sky clad'). The latter maintain that a Jain monk should wear no clothing and that a woman cannot reach liberation. The former preserve the Jain canon of written scriptures, while the Digambaras reject it.

Vardhamana's teaching has, despite this, been tremendously influential. The ideal of *ahingsa* has been absorbed into mainstream Hinduism, most notably in the twentieth century by **Mohandas Gandhi**.

BUDDHISM IN INDIA

There are three stages in the development of Buddhism in India. The early stage of Buddhism consists of the **Buddha's** teaching and its formulation by his immediate successors. The second stage is that of the Hinayana (or Theravada), which emphasized the negative aspects of Buddhism. This stage can be identified historically with the reign of King Ashoka, who promoted Buddhism widely in India and established a remarkable Buddhist state over a vast area. Gradually, however, a growing number of Buddhists came to feel that the Hinayana doctrine lacked emotional appeal. There were a great number of Buddhists who argued for a reform, and the schism resulted in Mahayana Buddhism. Mahayana means 'Great Vehicle', as opposed to the 'Lesser Vehicle' or Hinayana: the Mahayanists held that while the Hinayana would take a few hardy ascetics to their goal, it was insufficient for the great mass of humanity. The term Hinayana is, of course, a Mahayana one: the Hinayana Buddhists

The hands of the Buddha in the act of meditation.

would call themselves Theravadins meaning 'tradition of the elders' for their adherence to the Buddha's original teachings.

The main issue with Hinayanist Buddhism was its somewhat intellectual, negative and world-denying philosophy. There was very little in it that could inspire people's love and devotion and as a religion it was obviously lacking. Whereof the Buddha was unwilling to speak, Hinayana Buddhism was crystal-clear. Although it appears to be more faithful to the Buddha, the lack of ethical concern and compassion makes Hinayanism oddly unlike the Buddha that we find in the old *sutras* of the Theravada. Mahayanism, by contrast, developed a pragmatic acceptance of a broad range of religious approaches. Just as Krishna says 'however men approach me, even so do I welcome them, for the path men take from every side is mine', so Mahayana Buddhism accepts all comers on their own terms. While Hinayanism proposed the *arhat* as an ideal – an ascetic who turned away from the world to find the extinction of *Nirvana* – Mahayanism has the *Bodhisattva*, the Buddha-to-be who postpones his own liberation out of compassion for all beings. Mahayana Buddhism thus has more of the social concern that inspired the Buddha than the more doctrinally correct Hinayanism.

The two main branches of Mahayana Buddhism are the Madhyamika or Middle School of **Nagarjuna** and the Yogacara of **Vasubandhu**. The former is known as the Shunyavada, the Doctrine of Emptiness, and the latter as the Vijnanavada, the Doctrine of Consciousness. Each is considered in

detail in the chapters on those figures. However a few comments are worthwhile here. Although Vasubandhu is thought to be later than Nagarjuna, his philosophy is nevertheless regarded as less advanced. Vasubandhu's Doctrine of Consciousness holds that the only reality is consciousness, the mind. *Nirvana* is the extinguishing of all thoughts, merging with the single consciousness underlying all. That consciousness is undifferentiated and single. Nagarjuna's Doctrine of Emptiness accepts the contention that the material world is in some sense unreal and empty, but applies the same reasoning to the mind. He treads a 'middle path' between absolutely denying reality and absolutely asserting it. There is a strong case to say that Nagarjuna's philosophy is the genuine heir of the Buddha's.

In broad geographical terms, Hinayana Buddhism spread in South and Southeast Asia: Sri Lanka, Burma, Cambodia, Thailand, Malaysia and Indonesia. Mahayana Buddhism prospered in Northern India, Tibet, China, Mongolia, Korea and Japan. Hinayana Buddhism uses the Pali language of the early Buddhist Canon, while Mahayana Buddhism in India generally uses Sanskrit, and in other places uses local languages. Traditional accounts credit figures such as Kumarila Bhatta and Shankara with successfully putting down Buddhism, but the truth is that it lost its strength and was replaced by a reinvigorated Hindu religion and philosophy. Buddhism gradually died out in India, having made significant contributions to Indian thought and belief. Elsewhere it has continued to flourish down to the present day.

THE BUDDHA (SIDDHARTHA GAUTAMA)

b. between 480 and 430 BCE

The Buddha lived in a time of remarkable intellectual ferment. In northeast India, a new branch of Indian civilization was springing up along the Ganges and it found the teachings of the *Shramanas* or holy wanderers more attractive and accessible than those of the Brahmins. **Vardhamana**, the founder of the Jain religion, was a near contemporary of the Buddha and was known to the Buddhists. Gosala, the founder of the Ajivikas, a now extinct sect that lasted some eighteen centuries, was another

local figure. In the northwest of India, early Upanishadic literature had been composed by the Brahmins and new Upanishads continued to emerge. Across the wider world, a remarkable number of great thinkers – including, pre-eminently, **Confucius** in China and Socrates in Greece – flourished independently at about the same time.

The Buddha, which means the Enlightened One or the Awakened One, was born into the wealthy Gautama family and named Siddhartha. He is traditionally supposed to have lived circa 563–483 BCE, but recent research suggests that he was born sometime in the fifth century BCE. The main aspects of his traditional story are as follows. His mother had a prophetic dream the night before he was born in which a beautiful white elephant entered her side. Experts in dream interpretation and in the interpretation of marks on a child's body concurred that the baby would grow up either to be a universal ruler or a Buddha. The prophecy stated that he would follow the former course if he stayed at home and the latter if he left home. Fearing that his son would become a wandering ascetic, Gautama's father raised him in great luxury and attempted to shield him from the realities of life.

Despite these efforts, at the age of 29 Gautama had the experiences that confirmed his resolve to follow a spiritual path. Following, it is said, the prophecy of a seer, while out driving in his chariot he saw first an old man, then on the next day, a sick man, and on the day after that, a dead man. While lost in the contemplation of this revelation of the suffering that characterizes life, Gautama chanced to see a saffron-robed ascetic and was struck by his peaceful appearance in the face of all the evils of life. He then resolved to discover that peace for himself. That night he

Departure of Buddha – Siddhartha leaves his father's palace and family after seeing the four signs (old age, death, sickness and a hermit) that were to persuade him to become an ascetic.

secretly left the palace and his sleeping wife and newborn son for the life of a mendicant ascetic.

Over the next few years, Gautama progressed in his education, studying with learned Brahmins and submitting himself to severe austerities. Eventually he decided that austerities could not give him what he wanted, whereupon his companion monks abandoned him, certain that he had abandoned the spiritual path. Shortly after this, however, Gautama did achieve Awakening while meditating under a bo tree. Now aged 35 and known as the Buddha, he set out to preach his *dharma* or teaching and established his monastic

community or *sangha*. He is said to have died at the age of 80.

What is certain is that the Buddha left a large body of oral teaching, which was written down after his death by a council of his followers. This teaching is known as the Theravada, as distinct from later additions that were subsequently declared to be orthodox because divinely inspired. Although the Theravada is in Pali, here we will generally use the Sanskrit terms for the sake of consistency with the other Indian thinkers and the Mahayana Buddhists. There are several striking aspects of the Buddha's original doctrine. In his first sermon, delivered to his companions

Buddha sits underneath the sacred Bo Tree in northern India. It is here that he gained Enlightenment and from where he set out to preach his dharma.

immediately following his awakening, the Buddha taught the Four Noble Truths, which are that all existence consists of suffering; that this suffering is caused by desire or thirst; that there is a way to end this suffering; and that the way to end suffering is to follow the Noble Eightfold Path of right views, right intention, right speech, right action, right livelihood, right effort, right mindfulness and right concentration.

Underpinning this deceptively simple teaching is a philosophy of remarkable subtlety. First there are his 'Three Characteristics of Being', which state that being is impermanent, has no self, and is made up of suffering. Although nothing is permanent, according to the Buddha, our thirst causes us to imagine the transitory objects we perceive as real and lasting. Chief among these transitory objects is the self: against the orthodoxy of the traditional Vedic religion of the time, the Buddha declared that there was no consistent self or Atman. This aspect of his doctrine is known as an-Atman (no self). The analogy is with fire, which appears to have a continuing existence but changes from moment to moment. Because of the transitory nature of being, it can never satisfy our thirst and therefore our existence is continuously filled with suffering.

These three characteristics of being, in turn, are derived from the fundamental insight of the Buddha, which is that of dependent origination (*pratitya samutpada*). Dependent origination states that everything has a cause and in turn is the cause of other things. This doctrine is described by the Buddha as being the middle way between those of the 'Eternalists', such as the orthodox Hindu thinkers, who maintained the eternal existence of being, and those of the 'Annihilationists', who denied not only existence but also causality. The Buddha denies that things really exist, but does not deny causality. This explains how, without a consistent self or God, the illusion of continuity is created through an endless chain of cause and effect. Buddha's successor **Nagarjuna** was to take up this idea and further develop it, founding in the process the influential School of Madhyamika (Middle Way).

Using his understanding of causation the Buddha developed the traditional Hindu concept of *karma* (literally, 'action'). According to the Buddha, a person is made up of five groups or *skandhas*: body, feelings, perceptions, impulses and consciousness. These five are configured according to past actions in a certain way, and will be reconfigured in a better or worse way in the future depending on the good or bad actions performed in the present. At death, the 'consciousness' *skandha* carries its karmic charge on to its rebirth in a new body. As with the Hindu thinkers, the aim of the Buddha's philosophy is to find a way to get off this cosmic merry-go-round (or perhaps, misery-go-round).

This brings us to the best-known distinctively Buddhist concept, that of *Nirvana*, 'extinguishing' – in Pali, *nibbana*. *Nirvana* is variously imagined to be either heaven or a form of annihilation, but its literal sense is the extinguishing of the flames of desire, hatred and delusion. The Buddha refused to be pinned down on what *Nirvana* might be, or what would happen to an enlightened soul after death, but he did posit an 'unoriginated' realm or substance beyond the illusion of existence, which promised a kind of escape.

There is considerable debate about the Buddha's true belief, centring on the three questions of whether there is an absolute reality, whether there is a permanent self and whether *Nirvana* is existence or annihilation. Perhaps these questions come to the same thing: did the Buddha believe that there was an ultimate reality? Though he refused to speculate about such questions, is it safe to assume he was an atheist? We noted at the start of the chapter that the Buddha lived in a time of great intellectual ferment. When his doctrines are compared to those of the Upanishads, they are seen to share a great commonality. Both aim at liberation, and both move away from the old Vedic tradition. There are many statements in the Upanishads that could be attributed to the Buddha. For example, the description of Brahman as 'not this, not that', or the idea of Brahman as silence could, if the word 'Brahman' were replaced with *Nirvana*, seem eminently Buddhist. What the Buddha does not do is use positive means of describing reality. The Upanishads make use of both negative and positive means of speaking of reality:

The wise realize everywhere that
which is invisible, ungraspable,
without source, without senses,
without body,
That which is infinite,
multiformed, all-pervasive,
extremely subtle and undiminishing,
and the source of all.

Mundaka Upanishad 1.i.6.

The Buddha uses only the negative, as when he says 'transient are all compound things...sorrowful are all compound things...all things are without self' (Dhammapada, 278–280).

The debate on this subject continues. A Buddhist scholar such as Walpola Rahula would categorically deny the Buddha had taught anything resembling Upanishadic ideas, and would argue that the fundamental assumptions of Buddhism are entirely the opposite of those in the Upanishads. On the other side, there are those who maintain that the Buddha's denial of the reality of the self or of an ultimate reality amounts to the same thing as Upanishadic denials about the possibility of being able to define an ultimate reality. Certainly in later forms of Buddhism, such as the twentieth-century Japanese Zen of **Nishida**, Upanishadic views predominate:

As emphasized in basic Buddhist
thought, the self and the universe
share the same foundation; or
rather, they are the same thing.

The view of Walpola Rahula makes sense when Buddhism is treated as an entirely exceptional teaching. Within the context of a survey of Eastern thought such as this, however, it seems much more appropriate to view Buddhist metaphysics as an exceptional expression of a familiar doctrine, rather than as a doctrine contrary to all others.

From this point of view, the Buddha's real distinctiveness is as an ethical teacher.

The Buddhist *sangha* or monastic community was far more democratic and equitable than that of the early Hindu culture it sought to break with. The Buddha rejects caste entirely, and his treatment of women is broadly equitable. Having said this, the creation of the monastic order, with its surrounding lay community of the faithful, sets up a hierarchy in Buddhist

Walpola Rahula

culture that is similar to that which it replaces. Although birth is irrelevant to Buddhism, it is necessary to convert to Buddhism and ultimately to give up worldly life and take up holy orders, which is the highest calling. We have in the reign of King Ashoka, who ruled most of India from 270–230 BCE, an example of an early Buddhist kingdom. It had many remarkably attractive aspects, including what is probably the world's first welfare state, universal tolerance of different beliefs, and a justice system based on Buddhist principles.

As can be seen from the widely varying philosophies of subsequent Buddhists elsewhere in this book, there is almost no doctrine that has not been imputed to the Buddha by his followers. Regardless of this, however, it is possible to distinguish a 'true Buddhism' throughout history, characterized not so much by consistency in doctrine as by universal compassion, equity and justice. The Buddha's ethical teachings are the earliest complete articulations of these ideals and, to this day, remain one of the greatest Indian contributions to world philosophy.

King Ashoka, India's first Buddhist king.

THE SIX ORTHODOX SYSTEMS OF INDIAN PHILOSOPHY

Traditionally there are six main systems of Indian philosophy that acknowledge the authority of the Veda. The word used to describe the systems is *darshana* (which can mean 'view' or 'revelation'). Already implicit in the idea of a *darshana* is the possibility of a range of alternative

The six darshanas are best seen as a reaction to views that were regarded as beyond the pale: the materialism of the Charvakas, the Jain viewpoint of Vardhamana and, above all, the way of Buddhism.

views. Alternative revelations are not necessarily contradictory in India.

The six *darshanas* are best seen as a reaction to views that were regarded as beyond the pale: the materialism of the Charvakas, the Jain viewpoint of Vardhamana and, above all, the way of Buddhism. The main point about these dissenting systems was that they attacked the traditional structure of Indian society: the caste system, the tradition of the Veda and the authority of the Brahmins. Against these vigorous attacks the Hindu orthodox had to develop their own philosophies, to define and refine the views they instinctively held. All of the *darshanas* share certain terms of reference. All erect a standard of external reality against Buddhist scepticism, called variously *maya*, *prakriti*, atoms or Brahman. All have a theory of the self. All have a cyclical view of cosmic history. All except Mimamsa aim at salvation or liberation of the soul.

The six are traditionally grouped into pairs. The usual order, based on a perceived logical progression, is Nyaya Vaisheshika, Sankhya Yoga and Mimamsa Vedanta. There are critics of this system who point out its many inadequacies. It has been retained, however, as useful to those wishing to get the broad outline of Hindu thought.

NYAYA VAISHESHIKA

Nyaya (see **Gautama**) is the philosophy most concerned with logic and epistemology, which examines the basis of knowledge. Vaisheshika is an allied development and is metaphysical, concerned with the nature of reality. Vaisheshika (see **Kanada**) includes an atomic theory of matter. It is thought by some authorities to be much older than Nyaya, which is reasonable given the example of other philosophies in which logic is usually a later development than metaphysics.

SANKHYA YOGA

MIMAMSA VEDANTA

Sankhya means 'enumeration': the system recognizes 25 categories of existence, with the highest being *purusha* (spirit). The other 24 are all divisions of *prakriti* (nature). It is the most unorthodox of the six systems as it is often regarded as atheistic and, indeed, some authorities rejected it on this account. The Yoga philosophy is a practical extension of Sankhya, involving a system of exercises designed to bring the practitioner to a state of knowledge of the distinction between the *purusha* and the *prakriti*. Yoga adds a 26th category, namely God.

Sankhya is considered in the chapter on **Kapila,** and Yoga in the chapter on **Patanjali**. Both are very important for the *Bhagavad Gita* and so for the later course of Indian philosophy in general.

The most orthodox of the systems are the Mimamsa (Purva Mimamsa), literally 'the study of the early part of the Veda', and the Vedanta (Uttara Mimamsa), or the 'study of the latter part of the Veda', that is of the Upanishads. However, the Vedanta maintains an attitude of respectful distance from the *Samhita* (Vedic hymns) and is, on the whole, opposed to the Brahmanas, so of the three parts of the Veda it is only the Upanishads that it regards as revelatory.

Mimamsa is examined in the chapter on Jaimini. Vedanta is the most important of all the six systems and is represented by **Badarayana, Gaudapada, Shankara, Ramanuja, Madhva** and **Vivekananda**. **Gandhi's** philosophy is also largely reliant on Vedanta.

A Brahmin performing pujah. *The Hindu orthodox had to defend their philosophy against those who denied the tradition of the Veda and the authority of the Brahmins.*

GAUTAMA
4th century BCE?

Nyaya's ('Right Reasoning' or 'Logic') history is very ancient, being mentioned in the *Laws of Manu* and by the philosopher Yajnyawalkya. Here we are concerned with the post-Buddhist Nyaya, founded by Gautama who wrote its first textbook, the *Nyaya Sutras*. His namesake Gautama, the **Buddha**, and **Mahavira** the founder of the Jain sect, had both mounted attacks on orthodox philosophy some two hundred years before. It is likely that Gautama set out to establish a robust logical system that could defend the Veda from their criticisms. Whereas Mimamsa regards the scriptures as the only reliable authority and Sankhya appeals to a supreme form of reason, Nyaya makes use of logic and experience, the principal bases of Buddhist and Jain attacks. Many writers have noted the similarity between Nyaya and Aristotle's syllogistic analysis, and some argue that there was direct influence, either from Greece to India or vice versa. There is no conclusive evidence of this, however.

Gautama assumes the Veda to be true and therefore accepts spiritual liberation as a reality. On this basis, he wishes to purge philosophy of false and sentimental arguments which can only be founded upon spurious doctrines. Only once we understand what can be known and how we know what we know, and have discovered legitimate means for advancing in our enquiries can true philosophical thought take place. Logic is not, for Nyaya, merely a process to be tinkered with. Gautama sets out the various forms of debate, including discussion aimed at finding the truth, debating to win an argument against an opponent, attacking a position without having a position of one's own, and so on. He emphasizes the importance of having the earnest desire to find the truth. Liberation is, according to Nyaya, the self moving beyond the pain and pleasure of existence to pure unconscious being, which is the Atman.

The main contribution of the Nyaya School to Hindu thought is its logical structure, which has been adopted with modifications by all the other schools. Its enumeration of logical fallacies has been useful. The later thinkers were able to refer to Nyaya concepts such as 'the argument in a circle', 'infinite regress' or 'mutual dependence' with no need to elaborate further.

It is thought that, although having apparently developed independently of each other, Nyaya and Vaisheshika subsequently merged and came to be known as Nyaya Vaisheshika. Whereas the main concerns of Nyaya are logic and epistemology (the philosophy of knowledge), Vaisheshika develops its thinking into metaphysics.

The modern school of Nyaya, called Navya Nyaya or 'New Nyana', was founded in about 1200 CE by Gangesha, who wrote in response to the numerous criticisms of the school by the Vedantin philosopher Shriharsha. Navya Nyaya is notable for its hair-splitting tendencies.

The cow is a sacred animal in India, a tradition going back to 3000 BCE. Here, a yogi and a crowned cow can be seen at the entrance of a Hindu temple.

WHAT IS A SUTRA?

'Sutra' *is a word used to describe learned writings in both Hindu and Buddhist traditions. However, it does not mean the same thing for both. In Sanskrit, the word literally means 'thread'. 'Pithy, unambiguous, laying out all the essential aspects of each topic, and dealing with all aspects of the question, free of repetitiveness and flaw – those learned in the* sutras *say that such is a* sutra'. *Such is the account given in the* Padma Purana.

In the Hindu tradition, the sutra *format was one of the earliest literary forms. A Hindu* sutra *is the model of brevity, consisting of a series of short phrases or verses, often with no apparent connection or argument. This is misleading, because the* sutra *was never intended to be studied alone, but to act as an* aide-memoire *or a series of headings on which the guru (sage) or* acharya *(teacher) would expound. Reading the key texts of Hinduism can be rather like reading the chapter headings of a book. The* sutra *is the 'thread' on which the gems of the teacher's learning are hung. It also often provides a subject for meditation: having heard and understood an exposition on a* sutra, *the student can reflect on its words. The* sutra *thus comes to represent the understanding of the subject arising out of oral discussion between teacher and student, rather than being itself a full discussion. There are numerous references in the Upanishads to the warm bond between teacher and student, as in the prayer, 'May He protect us both together. May He nourish us both together. May we both acquire strength together. Let our study be brilliant. May we not cavil at each other.'*

The key texts of the Hindu philosophies are contained in sutras, *for example the* Yoga Sutras *of **Patanjali**, the* Brahma Sutras *or* Vedanta Sutras *of **Badarayana** and the lost* Sankhya Sutras *of **Kapila**. This literary form was widely used for all forms of knowledge, ranging from the world's first grammar, written by Panini in* sutra *form around 500 BCE, to the famous sex manual* Kama Sutra *(the* Sutra *of Desire).*

The Buddhist sutra *(in Pali, a* sutta), *on the other hand, normally refers to words attributed to the Buddha. Thus, the* Fire Sutra, *the* Love Sutra *and the* Sutra *of Advice to Sigala* are examples of the recorded utterances of the Buddha. Later, Mahayana Buddhism accepted a much wider definition of* sutra. *Works of great wisdom produced by later Buddhists were accepted as the revealed teachings of the Buddha. They normally followed the format of a sermon or* sutra *given by the Buddha. For example, the* Diamond Sutra *sometimes attributed to Nagarjuna or the* Garland Sutra, *which inspired Huayen Buddhism in China. Most Buddhist traditions base themselves on a particular* sutra, *with the notable exception of Chan or Zen Buddhism, which repudiates the* sutra *tradition, relying instead on direct oral transmission of teaching.*

KANADA
3rd century BCE?

Kanada, whose name literally means 'atom eater', founded the Vaisheshika School of Philosophy. His real name may have been Kashyapa. His philosophy is very close to that of Nyaya, and the two complementary schools came to be regarded as one, called Nyaya Vaisheshika, from the eleventh century onwards. Nyaya deals with problems of logic and epistemology, while Vaisheshika is concerned with metaphysics. Vaisheshika is a realist school and regards the objects of knowledge as having a real existence independent of the knower and of the process of knowing, a view that has some affinities with the Buddhism of the time.

Accordingly, Kanada explores the nature of matter in great detail. Because the senses perceive real objects, each sense corresponds to an element. Thus smell corresponds to earth, taste to water, sight to fire, touch to air and hearing to the fifth element of ether or space. The inference of the fifth element is typical of Indian metaphysics. All of the elements, except for ether, are made up of indivisible, indestructible and eternal atoms. According to Kanada, atoms have no dimension, which is problematic because that leaves no explanation for the way in which a number of atoms come to add up to a quantity. Two atoms make a dyad and three dyads make a triad, which is the smallest thing visible to the human eye.

Undoubtedly Vaisheshika is a pluralist philosophy, which means that it regards things as being many. Each individual (Atman) has, according to Vaisheshika, a separate existence; matter is made of vast numbers of tiny atoms; time and space also are real and indestructible; even God (in later Vaisheshika) is simply the Paramatman or Supreme Self. The mind or *manas* is physical and atomic and has no dimension. It can apprehend more than one thing at a time because it has no size and so can move at infinite speed between two or more objects of thought. Thus even the mind is, in a sense, physical. Although Vaisheshika is proto-scientific in many ways, the mysterious force *adrishta* ('unseen') is there to explain everything that is not explained by the known objects of existence. Magnetism, the rising of fire and the journey of the soul after death are some of the many topics covered by *adrishta*.

It is doubtful whether Kanada's scheme includes God, but later Vaisheshikas felt the need to include a divine power. God is the efficient cause of the universe in that he ordains its creation, but not its material cause, as the objects of the universe are eternally present. God's role is to organize the universe such that it provides a moral space in which the Atmans or individuals may play out their destinies. It is assumed that the individuals already have an accumulation of good and bad action (*karma*) from before the beginning of a cycle of creation. It is these cycles that give form and structure to the universe.

KAPILA
7th century BCE?

Author of the sadly lost *Sankhya Pravacana Sutras*, Kapila is traditionally acknowledged to be the founder of the Sankhya philosophy. There is no evidence for his existence and he may be only a legend, but Sankhya is one of the most important and influential systems in philosophical history. Of the six orthodox Hindu philosophies, perhaps only Mimamsa is as old, or older than Sankhya. Nevertheless, it is more advanced than the Nyaya Vaisheshika system and its theories form the basis of much later Indian thought. 'Sankhya' literally means 'counting up' or 'number', perhaps because of its fondness for enumerating the many categories of existence.

If Kapila existed, then we know of his ideas only indirectly through the work of his successors. The later Upanishads, the law manual *Manu*, the Mahabharata and the *Bhagavad Gita* all contain Sankhya ideas and attest to its importance as a tradition in the last 500 years BCE. There are theories as to whether there was a 'primal Sankhya', but as with the other philosophies, it seems as though Sankhya

gained its sharpness and definition at a later date. Before then it seems to have existed as part of a general philosophical ferment with a more speculative than argumentative character.

Sankhya is generally identified today with the classical Sankhya of Ishvarakrishna (*c*. fourth century CE), who wrote in the *Sankhya Verses* a succinct distillation of a lost text called the *Sixty Themes* (with an obligatory nod to Kapila). Ishvarakrishna's philosophy is spiritual, but seemingly atheistic. The argument as to whether Sankhya really is atheistic continues. In its early expression, it seems to sit well with theistic doctrines – most notably in the *Bhagavad Gita*. It may be that it was originally theistic, but that in the struggles with early Buddhists, it was found that the existence of God could not be proven. By removing God from the argument, the Sankhya philosophers were able to strengthen their position. Whether or not a belief in God was originally part of its tradition, it later became so: the influential sixteenth-century Sankhya writer Vijnanabhiksu also accepts the existence of God, as does the Yoga philosophy that has close links to Sankhya. The question is not as significant within the context of Indian thought as it would be in the West, because the spirit or *purusha* fulfils many of the functions attributed to God, and the existence of 'gods' is not in question either. What Sankhya seems to deny is the reality of an Ishvara or Lord, a paternal deity presiding over the realm of nature.

Sankhya enumerates 25 categories of existence, of which the first is the *purusha* or spirit and the other 24 aspects of *prakriti* or nature. These are too complex to enter into here, but the important point is that Sankhya is a dual philosophy, the division between *purusha* and *prakriti* being more fundamental than for any of the other subdivisions. *Purusha* is related to the English root word for 'person' but also carries a masculine connotation, whereas *prakriti* is generally thought of as female (i.e. Mother Nature). One important Sankhya allegory related by Ishvarakrishna is of *prakriti* as a dancing girl:

As a dancer ceases from the dance after having been seen by the audience, so also prakriti *ceases after having manifested herself to the* purusha.

*She, possessed of the qualities (*gunas*) and helpful in various ways, behaves selflessly for the sake of him, who is without the qualities and who plays no helpful part.*

It is my thought that there is nothing more delicate than prakriti, *who says to herself, "I have been seen," and never again comes into the sight of* purusha.

Sankhya Verses 59–61, translated by Larson

When *purusha* comes into contact with *prakriti*, the insentient nature of the latter is animated and given shape, and the cycle of life begins. Liberation is effected through the analytical realization of the difference between these two – between what is conscious and passive, and what is inanimate and active. It is our ignorance that binds us, while knowledge is the route to freedom. An unusual characteristic of the classical Sankhya system is that the *purushas* are at once the eternal self and multiple. While multiple individual souls (normally called the *jiva* in India) are easy to conceive of, a universe with millions of eternal *purushas* is more problematic.

In Sankhya, as in much of Hindu thought thereafter, the intellect or *buddhi* is counted not as *purusha* but as *prakriti*. A key error, according to Sankhya, is to confuse the *purusha* with the *buddhi*. Sankhya views all individuals as identical mechanisms. The apparatus of mind is animated by consciousness but is not that consciousness. The fundamental division is not between mind and matter, which is a quintessentially Western concern, but between the conscious and the mechanical. Another way of looking at Sankhya philosophy is to regard it as an exploration of subject-object dualism. The subject is conscious, the object unconscious. It is not subjectivism such as we find in the Consciousness-Only School of Buddhism (see **Vasubandhu**), because the reality of the object is not denied. Sankhya avoids the problem of egotism by distinguishing between the *purusha* and the *ahankara* or 'self-sense', which gives a sense of identity to all the elements of *prakriti*.

Another important and influential concept of Sankhya in Hindu thought is its analysis of *prakriti* as composed of three qualities (*gunas*): *sattva* (light), *rajas* (energy) and *tamas* (darkness). An account of the *gunas* is given on page 43. Recent research suggests that strong links may have existed between Greek and Indian philosophy from the earliest times. According to Professor Thomas McEvilley, links were particularly strong in the pre-Socratic period (545–490 BCE). If this is so, we can distinguish in Plato's philosophy the influence of Sankhya, particularly in his description of a human being as having three aspects, which is very close to the *guna* theory.

PATANJALI
2nd century BCE?

The name Patanjali is a pseudonym and may belong to several individuals who contributed to the literature on Yoga and other subjects. Patanjali is credited with two great works, the *Yoga Sutras* and the *Mahabhashya* ('Great Commentary'), which is a defence of the grammarian Panini against his critic Katyayana. It is probable that these two works are by different authors. Even the *Yoga Sutras,* which we will consider here, are regarded as being the product of several hands, with the earliest being composed in the second century BCE and the latest around the fifth century CE.

As the supposed author of the *Yoga Sutras,* Patanjali is the greatest figure in the Yoga system, which is related to and traditionally twinned with **Kapila's** Sankhya philosophy. Yoga is less theoretical, however, and to Kapila's conception of knowledge as a means to liberation it adds physical and mental disciplines. Patanjali also assumes the existence of a personal, all-powerful and all-knowing God and gives four traditional yogic proofs for God's existence. Liberation, as with Sankhya, is effected by disentangling the self from its identification with the psychophysical organism and understanding the separate natures of *purusha* (conscious self) and *prakriti* (unconscious nature). The process is very different, however, and involves not only reasoning but also disciplining the attention so that an intuitive realization is arrived at.

Patanjali's introduction of God to the atheistic or agnostic Sankhya system is intriguing. God is not necessary to Yoga, but Patanjali rather generously says that by devotion to and meditation on the eternal, infinite deity an individual may achieve liberation by an easier route than the arduous exercises and disciplines of Yoga.

According to both Sankhya and Yoga, the first step in the downward evolution of man is *buddhi* (sometimes also called *chitta*), which stands for both intellect and reason. Everything else having to do with man (the senses, the body, etc.) is a modification of reason, which should not be understood as a purely logical function, but as having emotional, physical and even mystical aspects. This is how Plato also understood reason. Thus, because Yoga gives the practitioner mastery over reason – which is the foundation of the mental and physical worlds – yogis can develop apparently supernatural powers. While Patanjali does describe these, he cautions against them as a distraction.

Although the popular conception of Yoga is as a system of physical exercises, these are not mentioned in the *Yoga Sutras.* Instead, Patanjali speaks of control of the breath and mental exercises for refining the attention. The final deliverance of the Eightfold Path is the complete cessation of the activity of the intellect. Even the final stage, *Samadhi*, in which the identification of the mind with the object of its attention is total, needs to be transcended since here the mind is still taken with the object.

The influence of Yoga, like Sankhya, is very broad. In the wider sense of the term, 'Yoga' can be used to describe a 'way', as in the *Bhagavad Gita* where, for example, *Jnana Yoga* is 'the Way of Knowledge' and *Karma Yoga* is 'the Way of Action'. Even in the restricted sense of a system of exercise or meditation it is found in both Hindu and Buddhist traditions.

Yogi in yogic meditation.

JAIMINI
c. 400 BCE

Perhaps the earliest recognizable Hindu philosophy is Purva Mimamsa ('the study of the earlier [part of the Veda]'), which is thought to have developed in its early form before 500 BCE. Whether or not it did pre-date the other schools is a matter of debate, but it makes logical sense to regard the Purva Mimamsa as the earliest because the subject of its study is the older parts of the Veda. The Vedanta philosophy is sometimes known as Uttara Mimamsa ('the study of the later [part of the Veda]'). For simplicity, however, 'Mimamsa' will refer here to the Purva Mimamsa, while 'Vedanta' refers to Uttara Mimamsa.

Mimamsa is an activist philosophy, which means that it regards action as the primary reality of the universe. Accordingly, it is concerned mainly with *dharma* (duty or right action) as opposed to contemplation. Only through continual observation of *dharma* and correct performance of ritual can man reach heaven. This associates the Mimamsa with the Brahmins, because the sacrifices and rituals can only be carried out under their auspices. Although Jaimini, who lived around 400 BCE, inherited perhaps a millennium of philosophical speculation, he is generally regarded as the father of Mimamsa. He codified and developed its ideas in his *Purva Mimamsa Sutra*. Jaimini attacked the view of an earlier Mimamsa scholar, Badari, who held that the injunctions of the Veda were to be carried out regardless of their results. His view, and that of Mimamsa after him, was that the Vedic rituals were designed specifically to allow their performer to reach heaven. The Vedas propound a life of action and

ritual. Statements in the Vedas that contain injunctions to act are therefore treated by Mimamsa analysis as primary, and those that do not are secondary. The lowest class of shudras, as well as those outside the caste system, are barred from the sacrifices[4].

All of this may sound very much like a particularly ritualistic and hidebound form of religion, but the philosophical aspect of Mimamsa is fascinating. Of the various means of discovering knowledge, Jaimini accepts only scripture (that is, the Veda) as authoritative on the subject of *dharma* (right action). Interestingly, although Jaimini claims that the Veda is not written by a human author, he does not claim that it is the word of God. His view is that 'the relation of the word to its meaning is eternal'. The scriptures, articulated in the pure medium of Sanskrit, are the perfect and unassailable truth. The sound of the words and their meanings and the effect of hearing them are inextricably linked forever. Any word carries its meaning within itself; if we do not know and understand a word on first hearing it, this is due to our own deficiency. Even apparently inarticulate sounds – noises – are said to be letters, each with its own Vedic meaning. The theme of the relationship between the fabric of the universe and *shabda* (which means 'sound' and also the 'testimony' of others or of the Veda) is one that will recur throughout Hindu thought down to the present day.

From the Mimamsaka emphasis on ritual develops an intriguing activist theory of linguistics: the verb is the main part of the sentence, and the primary form of the verb is the optative form commanding one to undertake an action, such as a ritual or sacrifice. Closely related to Mimamsa in this respect, although more extreme, is the Nairukta or Lexiconist philosophy that regarded the

Atman, the only reality, as a kind of eternal activity: the Great Verb in the sentence or book of the universe.

Mimamsa is the most orthodox of the Hindu philosophies and it is mainly against the ideas of Jaimini's

Jaimini wrote at a time when opposition to his culture was growing...the Brahmin monopoly of religion was unacceptable to those who had spiritual leanings but were debarred from taking part in Brahmin ritual.

predecessors that the unorthodox schools such as the Buddhists, Jains and Charvakas directed their early attacks. It is easy to see why: the Brahmin monopoly of religion was unacceptable to those who had spiritual leanings but were debarred from taking part in Brahmin ritual. The Upanishads – the earliest of which pre-date Jaimini – are similarly unimpressed by the ritualized culture of the Veda and attempt to supersede it. Jaimini wrote at a time when opposition to his culture was growing, from both within and without. His work can therefore be seen as an attempt to clearly define the practices of the old Vedic culture and defend it from opposition. All of these factions developed arguments in opposition to Mimamsa; and the friction probably contributed much, not only to their development but also to Mimamsa itself and subsequent Hindu philosophies.

The relationship of Mimamsa to Vedanta is interesting; while the former regards action as the means to liberation, Vedanta tends to favour contemplation. The analogy with Christian debates about faith versus good works is a tempting one, although it should be noted that the 'good works' of Mimamsa ritual are generally aimed at personal gain. With respect to action, Vedanta agrees with Jaimini's *bête noir*, Badari, that it should be carried out without regard for results. The first Vedantin text, the *Brahma Sutras*, was written by **Badarayana**, regarded by some scholars as a near contemporary of Jaimini. Whereas Jaimini is concerned with right action and Atman (the individual soul who will receive the heavenly reward for its sacrifices), Badarayana's main concern is the nature of Brahman or the ultimate reality, the universal form of God. Mimamsa does not regard Vedanta as a philosophical enemy such as Buddhism, however. Vedanta is cited by the Mimamsakas as useful for understanding the Atman.

Jaimini's successors are Sabara, who wrote a commentary on Jaimini's work in about 400 CE, and Kumarila Bhatta and Prabhakara, two philosophers from around 800 CE, who commented on both Jaimini and Sabara, each thus founding a different school of Mimamsa philosophy. Prabhakara also supports Badari, but his was to be a less popular branch of Mimamsa than was that of Kumarila. Kumarila is traditionally said to have been instrumental in the final defeat of Buddhism in medieval India, but this neat end to the struggle between Mimamsa and unorthodoxy seems to be an invention.

BADARAYANA
1st century CE?

An indication of the prestige of Badarayana, sometimes known as Vyasa, is that he is traditionally conflated with the mythical sage Vyasa who compiled the Vedas, the Mahabharata, the Purana and other sacred texts. However, as the name Vyasa means simply 'compiler' this may be the source of the confusion. The historical Badarayana lived possibly in the first century CE[5] and was the author of the *Brahma Sutras* or Aphorisms on Brahman. Of his life almost nothing is known but he seems, unusually, to have been a lay person rather than a Brahmin.

Although the *Brahma Sutras* are sometimes spoken of as one of the three great pillars of Hinduism, together with the Upanishads and the *Bhagavad Gita*, they are better seen as the founding work of Vedanta philosophy. The *Brahma Sutras* are also known as the *Vedanta Sutras* because they principally comment on the Upanishads, which are the 'Veda-anta' or 'that which comes at the end of the Vedas'. There is a possible reference to the *Brahma Sutras* in the *Bhagavad Gita* (XIII, 4), but most Hinduism scholars believe that the *Gita* pre-dates Badarayana.

Like the Vedas, the *Brahma Sutras* are better known in India by their reputation than through a direct reading of the text. A *sutra* (see box p. 34) is a concise aphorism, written in unbelievably dense and economical language. One result of this brevity is that it is almost impossible to understand the *Brahma Sutras* without a commentary to accompany them. Badarayana assumes the reader (or perhaps listener) to have an intimate knowledge of the Vedas and the Upanishads as well as contemporary philosophical discussions, and it may be that the intention is for them to remain mysterious to anyone without a well-versed Brahmin teacher to instruct them. The entire work is only 555 sutras long and could be printed in just a few pages, but commentaries can be vast. The English translation of **Shankara's** commentary is some 900 pages long. Badarayana manages to quarry a coherent philosophy from the bedrock of Hindu tradition, while simultaneously succeeding in attacking rival views from other contemporary and traditional schools. But whereas Shankara's commentaries are appended to a particular text, Badarayana considers the entire scriptural and philosophical tradition. Generally, in keeping with the obsessively economical *sutra* form, he neglects to say even what part of the tradition he is speaking of.

The first two of the four sections of the *Brahma Sutras* are a consideration of the scriptural references to Brahman, showing the Vedic tradition to be non-contradictory and consistent. According to commentators, he expounds his view of Brahman as the first and material cause of the universe and attacks at length the opposing Sankhya philosophy, with more cursory arguments against, among others, the Vaisesika, Buddhist and Jain viewpoints. Having established this, he goes on to consider all of the ways in which Brahman is spoken of within the tradition: the Blissful One, the Being Inside, space, *prana*, light, the Eater, the Internal Ruler, the One that is Unseen, the Infinite, and so on. Other sections concerned with more ritualistic aspects are of less interest here.

If the *Bhagavad Gita* is a work of poetry of a devotional and inspirational

THE THREE GUNAS

There has been from the earliest times in Indian philosophy a concept of a three-fold reality. Some believe this may have been connected to the seasons of India – the dry season, the rains and the harvest. Because the Indians experienced the year in this way, they were accustomed to thinking not in opposites but in a tripartite cycle. The Vedas and the earliest Upanishads explore metaphysical questions repeatedly in a triadic way. In the Chandogya Upanishad, *for example, there are said to be three colours (*rupas*) that underlie reality: the red, the white and the black. When one gains an understanding of these three, then one will no longer see the outward manifestations, such as the sun, moon, fire and so forth, but only the three colours. Similarly, in the* Brihadaranyaka *Upanishad, the creation story moves in a series of triple evolutions. Throughout the early texts, the threeness of things is continually stressed as essential to an understanding of underlying reality and interrelation, as well as to the processes of evolution and creation.*

In about 600 BC, a more developed theory emerged in Sankhya philosophy (see **Kapila***) that there were three qualities, essences or forms of being called the 'gunas', literally 'strands' or 'threads'. The word first appears in the Atharva Veda: a golden treasure chest in heaven is described as being like a wheel with three spokes or strands, called the* triguna. *The gunas have a part in all of the orthodox Indian systems and are commonplace ideas today. In Sankhya, the three* gunas *are* sattva *(light, buoyancy),* rajas *(activity, energy) and* tamas *(darkness, sleep). All three have an equal part to play in generating the cosmic dance of creation. The gunas also have a psychological or moral aspect. This comes through strongly in the* Bhagavad Gita, *where several chapters are devoted to the subject. Whereas in their cosmic role the* gunas *are regarded as equal, in their psychological or moral role there is a definite hierarchy. Put simply,* tamas *represents all that is ignorant, dark and false;* rajas *is linked to desire and is as such dangerous and unpredictable; and* sattva *is pure and true. All three are regarded as merely aspects of nature and the* purusha *or spirit is totally free from them, but* sattva *needs to be cultivated as the most propitious of the* gunas *for spiritual liberation. In the* Gita, *the* gunas *are associated with the three main castes: the sattvic Brahmins, the rajasic Ksatriyas and the tamasic Sudras. As Krishna says:*

When the light of knowledge shines through all the gates of the body,
Then it should be known that sattva *is dominant.*
Greed, activity and the undertaking of actions, restlessness, desire;
These are born when rajas *is dominant, Arjuna.*
Darkness and inertness, heedlessness and confusion;
These are born when tamas *is dominant, Arjuna.*

Bhagavad Gita, XIV, 11–14.

nature, and the Upanishads have a mystical turn, the *Brahma Sutras* are more purely philosophical in the Western sense. This is why they are known as the Nyaya Prasthana or logical aspect of the Hindu canon. Badarayana was *astika* (orthodox) in that he accepted the absolute authority of the Vedic hymns, the Upanishads, the *Bhagavad Gita*, and so on. Taking this as his starting point, Badarayana seeks to explain what it is that the scriptures are really saying. In doing so, he sets the pattern for the great commentators of the medieval period, but because of the gnomic style of the *sutras*, he himself became the subject of commentary. The earliest known commentary is by Shankara who found in Badarayana's great work the ideas of Advaita Vedanta. Subsequent commentaries, often in response, were written by **Ramanuja**, **Madhva**, Nimbarka, Vallabha and others, all of whom were able to fashion from the *Brahma Sutras* a confirmation of their own interpretation of the Vedanta tradition. There are more than a dozen major commentators on Badarayana's *Brahma Sutras*. Shivananda, a modern commentator, indicates the prestige of the work when he says that 'if any [teacher] wishes to establish his own cult or sect or school of thought, he will have to write a commentary of his own on the *Brahma Sutras*. Only then will it be recognized'.

Shivananda, a modern commentator on Badarayana's Brahma Sutras.

THE BHAGAVAD GITA
Author unknown,
between 5th and 2nd century BCE

Lord Krishna imparting the message of the Bhagavad Gita *to Arjuna.*

The vast epic Mahabharata tells the story of the war between two branches of the Bharata family, the Kauravas and the Pandavas. It is easily the longest work of epic literature in any culture, being, for example, seven times longer than Homer's *Iliad* and *Odyssey*, and three times longer than the Bible. It is a repository for all aspects of Indian culture, history and thought. Far and away its most important section, however, is the *Bhagavad Gita* or 'Song of the Lord'. It is not known whether the *Gita* is an integral part of the Mahabharata or an interpolation. The *Gita* is a discussion on the battlefield between Arjuna, the greatest warrior of the Pandavas, and Krishna, his charioteer. Arjuna sees his friends, cousins and teachers in the enemy lines and protests that he cannot fight against them. It would be better to die than to kill these men. Krishna's advice to him in eighteen short chapters amounts to a complete philosophy.

This is not the place for a detailed account of the philosophy of the *Gita* and so our main purpose here is to indicate its position in the history of ideas. The *Gita's* thought is derived from the classical Upanishads but is different in its emphasis. The principal difference is that it is a more religious work. The new element in the *Gita* is the ideal of devotion or *bhakti* to the Supreme Lord Ishvara, who turns out to be reincarnated as the charioteer Krishna. The traditional view of the relation between the two is that 'the Upanishads are the cows, Krishna is the milker, Arjuna the calf and the nectar-like *Gita* is the excellent milk'. Some verses in the Upanishads are also found in the *Gita*, in particular those of the *Katha* Upanishad, suggesting that the *Gita* may pre-date that and other of the later principal Upanishads.

Strictly speaking, the *Gita* is not classed by Hinduism with the great Upanishads as *shruti* ('heard') or divinely revealed teaching, but as *smriti* ('remembered'), a lower class of important scripture. Its philosophy is perhaps not quite comparable to the Upanishads for richness and speculative daring, being more dogmatic. Despite this, no Indian philosopher or religious thinker can ignore the *Gita*. The *Bhagavad Gita* is the most influential book in Indian history. T.S. Eliot ranks it, together with Dante's *Divine Comedy*, as one of the two greatest poems ever written, by which he means that they both combine literary greatness with a consistent and systematic philosophy. Leaving aside their relative literary qualities, there is no doubt as to which is the more important as regards philosophy. The *Bhagavad Gita* has lost none of its power to surprise and stimulate, shock and console.

From among the Hindu orthodox philosophies, the most important ones for the *Gita* are the closely allied pair of Sankhya and Yoga. **Kapila** is mentioned in the *Gita* and many important Sankhya concepts including the *gunas* (qualities), *purusha* and *prakriti*, *buddhi*, *ahankara*, and so forth are used. An important early declaration of Krishna's is:

In this world there is a two-fold basis [of devotion]
Taught since ancient times by Me,
O Arjuna:
That of knowledge – the yoga
of the followers of Sankhya
And that of action – the yoga
of the yogins.[6]

III, 3.

According to Radhakrishnan, this should not be taken too literally as an endorsement of the twinned philosophies of *Sankhya Yoga*. 'Sankhya' can mean simply 'knowledge' or 'enumeration' and 'Yoga' is used in many different ways throughout the *Gita*. He would translate this verse less literally

than does Winthrop Sargeant here. Certainly there are significant differences between the classical Sankhya philosophy and that of the *Gita*, above all in their different views of God.

The remaining four other orthodox philosophies are less significant for the *Gita*. The Mimamsa in its preoccupation with ritualism is rejected:

The Vedas are such that their scope
is confined to the three qualities;
Be free from those three qualities;

II, 45.

'Veda' here means the early part of the Veda – the Vedic hymns and the ritualistic Brahmanas – and not the Vedanta or Upanishads. It is not clear whether the founder of Vedanta philosophy, **Badarayana**, is earlier or later than the *Gita*, but of all the six, it is the philosophy closest in spirit to that expressed here, simply because, as we have seen, the *Gita* also draws on Upanishadic thinking.

There are a great many later commentaries on the *Gita*. The commentary by **Shankara** is now regarded as probably the work of a later follower, but even so, the Advaita Vedanta philosophy is one of the important interpretations of the *Bhagavad Gita's* meaning. Its main rival, if we disregard the explicitly religious interpretations as being too extreme, is the Vishishta Advaita of **Ramanuja**. A crux occurs in chapter XII, when Arjuna asks about the relationship between those who worship Krishna as Ishvara or Lord and those who worship Him as Akshara or eternal and unmanifest. This question is vitally important later, because the Advaita view is that *Jnana Yoga* or the 'Way of Knowledge' is the greatest; while the Vishishta Advaita view is that *Bhakti Yoga* or the 'Way of Devotion' is better. Krishna's answer is a model of diplomacy: the devotees are the 'most devoted' and have the easier path:

> But those who honour
> the imperishable,
> the indefinable,
> the unmanifest,
> the all-pervading
> and unthinkable,
> the unchanging,
> the immovable,
> the eternal,
> controlling all the senses,
> even-minded on all sides,
> rejoicing in the welfare
> of all creatures,
> They also attain Me.

XII, 3–4.

The most fundamental message of the *Bhagavad Gita* is not its support for one or other *darshana* or 'view', but the figure of Krishna himself, who embodies better than any other figure in Indian culture the spirit of universal tolerance: 'however men approach me, even so do I welcome them, for the path men take from every side is mine' (IV, 11).

Thus, even someone who worships another god worships Krishna, and even someone who has lived an evil life can reach the Supreme. Of the ways advocated by Krishna, commentators have distinguished three as the most important. These are the way of *karma*, performing action while renouncing the results of the action; the way of *jnana*, that of knowledge; and the way of *bhakti*, that of devotion.

Krishna

NAGARJUNA

c. 150–250 CE

The dates of Nagarjuna's life are hard to determine, but most scholars place him between 50 and 280 CE. The earliest biography is that by the Chinese translator Kumarajiva in 401 CE. His works are known in Chinese, Tibetan and Sanskrit, and although many are undoubtedly the work of others, the historical Nagarjuna certainly wrote two highly important texts, the *Fundamental Middle Way Verses (Mula Madhyamaka Karika)* and *Refutation of the Objections (Vigrahavyavartani)*. As such, he emerges as the first major figure of Mahayana (Greater Vehicle) Buddhism. The fact that Mahayana was a reinterpretation set it apart from the earlier form of Theravada or Hinayana (Lesser Vehicle) Buddhism. These names signify the Mahayanist view that their tradition would be able to carry a far wider populace into the Buddhist community. The Mahayanist School of the Middle Way *(Madhyamika)*, founded by Nagarjuna, takes its name from the idea, central to its teaching, that the **Buddha** treads a 'middle path' between total affirmation and a total denial of certain things. Although Nagarjuna seems to have been earlier than **Vasubandhu**, the central figure in Yogacara, the other main branch of Mahayana Buddhism, philosophically his ideas would seem to be an advance. It may be that Vasubandhu formulated ideas that had been around for many centuries, and that the two systems developed side by side.

Nagarjuna was influenced by the early Mahayana tradition expressed in the Perfection of Wisdom writing, where the idea of *shunyata* or emptiness is explored. He took the idea much further than anyone had before, however, in making it the whole basis of his philosophy.

The *Fundamental Middle Way Verses* are a remarkable document, composed in couplets, setting out a philosophy that is both austere and highly fruitful. Its key concept is *shunyata* ('emptiness'), and Nagarjuna's philosophy is also known as the Shunyavada. *Shunyata* is a famously difficult concept but one certainly worth spending time over to understand. It is variously misunderstood as a denial of the experience of life, or as a metaphysical void, or as some kind of mystical state. It is none of these, but is rather a technical term used to deny the Hindu philosophical concept of *svabhava* ('self-being' or 'self-existence'). The quality of self-existence is, according to most orthodox Indian philosophers, possessed by the Brahman and by the Atman or Inner Self. Some, such as the dualist Sankhya philosophers (see **Kapila**), hold that nature has a similarly self-existent quality, while the followers of **Charvaka** seem to have believed that matter alone possessed self-existence. Generally self-existence implies permanence.

Against this, the Buddha claimed that the Brahman, the Self and nature were not self-existent but *shunyata* (empty). Beneath the web of 'dependent origination, of cause and effect, there is emptiness'. Nagarjuna's verses are aimed at bringing the reader to an understanding of the nature of *shunyata:*

> *For him to whom emptiness is clear,*
> *Everything becomes clear.*
> *For him to whom emptiness*
> *is not clear,*
> *Nothing becomes clear.*[7]

To this end, Nagarjuna uses emptiness to undermine everything, not just worldly things or (as he would see it) Hindu misconceptions, but *dharma*, *sangha* (the Buddhist monastic community) and even the Buddha himself and his teaching. All are said to be empty. Thus, on the authority of the Buddha's teaching, the teaching itself is rendered empty and without a lasting basis. 'There is not the slightest difference between cyclic existence [*samsara*] and *Nirvana*', he writes.

Having shown *shunyata* to be the nature of everything, thereby dismantling the Buddhist teaching, Nagarjuna rebuilds it with his concept that the Buddha taught 'two truths: a truth of worldly convention, and an ultimate truth'. Conventional truth was created by the Buddha out of compassion to help those on the path towards the ultimate truth, but on a realization of the ultimate truth, the conventional was rendered

meaningless. This idea perhaps conflicts with the Buddha's assertion that he had no esoteric teaching, that there was nothing in the 'closed fist of the teacher'. On the other hand, Nagarjuna could argue that the esoteric truth was already present within the exoteric. Although, as some claim, Nagarjuna's tradition may indeed have influenced **Shankara** in his own use of a 'two-truths' theory, this had already been explicitly stated in the Upanishads[8]. In any case, the two-truths view allows Nagarjuna to show that although the principle of emptiness does indeed undermine everything, it provides a meaningful way of looking at concepts such as *Nirvana*. In order to understand the unconditioned reality that *Nirvana* represents, the concept of *Nirvana* itself must be shown to be empty, like all other concepts. Only by understanding emptiness as it really is – the Buddha's higher truth – can the Buddhist come to enlightenment.

The subtlety of Nagarjuna's application of *shunyata* lies in his adherence to the Buddha's principle of *madhyamika* – maintaining a middle course between denial and affirmation. Nagarjuna's 'position' is to take no position. *Shunyata* should not be seen therefore as a negative principle; it neither completely denies nor completely affirms anything. Its denial is of the lower truth only; its affirmation is of the higher truth only, and cannot be applied in the context of lower truth. Its use is analogous to modern mathematicians' use of irrational numbers such as the square root of -1. Though it is impossible to conceive of *shunyata*, it proves to be a practical tool for certain otherwise impossible problems.

Nagarjuna's system is superior in many ways to that of Vasubandhu.

While Vasubandhu maintains that the material world is illusory and that consciousness is the fundamental reality, Nagarjuna calls into question the mind as well. Vasubandhu says that because the physical world is unintelligible, it is unreal. Nagarjuna says that the mind is itself unintelligible, in the sense that we have no way of knowing it, and therefore it is unreal, empty. Paradoxically, it is the very emptiness of everything that makes things possible. Nagarjuna argues that in a perfect, real and eternal universe there would be no possibility of change. All of the Hindu systems and the Yogacara system deal with this by the introduction of an extra element, usually *avidya* (ignorance). In the Sankhya system, it is the stored-up potentiality of the past actions of the eternal souls that restarts the creation and the play of the *prakriti* (nature). This extra residue, like a grain of sand in the oyster, causes the evolution of the universe. Nagarjuna has no need for such an extra element. The universe is empty of self-existence and has only a conditional reality. This is why it is able to change.

The development of Buddhism has been compared to that of British rationalism, moving from the naive realism of Locke, which accepts a common-sense view that the senses give us real information about real things, to the sceptical idealism of Hume, who destroys all certainty. Russell notes that, according to Hume's philosophy, if I believe myself to be a poached egg, all that could be said of this view is that it is a minority one. Nagarjuna's philosophy is open to the same charge. In consistency and rigour, it is second to none, but in terms of practicality and as a system to inspire people to practise Buddhist compassion, it has serious drawbacks.

Nagarjuna's *shunyata* is a way of conceiving of the absolute truth or *Paramartha* of which the Buddha spoke, without reducing the absolute to human terms. To all intents and purposes, *shunyata* is the Brahman of the Upanishads, the ultimate reality that surpasses understanding. As Radhakrishnan says, 'From our point of view, the absolute is nothing. We call it *shunyam*, since no category used in relation to the conditions of the world is adequate to it.' He also quotes Duns Scotus, 'God is not improperly called nothing.' If *shunyata* is God, then what has happened to the atheism of the Buddha? By defining the ultimate reality as *shunyata* in its essence and *Nirvana* in its experience, Buddhism in the end creates a conception of God as nothing short of transcendental and absolute. Nagarjuna's philosophy may be mind-bendingly difficult, but it is faithful to the Buddha's mistrust of metaphysical speculation, unlike the more florid Yogacara and later elaborations such as the Chinese Huayen. It has affinities to later Buddhism and also to Zen, but is much closer to Advaita Vedanta as developed by **Gaudapada** and Shankara, stripped of its dependence on the Hindu scriptures. Understandably, this is a comparison that neither the Madhyamika Buddhists nor the Advaita Vedantins would have enjoyed.

VASUBANDHU
4th or 5h century CE

Mahayana (Great Vehicle) Buddhism, the most widespread and important branch of the religion, is itself divided into two main sub-branches. These are the Madhyamika, the central figure of which is **Nagarjuna**, and the Yogacara of Vasubandhu. The Madhyamika is characterized by its basic doctrine of *shunyata* or emptiness. Yogacara Buddhism, on the other hand, is monistic (meaning that it believes reality to be one) and idealistic (meaning that it believes the one reality to be the mind).

Vasubandhu is a controversial figure because there is some doubt as to whether the historical account refers to a Vasubandhu different from the one that is important to Buddhism. The traditional account given by Paramartha (499–569 CE), which has been questioned but not disproved, is that he was the younger brother of a

Mahayanist called Asanga. Asanga perceived his brother's great abilities and feared that he would use them to attack the Mahayana. He pretended to be ill, and when Vasubandhu returned home to visit him, he used the opportunity to convert him to Mahayanism. Asanga was himself an important thinker, making them one of the very few examples of 'brother philosophers'[9]. Vasubandhu went on to write commentaries on the Mahayana scriptures (he was already credited with a famous commentary on the Hinayana text, the *Abhidharma*), including the Perfection of Wisdom verses[10], the *Garland Sutra*[11], the *Nirvana* and the Vimalakirti. He also wrote a number of important texts expounding his Yogacarin ideas.

As has already been said, Yogacara Buddhism is based on the assumption that the mind is the only true reality. It is thought to have developed out of a criticism of the theories of the two main Hinayana (Lesser Vehicle) schools. The first point of view is that the world we perceive is straightforwardly real, which is called naive realism. That is to say, if I see a tree, what I see is a real thing called a tree. The second school believes that the world we perceive is real, but that we have no direct connection with it through perception. That is to say, there really is a tree, which I infer from my visual impression of a tree, but what I see is a mental image, not the tree itself. Vasubandhu's philosophy is an extension of the second Hinayanist point of view. It is not a great leap from the idea that our perceptions merely relate to external reality, to the view that there is no external reality. Both Hinayanist views are dualistic in that they believe in the reality of both the mind and of the world. Vasubandhu

Vasubandhu with his brother, Asanga.

argues on the other hand for a monistic view in which the only reality is the mind. This is close to the idealism of Berkeley. I may have a perception of an apparent tree, or imagine a tree, or dream of a tree, but there is no tree. Another name for Yogacara is Vijnanavada or 'Idealism'. A simple formulation of its philosophy is that 'the world is entirely intellectual'.

Vasubandhu, like any idealist[12], faces the problem of how to account for the apparent consistency and

*Vasubandhu argues that
we may awake from
ordinary waking consciousness
and see that
the material world
is illusory.*

independence of the material world. Comparison is made between dreams and the waking state: when we awake, we see our dreams to have been illusory. Vasubandhu argues that we may awake from ordinary waking consciousness and see that the material world as we have seen it in our dreams is an illusion. One of the great critics of Buddhism, **Shankara**, points out that when we wake up from a dream we know that it is illusory because we experience the greater reality of the physical waking world. The question that faces Vasubandhu is this: if we wake up from the ordinary world, what is the greater reality that allows us to see that previously we had only dreamt? One solution would be that there is a higher level of consciousness that is ultimately and eternally real, and which reveals the lower levels as merely conditional realities. This is the solution of the Hindu Vedanta philosophy[13]. However, the **Buddha** declared that everything changes, that permanence does not exist. As an alternative, Vasubandhu endows the mind with a complex structure.

Vasubandhu distinguishes eight types of consciousness, the most fundamental of which is the great 'storehouse of consciousness', the *alaya Vijnana*. The *alaya* corresponds to the unconscious of Freudian psychology. In our unenlightened state, we are aware of only a tiny proportion of the storehouse; the rest is totally unconscious. Within its storehouse all knowledge exists, but beyond the reach of ordinary awareness. This serves to explain the operation of *karma*: the consequences of our mental actions are stored in the *alaya*, awaiting the right time to re-emerge. Underlying the *alaya* is the ultimate reality of *tathata*, the true nature. *Alaya* is *tathata*, but with the addition of *avidya*, or ignorance.

Tathata is similar to the idea in the *Mandukya* Upanishad of *prajna*, the undifferentiated consciousness of deep, dreamless sleep. There is pure consciousness without duality, 'one without a second'. The experience of *tathata* is what falsifies the lower consciousness of illusion, *skandha Vijnana*. The practice of Yoga is advocated to cleanse consciousness of its defilement by *skandhas* or elements of illusory existence. When consciousness arises out of its preoccupation with the material world and rests in pure consciousness, without subject or object, then the world of ordinary consciousness, with all of its troubles and suffering, is transcended. The seeds of past actions within *alaya* are then allowed to play themselves out and are not replaced with new ones, liberating the soul from rebirth. *Nirvana* is the state of dwelling in reality and is negatively defined as the cessation of ignorance and false perception.

A good question to ask is whether this theory really provides an alternative to Vedantin metaphysics, or whether it merely conceals the same old answer. In the same way that the

Siddhartha Gautama in meditation.

Aristotelian cosmology adopted by Muslim thinkers sought to finesse the problem of how God creates by proposing a hierarchy of divine agents[14], Vasubandhu's philosophy seems to be based on a non-Buddhist

Brahman or ground for reality, with which the Self or Atman can be united. Radhakrishnan writes that 'the philosophical impulse led the Yogacarins to the Upanishad theory, while the Buddhist presuppositions made them halting in their acceptance of it.' It is only fair to comment that the Buddha's own teaching does not rule out Yogacarin metaphysics. He refused to speculate on metaphysical matters, but hinted at times at an 'unoriginated' ground of existence, a realm to which *Nirvana* promised escape. If we understand the Buddhist critique of self, God and absolute reality to be an attack on our psychological understanding of such concepts, then they in fact are not denied. It is not that there is no self, but that being the self is radically different from thinking about it. Such an interpretation could not be described as orthodox Buddhism, but as discussed in the chapter on Buddha, it seems to be the only philosophically reasonable view.

Ironically for a system which is aimed at bringing us to a state of pure consciousness of nothing at all, the Yogacara philosophy of Vasubandhu has an elaborate complexity which is only hinted at in the foregoing sketch. It foreshadows the still greater complexity of the Chinese Huayen system[15] and is in many ways an admirable psychological picture that foreshadows developments over a thousand years later in the West. But as Vasubandhu says, the very idea that 'all this is perception only' is itself an idea. The final deliverance of Yogacara is to move beyond the ideas presented by its philosophy to the experience of reality.

GAUDAPADA
d. c. 700 CE

The first of the major commentaries on the Upanishads is the *Karika* or Verses of Gaudapada on the *Mandukya* Upanishad. **Shankara** speaks of Gaudapada as his teacher Govindapada's teacher, but he may have died almost two hundred years before Shankara. Not much is known about Gaudapada the man, although it is conjectured that he may at one time have been a Buddhist. Certainly, his thought and language owe much to Buddhist works, although as we will see he adapted them to the Advaita (non-dual) Vedanta philosophy.

Gaudapada was the pioneering example for Shankara's method of furthering philosophy by commentating on the scriptures. Indeed, Shankara wrote a commentary on the *Karika* itself, including it as part of his commentary on the *Mandukya*. The *Karika*, which is written in the *shloka* verse form consisting of sixteen-syllable couplets that is also found in works such as the *Bhagavad Gita*, is the first clear statement of Advaita Vedanta.

One important teaching in Gaudapada's philosophy is *ajata* (non-becoming). Gaudapada denies the idea of creation: the universe is not a play, or the will of Brahman, or a divine illusion, but simply the unchanging nature of Brahman: 'what desire can one have whose desire is always fulfilled?' He is also a proponent of *vivarta* (illusionism). The universe is an illusion born out of ignorance, so vast and entrancing that even the Brahman is apparently taken in. Gaudapada says, 'This is the *maya* [illusion] of that God by which He Himself is deluded'. This surprising statement is one which Gaudapada is compelled to make as a consequence of his radical non-dualism: because there is only one unchanging reality, the person who is suffering from the delusion is, in some sense, the Brahman. Most thinkers after Gaudapada have regarded this as too extreme. Radhakrishnan in *Indian Philosophy* sums up this very criticism by Gaudapada when he says:

The theory which has nothing better to say than that an unreal soul is trying to escape from an unreal bondage in an unreal world to accomplish an unreal supreme good, may itself be unreality.

Shankara's explanation is that the delusion of the Brahman is only an apparent one: the most important illusion is not the *maya*, but the illusion that He is in fact fooled by it. In this he departs from the view of Gaudapada.

It is interesting that Gaudapada should have chosen the *Mandukya* Upanishad as the basis of his commentary. Among all the classical Upanishads the *Mandukya* is the most purely abstract, its twelve short verses encapsulating a philosophy of static, eternal majesty in which the entire universe is the primal sound AUM, which is Brahman. By contemplating this single word, the aspirant may attain enlightenment. A poetic translation of *Mandukya* is 'the frog', because with three jumps, a frog can go from the parching heat of the day (representing the illusion of life) to the cool deeps of the water (representing the peace and joy of knowledge). These three jumps are the three letters of AUM, representing respectively the states of waking, dreaming (or thinking) and deep sleep. Understanding any one of these brings great benefits; understanding the Primal Word in full brings liberation, which corresponds to a fourth state known as *Turiya*. The Upanishad represents a kind of auditory equivalent to Plato's great vision of the universe from beyond time in the Timaeus. It is worth noting that in the Eastern tradition, we do not find such a preponderance of visual metaphors for knowledge as in the West. The *Mandukya* Upanishad is one of the key texts expounding the Hindu idea of God not as light (*jyotir*) but as sound (*shabda*).

The short Upanishadic text is the basis for Gaudapada's *Karika*, which, although concise and pithy, is almost twenty times as long. In fact, only the first chapter is a direct commentary, the remainder being a remarkably clear and readable exposition of early Advaita Vedanta. The fourth and longest chapter, consisting of 100 *shloka* verses, is entitled *Alatashantiprakarana,* which means 'Quenching the Firebrand'. This is a common Buddhist illustration: just as a firebrand moving in the dark appears as an arc, so consciousness appears to vibrate between subject and object. When realization of the truth occurs, all objects disappear and consciousness shines by itself, illuminating nothing as there is nothing other than itself to illuminate. Arriving at this state, the individual should pretend to still be ignorant, but will naturally live modestly and with restraint. Gaudapada argues throughout the *Karika* that the waking and dreaming states are equally illusory: when we are awake, we see things that we cease to see when asleep, and vice versa. Because Gaudapada holds reality to be permanent and unchanging, this demonstrates their illusory nature.

In the closing *karikas*, Gaudapada makes repeated use of the word '**buddha**' meaning 'awakened', finally stating:

The knowledge of the awakened man [a 'buddha'], who is all-pervasive, does not extend to objects; neither do individual souls reach out to objects. This view was not expressed by the Buddha.

Gaudapada has throughout the *Karika* made frequent use of Buddhist terminology and arguments. Here, in the penultimate verse, he protests that his philosophy is not Buddhism. Just as the **Buddha** questioned Hindu terminology (for example, he compared a 'true Brahmin' who showed fine qualities to one who was merely born into a Brahmin family), Gaudapada contrasts a true buddha or 'Awakened One' with the historical Buddha whose knowledge, he implies, was incomplete. In Gaudapada's view, the knowledge of one who is awakened is of the self, the subject, as opposed to objects. The emptiness expounded by Buddhists such as **Nagarjuna** finds its parallel in Gaudapada's negation of objective reality. But whereas the Buddha declined to discuss the nature of *Nirvana*, Gaudapada states that it consists in a consciousness that corresponds to reality, that is, an awareness that no longer reaches out to illusory objects but which rests in the contemplation of itself: in his words, 'a knowledge comparable to infinite space'.

write commentaries on Vedantic literature, most notably on some of the Upanishads and the *Brahma Sutra* of **Badarayana**. Other than this, his *oeuvre* is extremely doubtful: a vast literature is credited to Shankara, but modern scholarship based on linguistic research regards much of it as being the later work of others. His successors at four monasteries in India over the past 1,200 years are known as *Shankaracharyas* (Shankara Teachers) which, added to the relative disregard in India for historical dates and persons, perhaps explains the great bulk of Shankarist works. Among

SHANKARA
c. 700–750 CE

*'Brahman is truth,
the world
is untruth,
the individual self
is not different
from the
Brahman.'*

Shankara was born, according to tradition, in the south Indian region of Kerala. One tradition dates his birth to 788 CE, but some experts now believe he was born almost a century earlier. As a teenager, he is said to have resolved, despite his mother's opposition, to become a Sannyasin monk. He travelled to Badrinath, where he became the disciple of a sage called Govindapada. Not much is known about Govindapada, but he certainly was a follower in the tradition of **Gaudapada**, who wrote the first known Upanishadic commentary, his *Karika*, on the *Mandukya* Upanishad. Following the example of Gaudapada, Shankara proceeded to

the questionable texts are his commentary on the *Bhagavad Gita*, his *Vivekacudamani* (Crest Jewel of Wisdom) and many devotional hymns. Leaving apocryphal texts aside, a philosophy of greater clarity emerges.

Shankara lived in a time of flux for Indian culture. Of the unorthodox systems, Jainism seems to have been at its height, while Buddhism, as reported by a Chinese visitor of the time, was in obvious decline. Of the orthodox systems, Mimamsa, with its emphasis on ritual, failed to satisfy either emotionally or intellectually. Brahmanism, the old religion based upon the Veda, was beginning to give way to Hinduism as we know it today, with the rise of Shivaism (worship of Shiva), Vaishnavism (worship of Vishnu), Shaktaism (goddess worship) and of a thriving culture of temple worship. Shankara's aim was to revive the study of the Vedanta or

Shiva the Destroyer, the most powerful god of the Hindu pantheon and one of the godheads in the Hindu Trinity.

Upanishads, founded by Badarayana and continued by Gaudapada, and to steer Indian culture away from the influence of the later works such as the Puranas. At the same time it would be totally wrong to regard Shankara

as an opponent of tradition. His view of the Indian orthodox religion of the earlier part of the Veda is the same as that expressed in the Upanishads: profound respect, mingled with a far greater respect for pure philosophy.

Shankara's philosophy purports to be no more than a transmission of that of the Upanishads, the Vedanta. This is, in one sense, perfectly true. Radhakrishnan in *Indian Philosophy* quotes Jacob, 'It may be admitted that if the impossible task of reconciling the contradictions of the Upanishads and reducing them to a harmonious and consistent whole is to be attempted at all, Shankara's system is about the only one that could do it.' It is not that Advaita Vedanta is the philosophy of the Upanishads, but that it is the most consistent philosophy that could be derived from them. The only serious rival to this claim is the view of Ramanuja, whose Vishishta-Advaita or 'Qualified Non-Dualism' emphasizes the devotional and theistic elements in the Upanishads. Most scholars regard Ramanuja's view, examined in the next chapter, to be a valid extrapolation of the Upanishads, but closer still to that of the *Bhagavad Gita*. Although Shankara's philosophy owes something to the Madhyamika Buddhism of Nagarjuna, his debt is far less than that of Gaudapada. The charge that Advaita philosophy is 'purified Buddhism' or 'secret Buddhism' is not simply justified in Shankara's case. Both Buddhism and Advaita bear strong resemblances to the Upanishads, but Shankara's link to the wider Hindu culture is strong and genuine.

The central tenet of Shankara's system, Advaita, means literally 'not-two' or 'non-duality'. 'Advaita Vedanta', the name of his philosophy, therefore means the non-dualistic interpretation of the Vedantic tradition. Advaita Vedanta has been hugely influential down to the present day and has in the past two centuries assumed a pre-eminent position in India, partly due to its adoption by Western thinkers. This fact tends to obscure the existence of alternative forms of Vedanta and of the other Indian philosophies. The power and appeal of Advaita Vedanta principally arises from the clarity of its essential doctrine. It depends on a handful of pithy statements, all of which are taken from the Upanishads. The positive aspect is *'sa atma tat tvam asi'* ('you [Brahman] are that self') or *'aham Brahmasmi'* ('I am the Brahman'); the negative is *'neti, neti'* ('not this, not that'), meaning that nothing that is experienced is the Brahman. Shankara's genius was to apply these ideas rigorously. His doctrine can be summarized in the sentence *'Brahma satyam, jagan mithya, jivo Brahmaiva naparah'* ('Brahman is truth, the world is untruth, the individual self is not different from the Brahman.'). A story told of Shankara as a boy communicates something of the attractive drama of Advaita Vedanta. Some boys were arguing over how many seeds were in a melon. Shankara said that the number of seeds in this melon was equal to the number of gods that created the universe. When the melon was cut open, it was found to contain only one seed.

From Gaudapada, Shankara took the idea of *vivarta* or illusionism, the idea that all of apparent existence is an illusion (*maya*) or dream founded on ignorance. He also made use of Gaudapada's concept of a higher and a lower level of truth or knowledge.

Shankara does develop this scheme, however, distinguishing three levels: lowest of all is the world of illusion, as when we mistake a coil of rope for a snake; next is the world of everyday appearance, as when we recognize the rope for what it is; finally, there is the ultimate reality of the Brahman. Shankara's view is that with the recognition of a higher level of truth, the lower level is totally cancelled out or sublated (*badha*). This means not only that an error has been corrected, but also that the reality of the previous, lower truth is utterly rejected in favour of the latter, new truth. The dramatic shift between each of the three levels of reality is altogether more radical than is found, for example, in Plato's four-level reality in *The Republic*. Whereas for Plato a physical body's shadow or reflection tells us something about the appearance of that body, and the body in turn is a 'shadow' of its 'form' or 'idea', for Shankara there is no such relationship. A lower level may indeed lead on to a higher, but when the higher is manifest, the lower is discarded. The classic example of a rope that is mistaken for a snake is useful in illustrating this. When the rope is seen as it is, the fear and ideas associated with a snake are of no further use. In just this way, we are to understand the realization of the non-dualistic nature of the Brahman and of the *jiva* or individual soul. Following the recognition of the reality, there is no reference back to the knowledge of the apparent duality that preceded and led up to it.

The evidence that Shankara's work includes a number of interpolations by other Shankara Teachers serves to clarify certain issues. The details of this controversy are beyond the scope of this introduction, but just to give you an example, in the commentary on the *Isha* Upanishad 'Shankara' imports an additional negative 'a-' into verse 14, blandly remarking that this meaning fits better with his interpretation. A subsequent commentator from a rival tradition remarks sarcastically, and with some justification, on his 'unprecedented skill in grammar'. The general view of the original Shankara's scholarship is that it is generally careful and accurate, as well as characterized by a vision and subtlety unrivalled in Indian thought. Shankara's commentaries are an impressive achievement, and were a benchmark against which subsequent Vedanta thinkers tested their mettle.

Shankara is also said to have travelled extensively in India. He seems to have focused his initial efforts on rural areas as the cities were strongholds of rival philosophies. His commentaries reflect this, being punctuated with semi-dramatized debates between Shankara and an objector, and there are many stories about Shankara taking on and defeating local pundits, who by tradition, were then bound to become his disciples. This custom gave Shankara, who was a supreme debater, the opportunity to spread his doctrines across India. His most famous victory in debate won him his greatest disciple and interpreter, Sureshvara, who was then appointed as the head of a monastery or *ashram* that he founded at Sringeri. Shankara's work in founding monasteries was socially important because it satisfied the need of those Hindus wishing to

Shankara surrounded by his disciples.

retreat from the world. Again, many people with this inclination would previously have been drawn towards Buddhism. He went on to found similar monasteries at Puri, Dvaraka and Joshimath. These four centres still exist today, led by sages known as *Shankaracaryas* (Shankara himself is

> *By rooting his philosophy*
> *in the Vedic tradition,*
> *Shankara was able to exert*
> *a much broader*
> *and deeper influence,*
> *emotionally, intellectually*
> *and politically than*
> *would otherwise have*
> *been possible.*

sometimes known as *adi* Shankara, the first Shankara) who are acclaimed as Jagadgurus or 'World Teachers'.

At this point, it is worth mentioning Shankara's contemporary, Bhaskara, who was concerned with re-establishing the importance of the traditional Brahminical *dharma* or rule of life against the potentially corrosive otherworldly Advaita. Bhaskara was the greatest proponent of the philosophy known as Bhedabheda: the view that God is both divided, in manifesting in the world, and non-divided. The analogy is with the waves of the ocean, which are real, although part of a greater reality (i.e. the ocean). If the world is an aspect of God, rather than an illusion founded on ignorance, then our behaviour in it is highly significant. Shankara was able to defeat this doctrine on both logical and theological grounds, but it is an interesting

precursor to the challenge of **Ramanuja** some three centuries later. Advaita Vedanta is, as outlined by Shankara, essentially concerned with *jnana* (knowledge). Although Shankara's achievements included the restoration of Hindu culture and religion to a central place in India, his doctrines are intellectually based. Those for whom the two alternative paths of *karma* (action) or especially *bhakti* (devotion) held greater attraction would never be fully satisfied by Shankara's philosophy.

It is possible to make the criticism that Shankara's philosophy has no need of its reliance on scripture. If there is only one self, identical with Brahman, it seems absurd to regard knowledge of the Upanishads as essential to its self-realization. The self is not a historical concept. It is likely, however, that the importance Shankara places on scripture is part of his overall aim to absorb and build on tradition rather than to emphasize his own importance. In any case, its effect was to inspire a revival of Indian thought through the genuine study of its key texts. By rooting his philosophy in the Vedic tradition, Shankara was able to exert a much broader and deeper influence, emotionally, intellectually and politically than would otherwise have been possible.

This may be behind the legend of Shankara as we find him within the Shankarist tradition, as a kind of Hindu Renaissance man. More religious than the devotee, more intellectual than the scholar and more heroic than the greatest Hindu generals, Shankara's symbolic significance belies the traditional 32 years of his life. Radhakrishnan's comment that 'in a few years, Shankara practised several careers, each enough to satisfy an ordinary man' has to be taken in the context of later studies that have revealed the extent of confusion about whether a particular '*Shankaracharya*' is Adi ('the first') Shankara or not. The Shankarist tradition became synonymous with the re-establishment of Hinduism as the central faith and philosophy of India, which took place in succeeding centuries. Thus Shankara, as its figurehead, is supposed to have been a military leader when necessary, defeating enemies who could not be won over by reason. There

'Love is greater than law.'

are many legends surrounding Shankara, including a number of miracles associated with him from boyhood onwards, indicating his dual significance, both as philosopher and as religious figure. Although it is difficult to know what truth there is in such stories, some do seem to provide a useful indication of his significance to India. The most common traditional story told about Shankara has the ring of authenticity. Although a Sannyasin and therefore bound to observe the principle of non-attachment to other beings, Shankara returned to his mother's house in the last days of her life and, after her death, built and lit her funeral fire. In this, too, he violated Sannyasin code, which forbade the kindling of fire. One of Shankara's twentieth-century successors, Shantananda Saraswati, related that when challenged by the local orthodox pundits Shankara replied simply, 'Love is greater than law'. In another story Shankara met with a Chandala (Untouchable) in the street, from whom he drew back.

The Chandala accused him of failure to adhere to his own principles of non-duality, whereupon Shankara composed a hymn with the refrain, 'He who has learnt to look on phenomena in the light of Advaita is my true Guru, be he a Chandala or be he a Brahmin.' Advaita Vedanta does not in itself have a socially radical import, but the idea of there being one Self that is also Brahman is clearly erosive of rigid caste boundaries. This was certainly a legacy of **Ramanuja** and **Madhva**, each of whom developed versions of Vedanta with more explicit ethical concern.

The tradition of *Shankaracharyas* has added much over the centuries to what is certainly there in Shankara himself. It is difficult to trace a historical development of Shankarism, but it today includes a substantial ethical element as well as a devotionalism akin to that of **Ramanuja**. It would be wrong to suppose, however, that Adi Shankara, the first Shankara, has been entirely hidden by the hagiographers and the later *Shankaracharyas*. His essential doctrine of Advaita, shorn of its religious trappings, has in the past two centuries established itself both as the principal philosophy within India, and as India's main philosophical export other than Buddhism. Its influence on the West has been particularly marked.

RAMANUJA
c. 1017–1137 CE

Ramanuja took **Shankara's** Advaita Vedanta or non-dualism in a theistic direction. In this he was influenced by his upbringing in the Tamil tradition of devotional hymns to the god Vishnu, in particular those of the Alvar Saints. Ramanuja's life is known to us only through his hagiographers, but legend has it he was born into a pious Brahmana family and studied with Yadvaprakasha, a Shankarist teacher. His brilliance was evident from early on in several instances where he challenged his teacher's interpretations, to the point where he eventually broke with him. Ramanuja's questioning was, however, based on the deeply reverential love that he felt for Vishnu, of whom he

subsequently had a vision. Ramanuja became a temple priest at Kancipuram and was summoned by Yamuna, the great Vaishnavite teacher himself, then on his deathbed, to be his successor at Srirangam. Ramanuja is also said to have made a 20-year pilgrimage around India in which he displayed his matchless debating skills against different opponents. He converted King Bittideva at Mysore to Vaishnavism (worship of Vishnu), which increased his influence manifold. On his return, he continued his work, establishing 74 monastic centres before dying, according to tradition, at the age of 120.

Ramanuja succeeded in founding a new and powerful form of Vedanta philosophy, Vishishta Advaita, which built on Advaita's strength while making room for a warmer and more devotional approach. The main problem of philosophy for Ramanuja is not ignorance, as with the more intellectual schools, but unbelief. He disputed with the logical tradition of the Nyaya philosophers (see **Gautama**), for whom the divine is reached through reasoning. Wishing to strengthen the essence of faith, Ramanuja systematically attacked arguments which attempted to prove the existence of God. By demolishing such proofs, Ramanuja established his view that Brahman transcends all human reason. The parallels with Christian belief are evident, although Ramanuja's arguments intriguingly foreshadow modern Western rationalist philosophy.

His greatest influence, and also in some ways, his greatest adversary, is Shankara. Ramanuja wanted to establish a philosophy centred not on knowledge, as in Shankara, but on devotion. According to Ramanuja's view, the paths of *Karma Yoga* (the 'Way of Action') and *Jnana Yoga* (the

'Way of Knowledge') are merely preparations for *Bhakti Yoga* (the 'Way of Devotion'). This may seem like a scholastic quibble, but its implications are important and fascinating and will be considered in more detail below. The intellectual underpinning that Ramanuja lent to **Bhakti** has been very influential in Indian philosophy. The key to this is his conception of God, not as the infinite transcendent **Nirguna** ('without qualities') Brahman, but as the manifest **Saguna** ('with qualities') Brahman. The qualities of Brahman are principally knowledge, consciousness and bliss, and these are identified in

Ramanuja with the personal God, specifically Vishnu, the sustainer, whose *avatars* include Rama and Krishna. Vishnu and Siva are the two personifications of God that have traditionally attracted the most worshippers in India.

Vishishta Advaita means literally 'qualified non-duality'. Ramanuja holds that there are three orders of existence: God, soul and matter. He adopted this idea from Bhartriprapanca, a philosopher older than Shankara. Ramanuja holds that at the level of God, everything is God and there is no other, but at the lower orders, the substance of God is 'qualified'. The analogy is with the soul

Rama (pictured), the seventh incarnation of Lord Vishnu, was said to have taken birth on earth in order to annihilate the evil forces of the age.

and the body: the body is said to be the servant of the soul, and to have no reality separate from it, and yet it retains its own character as a body. Another important aspect of Vishishta Advaita is that it attributes reality to the world. In this he follows Bhaskara, a younger contemporary of Shankara, who promulgated the view that God was both divided and non-divided (*bhedabheda*), just as the waves of the ocean are real, although part of a greater reality (i.e. the ocean). Shankara had attacked *bhedabheda* on logical grounds, pointing out that it ascribed mutually contradictory attributes to the same thing. Ramanuja resolved this and other problems with *bhedabheda* by arguing that reality does not necessitate independence. The souls are real but their existence is dependent on God; they are its body. Similarly, the material universe is also real, though dependent. It is important to recognize that there is no duality (as in the Sankhya philosophy – see chapter on **Kapila**) or multiplicity (as in the Vedanta of **Madhva**) in Ramanuja's teaching. He must make room for a kind of subject-object relationship in order to satisfy the need for worship, but his theories adapt non-dualism rather than shatter it. Ramanuja allows for the possibility of release through unity as described by Advaita, but gives it a secondary position to the pure joy of adoring God in heaven, which is true *moksha* or liberation.

Ramanuja's philosophy developed through his commentary on and re-interpretation of the traditional Vedanta texts including the Upanishads, the *Brahma Sutras* and, late in life, the *Bhagavad Gita*. The *Vedarthasangraha* established Ramanuja's philosophy with its closely argued examination of apparently contradictory statements in the Upanishads. Ramanuja argued that

only Vishishta Advaita could make sense of these contradictions. The most important of Ramanuja's commentaries is, however, that on the *Bhagavad Gita*. Despite the difficulty of dating Hindu works, it is certain that the *Gita* adds something new to what is already present in both the ritual religion of the Veda and the philosophy of the Upanishads. That new element is *bhakti* or devotion. If it was Shankara's genius to perceive the importance of non-dualism for the Upanishads, it was Ramanuja's to expand on the devotionalism of the *Gita*.

Ramanuja's interpretation of the *Gita* is that it puts forward a vision of devotion to the Lord (in this case, Krishna) that is a higher ideal than the self-realization (*atma jnana*) of pure Shankarism. Brahman is not the Supreme Lord, but is the *atmatattva*, the 'soul-stuff' which is the true nature of a human being. When a human soul realizes its identity with the Brahman, it becomes purified of its association with lower things, such as the body and the individual ego. This stage, which is the highest ideal for Advaita, is merely preparatory for Vishishta Advaita. The soul then becomes fit for the divine vision of the Lord, with whom it has a 'supreme likeness' in the words of the *Mundaka* Upanishad. The love of the soul for God and of God for the soul becomes a self-perpetuating and blissful union, which is the highest heaven. Indeed, Ramanuja regards self-realization as a slightly dangerous aim for the average person, who he advises 'to engage in actions without regard for their fruits: let him forget about self-realization if he would reach his goal[16]. Ramanuja's analysis of the *Gita* is a powerful and persuasive one, and is regarded by many scholars as the closest to the intention of its unknown author. It relates self-realization to the Sankhya and Yoga philosophies (see chapters on **Kapila** and **Patanjali**), in which the aim is to separate the conscious element in man from the unconscious or natural part, as well as to Vedanta. Ramanuja was able to demonstrate that devotion to *Saguna* or manifested Brahman was not of lesser importance, as Shankara had argued, but the final aim of philosophy and religion. His philosophy incorporated the insights of his predecessors and overlaid them with the devotionalism of his Tamil homeland.

Ramanuja is generally thought to be the most credible opponent of Shankara. His system is analogous to the mysticism of the Sufis, which like his is devotional and religious in direction[17]. There is justification for regarding it as the counterpart of Advaita Vedanta: while Shankara eliminates

from his system all that is not absolute Brahman, Ramanuja builds towards a conception of **Ishvara** (the Lord) through an appreciation of his divine qualities. Both approaches are validated by different aspects of the tradition that also includes the Upanishads.

Ramanuja's influence in India today can most clearly be seen not in philosophy but in religious organization. The Hinduist Shri Vaishnavism (Devotees of Lord Vishnu) sect, inspired by his teachings, is still the largest. It derives much of its popularity from Ramanuja's assertion that anyone, regardless of caste, can reach Vishnu. This statement alone represents a significant contribution, as traditionally the lowest Shudra caste was barred from many religious activities. The two main centres of Sri Vaishnavism in India are at Srirangam in the South and at Tirupati in the North.

Lord Vishnu

MADHVA
1197–1276 CE

Increasingly the most prominent of Hindu philosophical systems, as well as another branch of Vedanta, Dvaita Vedanta was created by Madhva in the thirteenth century. His position is in many ways opposed and antithetical to that of **Shankara**, so instead of Advaita Vedanta, we have the doctrine popularly known as Dvaita Vedanta, the doctrine of duality. Madhva (also known as Ananda Tirtha) was acclaimed even while alive as a divine incarnation sent to combat the evil incarnated by Shankara and his allegedly deceptive teaching. Madhva's life story, as traditionally narrated, also contains many parallels with that of Jesus, including miracles such as walking on water and feeding the hunger of a multitude with loaves and fishes. This is probably due to Christian influences in Southern India.

The Upanishads contain several key statements generally thought to confirm non-duality. Madhva held the Upanishads to be revealed truth, and yet espoused an opposite view. To do this, he interpreted the Upanishads in a new, very unorthodox way. In the chapter on Shankara, we saw how he did not hesitate to propose alterations to the received Upanishadic text in order to support his own viewpoint. Madhva, perhaps following in his adversary's footsteps, used similar techniques to reverse the meaning of key statements in the Upanishads. For example, *'Sa atma tat tvam asi'*, 'You [the Brahman] are that self', becomes 'You are not that self'. Madhva claims that a negative prefix 'a-' is hidden in the statement, which is not grammatically impossible. The resulting argument is just about feasible but not widely accepted.

However, from a philosophical point of view, the question of correct interpretation is perhaps less important than the reasons behind Madhva's approach. His system is more complex than mere duality and the term Dvaita Vedanta is, though convenient, somewhat misleading. Madhva's followers today prefer the term *Tattva-vada*, which means, more or less, 'Reality-ism', but a more precise term is *Bheda-vada,* or 'Difference-ism'. Madhva's essential doctrine of differences is that God (identified with Vishnu), the Self and matter are real, separate and different. In addition, there are multitudes of selves and multitudes of material objects, all different and separate. Only

Vishnu is independently real, however, while all other things depend on him for their existence. Much of Madhva's thinking is drawn from the Sankhya philosophy (see chapter on **Kapila**). Vishnu is the efficient cause of the

Lakshmi, Vishnu's consort, is the goddess of wealth and of prosperity, both material and spiritual.

world, but its material cause is nature or *prakriti*, identified with Vishnu's consort Lakshmi. Vishnu's contact with Lakshmi animates the world and sets into motion the three *gunas* or qualities.

Another influence on Madhva is thought to have been the arrival of Christianity in India. It is widely acknowledged that St Thomas, one of the Apostles, travelled to the subcontinent and founded a mission that was still influential in southern India in Madhva's time. Because of the tolerance shown by Indian culture for

doctrinal heterodoxy, Christianity was allowed to co-exist alongside as well as influence Hinduism over hundreds of years, although interestingly, conversion has never been a large-scale phenomenon. Western readers will easily recognize in Madhva's cosmology millions of souls, fashioned from common matter but presided over by a transcendental God – echoes of Christianity, even if it had its beginnings in Sankhya. Intriguingly Madhva also posits a version of predestination that is similar to that developed by John Calvin in sixteenth-century Europe, although for different reasons. It is part of the Sankhya system that at the beginning of a cycle of creation souls start with a certain karmic disposition. Creation is set in motion by the Lord as a mechanism for the playing out of these dispositions. Madhva's view of souls as particular individuals causes him to imagine their several fates. Some are fated to find liberation from the cycle of *karma* through union with Vishnu in Heaven. Others will continue to follow the path of birth, death and rebirth, which is his version of Purgatory. Others still (and here we find Western influence, as he differs from all other Indian thinkers) are destined for eternal suffering and damnation. This vision of the universe is highly mechanistic and demonstrates parallels with some of the Western philosophies that emerged with the rise of science. Commentators have noted that it paradoxically weakens the power of God, who is reduced to a superintendent-like role by the requirement of *karma* to play itself out in individual souls. Like **Ramanuja**, Madhva argued that devotion and not the scriptures was the only true route to God, but he was less antagonistic to logic and provided several proofs for his existence.

VIVEKANANDA
1863–1902

It is only over the last 200 years that Indian thought has been widely available to the West. The most immediately attractive forms, namely Buddhism and Advaita Vedanta, were also the most sophisticated. This book is not the place to review the impact of the translations of Indian texts on late eighteenth- and nineteenth-century European cultures. Suffice it to say that practically every major figure in philosophy and the arts, who was active between 1790 and 1850, was an enthusiastic reader of the Upanishads, the Buddhist canon and Sanskrit literature in translation. The work of German philosopher Schopenhauer, to take one example, has even been described as a popular version of Buddhism. This trend continued well into the twentieth century through figures like the poets T.S. Eliot and W.B. Yeats. What could

be regarded as the first wave of Indian influence has now considerably abated: contemporary philosophers, novelists and poets no longer quote the Upanishads. The second wave, which spread its influence more widely through society, came with the arrival in the West of a number of authentic teachers from different Indian traditions. The first, and perhaps most dramatic of these visitors, was Swami Vivekananda.

The scene for Vivekananda's appearance was the World's Parliament of Religions in Chicago in 1893. At the age of 30, Vivekananda took to the stage as the Hindu representative and electrified his audience with an account of Advaita Vedanta. A newspaper account of the day called him 'an orator by divine right and undoubtedly the greatest figure at the Parliament.' Vivekananda had only uttered the words 'Sisters and Brothers of America' when he was drowned out by a two-minute ovation, a reception not given to previous speakers from the Greek Orthodox, Confucian, Buddhist and reformist Hindu Brahmo Samaj speakers. He continued thus:

It fills my heart with joy
unspeakable to rise in response
to the warm and cordial welcome
which you have given us. I thank
you in the name of the most
ancient order of monks
in the world. I thank you in the
name of the mother of religions,
and I thank you in the name of
millions and millions of Hindu
people of all classes and sects.

Vivekananda's message, however, was obviously not just about the greatness of his own tradition:

*The present convention, which is
one of the most august assemblies
ever held, is in itself a vindication,
a declaration to the world of the
wonderful doctrine preached in the
Gita: 'Whosoever comes to Me,
through whatsoever form, I reach
them; all are struggling through
paths which in the end lead to Me.'*

Vivekananda's statement that 'all religions are true' seemed to encapsulate the very spirit of the conference. His powerful oratory skills and spiritual depth had an intensity that went far beyond the rhetoric of watery ecumenism. Vivekananda's personality and ideas entranced America. On the one hand, he was a highly educated and talented individual, well versed in Western and Eastern thought, acclaimed by a British professor as the most brilliant student he had ever met. On the other, he was the favourite disciple of Ramakrishna, the extraordinary Hindu saint who died in 1886. These two aspects were reflected in the name chosen for Narendranath Datta (his real name) before he left for America. Vivekananda means 'the bliss of *viveka* (reason)'. The combination of intellect and genuine spiritual experience enabled Vivekananda to deliver a message that resonated widely with audiences: 'only the man who has actually perceived God is religious...religion is not in books and temples. It is in actual perception'. After the Parliament, he agreed to conduct a lecture tour of the United States, taking to the same gruelling round of lectures in cities and one-horse towns that entertained figures such as Dickens and Wilde.

Having travelled in the West, he returned to a hero's welcome in India. His health was undermined by exhaustion, however, and except for one brief visit to America to open some centres devoted to the study of Vedanta and Ramakrishna, he remained in India, returning to the austere life of an ascetic monk. The Ramakrishna and Vedanta societies he founded still thrive today, complemented by many other organizations dedicated to the understanding and study of Advaita.

The Advaita Vedanta philosophy promoted so successfully by Vivekanand is covered more fully in other chapters so we will not consider it in any great detail here. It is worth noting, however, the particular emphasis given to Advaita, reinterpreting it for the modern era. According to Vivekananda, there are two sources of knowledge: science and the Veda. Science is the knowledge arrived at through the senses, while the Veda is 'that which is known through the subtle, supersensuous power of Yoga'. The Veda is normally regarded as the collection of hymns, rituals and Upanishadic philosophy on which Indian thought is founded. Here Vivekananda posits a higher, transcendent Veda, analogous to Islamic notions of the Quran and to the Word or *logos* of Greek philosophy. This transcendent Veda is reflected, above all, in the Vedanta or Upanishads. This is *Sanatana Dharma* or Eternal Religion. Thus Vivekananda succeeds in articulating a vision of Hinduism that is both loyal to its own spirit and answerable to the need for a global spiritual faith.

MOHANDAS GANDHI
1869–1948

Gandhi was born in Porbandar, Gujarat, into a political family with deep religious convictions, both Hindu and Jain. His father was prime minister of Porbandar. Gandhi was married at the age of 13 and was sent to England at 19 to complete his education and train as a barrister. He returned three years later in 1891 but was unable to find work in India. In 1893, he accepted a one-year post at an Indian law practice in Natal, South Africa. Gandhi's experience of racial oppression there inspired him to pursue political activity and the development of *satyagraha*, his personal technique of non-violent protest, literally 'holding on to truth'. Gandhi distinguished *satyagraha* from passive resistance, as practised by activists

such as the English suffragettes, because unlike them, he rejected all violence. He stayed in Natal until 1913, when he returned to India. At that time, India was under the Raj or British rule. The injustice of a piece of British legislation moved Gandhi to take to the political stage once more. He dedicated the rest of his life to political struggle and to *swaraj* or self-rule, the cause of Indian independence. The movement was finally successful, but Gandhi fell victim to the deep divisions between Hindus and Muslims and was assassinated by a Hindu fundamentalist in New Delhi in 1948.

Members of Gandhi's ashram *gather around his body after his assassination.*

Gandhi's work as a political activist was deeply infused with religion and philosophy. As has already been indicated, there were both Hindu and Jain influences in his upbringing. His Hinduism was essentially that of Advaita Vedanta, the non-dualist philosophy perfected by **Shankara** and which came to be the predominant form of Indian thought. Gandhi's Advaita emphasized truth (*satya*) as opposed to Brahman, perhaps because it carried less sectarian associations. His Truth carries essentially the same meaning: 'Truth alone is eternal, everything else is momentary'. The motto adopted by

Gandhi lying in state after his shocking assassination. The violent manner of his death was in stark contrast to his peace-loving philosophy.

India after Independence shows this influence: *'Satyam eva jayate'* (Truth alone conquers)[18]. Gandhi added Jain ethics to Advaitin philosophy, especially the principle of *ahingsa*, ('harmlessness' or 'non-violence') or, as he sometimes translated it, 'Love'. Gandhi taught that Love, Truth and God are interchangeable terms and developed techniques to resist oppression that involved arousing compassion in the oppressor by the acceptance of suffering. Gandhi's assumption was that love, being more fundamental than injustice, would eventually win.

Essential to Gandhi's work was his personal asceticism, which included the practice of poverty, chastity and spiritual endeavour to cleanse the individual of any impurities associated with egotism. Gandhi believed that the best way to promote a philosophy was to be the living example of it. The lofty ideals of Gandhian philosophy would be impossible if the *satyagrahi*, its practitioners, were subject to fear and personal concern. Imprisonment, abuse and physical suffering could hold no terror for one who had conquered himself.

Another crucial principle for Gandhi was *sarvodaya* ('the good of all'). Like **Vivekananda**, Gandhi was aware of, and rejected, the Western nineteenth-century philosophy of utilitarianism. Utilitarianism is based on the assumption that to do good to one involves the deprivation of another. Its highest ideal is the happiness of the greatest number, defined materially. For Gandhi, this is an impoverished and 'heartless' philosophy because 'in order to achieve the supposed good of fifty-one percent, the interest of forty-nine percent...should be sacrificed'. *Sarvodaya* demands a more creative and compassionate form of accounting for personal happiness. Whilst including material prosperity, it is primarily concerned with self-realization. Gandhi founded several *ashrams* or spiritual centres to pursue

Gandhi sitting in his home weaving.

the ideals of *sarvodaya*. Politically, it inspired Gandhi 'to wipe every tear from every eye'. It led him to oppose discrimination of all kinds, whether based on race, sex, religion or caste. So, for example, although Gandhi upheld traditional gender roles, he believed that women should be accorded equal honour and respect. Again, Gandhi fought for the rights of the lowest castes, the Untouchables in particular, whom he lovingly called the *Harijan* or 'Children of God'. Again, *sarvodaya* draws on a wide range of Indian ethical traditions, including the universal compassion of Buddhism.

Gandhi's politics and economics were inspired by his philosophy and vice versa. He rejected the welfare state as an assault on the dignity of every individual's ability to be responsible for themselves. For Gandhi, the state should intervene very little in the lives of the people, but should create conditions for local self-government. The symbol he adopted to represent his ideal of village life was that of the spinning wheel or loom. He opposed rapid industrialization because he saw its ideal of endless economic growth to be inhuman and destructive. Gandhian 'small is beautiful' economics may have seemed backward at one time, but today seem relevant and prophetic.

Gandhi was not an original thinker as such; nor was his religious and philosophical synthesis entirely consistent. But to judge Gandhi on such criteria would be to deny the remarkable achievements of one of the twentieth-century's towering figures. He inspired future leaders like Martin Luther King and Nelson Mandela to oppose and defeat injustice. Even to mention the leading figures of the Communist struggle such as Stalin and **Mao** is to show how important Gandhi was as an alternative: providing a practical philosophy of life built not on hatred, conflict and division but on love, truth and the good of all.

Part Two

THE
MIDDLE EAST

ZOROASTRIANISM
AND ISLAM

ZOROASTER (ZARATHUSTRA)

*Zoroaster was not a prophet, a lightning conductor of God,
in the sense that Muhammad was, but he was nevertheless
an inspired poet and philosophical thinker.*

The traditional date for Zoroaster, derived from a Greek source, tentatively places him '258 years before Alexander', some time between 1700 and 1000 BCE. This indicates, together with other evidence, that Zoroaster was probably born around 628 BCE. However, there are problems with this dating. In particular, the language of the Zoroastrian Avesta and the *gathas* or hymns attributed to Zoroaster, has been found to be very close to that of the Sanskrit of the Veda. This, together with the many gods and concepts they have in common, suggests a joint background. The Rig Veda is thought to have been composed no later than 1200 BCE, possibly much earlier. Another theory suggests that Zoroaster might have been writing in a formal sacred language preserved, as Sanskrit or Latin is today, many thousands of years after its formation. This seems far-fetched. A much safer assumption is that the *gathas* are what they seem to be, effusions of an oral tradition much like Homeric Greek or the hymns of the Rig Veda. The later dating seems to have arisen out of confusion over the King Vishtaspa, who was converted by Zoroaster, and a much later king of the same name. His name is a later Greek translation of Zarathustra.

Zoroaster seems to have been one of the heirs to a folk religion underlying both the Avesta and the Veda. His role in the formation of the Zoroastrian tradition was that of a prophet. He was not a prophet, a lightning conductor of God, in the sense that Muhammad was, but was nevertheless an inspired poet and philosophical thinker. He selected and worshipped one of the Avestan gods, Mazda Ahura, above all the others. Mazda Ahura is the embodiment of good; his enemy is Angra Mainyu, the head of the *devas* and evil personified. It appears that Zoroaster viewed the *devas* as symbolic of the pillaging warriors who worshipped them, representing destruction, falsehood and violence. The *ahuras*, on the other hand, were the gods of a peaceful pastoral existence. They also exist in the Veda

war-like cattle thieves really was as Zoroaster portrays it. At one point, he speaks of himself as a refugee, crying out, 'To what land shall I go to flee, whither to flee?' He seems to have found refuge at the court of King

Baptism by fire, as practised by the Parsees of Bombay in India, followers of Zoroaster to whom fire is sacred.

relics, with the gods Varuna and Mitra classified among them, but elsewhere in the Veda, the *asuras* (as they are known in Vedic Sanskrit) are a kind of demon. Zoroaster is characterized in the *gathas* as being created by Mazda Ahura for the protection of the Ox and the Ox Keeper from the violence of 'the followers of the Lie'. It is not clear whether the divide in Aryan society between peaceful and righteous herds and

Vishtaspa, in an unnamed country where he composed the *gathas*.

A fundamentally important question concerning Zoroastrianism is whether it is monotheistic or dualistic. The description given above, characterizing the religion as an opposition of good and evil, brings out the latter tendency. The former is emphasized in the portrayal of Mazda Ahura as the One God of All. At one point in the *gathas,* Zoroaster speaks of the 'two primeval spirits, who reveal themselves as Twins...the Better and the Bad'. Spenta Mainyu (Holy Spirit) is the good counterpart to Angra Mainyu's Evil Spirit. Mankind is given free choice between the two, but it is suggested that Mazda Ahura is perhaps the creator of both, and that the twins have each chosen for themselves between good and evil. Another version that developed in the early centuries of the Christian era, but which is not based on the Avesta, is that both Mazda Ahura and Angra Mainyu are the children of a greater spirit called Zurvan. The debate continues, but a sensible approach seems to be one that regards the Zoroastrian tradition as somewhere between extreme dualism and a qualified monotheism. The former might be represented by Manicheanism, a Persian sect from the third century CE which was influenced by Zoroastrianism and which envisaged life as a continuing struggle between the opposing forces of good and evil, and the latter by Christianity, in which the Devil is real and part of God's creation.

To the picture of Mazda Ahura and his nefarious opponent are added the *amesha spenta*, six spirits or beneficent immortals created by Mazda: Asha Vahishta (Justice, Truth), Vohu Manah (Righteous Thinking), Spenta Armaiti (Devotion), Khshathra Vairya (Desirable Dominion), Haurvatat (Wholeness) and Ameretat (Immortality). These spirits can be seen either as entities or eternal qualities. Depending on the emphasis that is given, Zoroastrianism can seem either more or less polytheistic.

Zoroastrianism as a religion had its high point as the official religion of the Persian Empire between the third and seventh century CE. It was then supplanted by Islam when the Arabs conquered the Persians, and was persecuted as a form of worship. Around the tenth century CE, a community of Zoroastrians gathered in southern India, around the city of Bombay, where they were tolerated and became known as Parsis (Persians). Today there are an estimated 200,000 Zoroastrians living there. The original thought of Zoroaster is hard to make out, but as a religion, it is tolerant and peace-loving, upholding ideals of freedom, service, community life, courage and a sensuous and responsible feeling for nature.

Despite its dwindling numbers, the influence of Zoroastrianism has been great. The Christian and Islamic belief in the Resurrection of the Body was originally a Zoroastrian doctrine. In the eighteenth century, the discovery of the Avesta inspired a European élite hungry for revelations about the Orient. Zoroaster presented a tantalizing glimpse to European free-thinkers who were beginning to question the Church of a monotheistic, peaceful and ethically centred culture long before Christ. Perhaps because of the ambiguity of the Avesta, Zoroaster became something of a talisman. He was transformed by Mozart into the Sarastro of *The Magic Flute* and by Nietzsche into the prophet in his philosophical fable, *Thus Spake Zarathustra* – neither representation owing much to the original figure.

ISLAMIC PHILOSOPHY: INTRODUCTION

*Seeking knowledge
is an ordinance obligatory
upon every Muslim.*

A man praying and reading from the Quran in Iran.

The term 'Islamic Philosophy' has a strange sound to non-Islamic ears. Even before the recent rise in fundamentalism fuelled fresh prejudices against Islam, it was commonplace in the West to disregard its contribution to philosophy. The perception was that its importance was only as the transmitter of Greek philosophy to medieval Europe. Bertrand Russell's comment in his *History of Western Philosophy* that 'Arabic philosophy is not important as original thought' is typical of an attitude that existed until recent times. This view neglects the importance of Islamic contributions to rational philosophy as founded by the Greeks and – more importantly – the ideas that were original to Islamic thinkers.

Having said this, Western ignorance of Islamic philosophy does reflect a certain suspicion within the tradition itself. Muslim philosophers have frequently had to argue in favour of the validity of speculative thought.

The principal flowering of philosophy in the Arab–Muslim world took place in the 700 years following the death of the Prophet Muhammad in 632 CE, the period we examine in this book. There were three main aspects to Islamic enquiry: *kalam*, literally the 'word' of God and, by extension, theological work based on this; *falsafah* or philosophy; and mysticism or Sufism. This tripartite division is a useful one to bear in mind, even though the line between *kalam* and *falsafah* is not as simple as it might seem: *kalam* includes philosophical aspects, while *falsafah* has much that Western readers would regard as theological. For the purposes of this book, we will regard all three aspects as fertile sources of new thinking.

A major topic of discussion in the Islamic world is the extent and nature of knowledge that is necessary to be a Muslim. Advocates of both philosophy and theology could quote the Quran: 'Seeking knowledge is an ordinance obligatory upon every Muslim.'[19] While Muhammad speaks in many places of his high regard for knowledge, it is also true that he said such things as 'we seek refuge in Allah from useless knowledge.'[20] The debate as to what knowledge the Prophet regarded or would have regarded had it come to his attention, as valid and necessary, continues to this day. In the early years of Islam, much intellectual effort centred on the text of the Quran and later on the traditions of reports of the life of the Prophet (the *Hadith*) and the customary practices of Muhammad and his followers. Speculative thought was not encouraged and belief was regarded as more important in order to be a good Muslim. Comparisons with other traditions show that founding figures often focus on ethical matters and discourage speculation. The examples of **Confucius** and the **Buddha** elsewhere in this book show that this is no bar to their successors undertaking such activity.

After a time, it became obvious to Muslims that some questions were not dealt with specifically in the traditional sources, and that in its collision with other faiths and systems of thought, Islam needed to become more sharply defined. This brought about the development of *kalam* and later of the *falsafah* or philosophy that came from the sophisticated Greek cosmology, metaphysics and logic which dominated thought in the Mediterranean region of the time. Greek philosophy, transformed into *falsafah*, gave Islam a structure that allowed it to deal with the challenges of rival thought systems. The undoubted forefather of Islamic philosophy is Aristotle, but the influence of Plato and the Neoplatonists is also important. In time, some Islamic thinkers would come to regard *falsafah* as equal to or, in some cases, more important than the scholasticism of *kalam*. This did not

mean that the Quran ceased to be the reference point, however. It would be true to say that rational philosophy as such is generally a subsidiary pursuit of Islam, a means to the truth rather than an end in itself. Islamic philosophy set the tone for the Christian Middle Ages and the world of thinkers such as St Thomas Aquinas. Its theology and mysticism, though less directly influential, have much in common with that period in the Western tradition.

Sufism is the third important strand. It seems that there were already Sufis around at the time of Muhammad, wool-robed ascetics who made pilgrimages to Mecca and walked around the Ka'ba. Certainly this is the view of the **Ibn Khaldun**, an important Muslim historian of the Middle Ages. Whether or not this is true, by the time of the main flowering of Sufism, it had become a branch of Islam, albeit a highly exceptional one. There are three main schools of thought on the origin of Sufism, insofar as it is not just a natural effusion of spirituality such as that found in many cultures. Traditional Islamic view holds that it represents the esoteric or mystical teachings of Muhammad. Historically, there is not much evidence to support the Prophet Muhammad as a mystic and, on the face of it, his prophesy was principally concerned with ethical and social issues: essentially on how to be a good Muslim and a good person. Also, as we have seen, there is some evidence that Sufis pre-dated Muhammad. However, this view is the one held by most Sufis and there is no decisive evidence against it. The second school of thought holds that Sufism is a development of either Indian or Persian origin as a reaction against Judeo-Christianity. Certainly the Indian Vedantic philosophy[21] seems to have

The depiction of the natural world is forbidden in Islamic art, with a few exceptions. This led to the development of a rich tradition of decorative abstract art such as tilework.

influenced the later development of Sufism, but it cannot be proven to have been its source. Equally, the Persian theory is unsustainable although Zoroastrian elements influenced the Middle Eastern world as a whole. Thirdly, and finally, there is the view that Sufism sprang from Neoplatonism. This is historically plausible, given the extent of Neoplatonic thought available to the Arab world. Gibbon, in *Decline and Fall of the Roman Empire,* records that seven Neoplatonist philosophers were forced to flee Emperor Justinian to the Persian court in 532 CE.

Whatever its source, Sufism became an integral part of orthodox Islam, especially after the time of **al-Ghazali**, who was both a Sufi and the greatest Islamic theologian. His views are generally regarded as normative by most subsequent thinkers and his support for *kalam* and Sufism was equalled by his attacks on some of the *falsafyah* that preceded him. Al-Ghazali's great skill and

Devout Muslims praying in the direction of Mecca at a mosque in Cairo, Egypt.

authority succeeded in finding an accommodation between orthodoxy and Sufism, despite certain heterodox elements within the mystic tradition. Sufism has intermittently conflicted with orthodoxy throughout history, and this remains true to this day with the rise of 'fundamentalist' Wahabism which particularly disapproves of Sufism[22]. Although like *falsafah*, Sufism was persecuted periodically for perceived or actual unorthodox beliefs or practices, it is best seen as an integral part of Islamic history, which makes less sense without its mystic core.

Islam could be seen as a relative latecomer when compared to rival religious and philosophical traditions. The Prophet died in 632 CE, between six and eleven centuries after the key figures in most other cultures. But while most of Europe was plunged into the Dark Ages, Islam flourished, founding universities and theological colleges, translating the Greeks and developing the arts and science. From a Western point of view therefore the importance of Islamic *falsafah* primarily has been the preservation and transmission of the Hellenistic tradition of Plato, Aristotle and the Neoplatonists, principally Plotinus. Although vestiges of the old Classical civilization persisted in monasteries on the edge of the Atlantic, it owes much of its survival to the work of Islamic scholars. The rediscovery of the Greek tradition by the West was to have a decisive effect on the development of thirteenth-century Christianity, and on the proto-science that followed.

Western perspective emphasizes the work of the Aristotelians and of scholarly translators and tends to obscure that of others. The most important Islamic name for medieval scholastic thinkers was **Averroës** (Ibn Rushd) who translated his own commentary of Aristotle. **Avicenna** (Ibn Sina), though also a philosopher, was better known for medical works in the tradition of Galen. Islamic thinkers had influence on a number of other areas, in particular medicine and mathematics. Al-Khwarazmi translated a Sanskrit text in around 830 CE that, rendered in Latin in the twelfth century as *Algoritmi de Numero Indorum*, gave us both the mathematical term 'algorithm' and the 'Arabic' number system, although of course the system is Indian. Because the Western tradition did not value the thought of the Islamic world for itself, names such as **al-Ghazali** and **Ibn Khaldun** were not Westernized. The originality of their ideas has only recently been recognized.

This is not the place for a discussion of Islam as a religion, but a few comments are worthwhile and necessary. Firstly, it should be said that the modern Western perception of Islam as a war-like and intolerant culture is mistaken. It is true that war was an important part of early Islam and inspired the growth of an empire almost the equal of Rome; but it is wrong to imagine that 'Holy War' was part of the Prophet's message. Rather, it grew out of an Arab culture older than Muhammad in which raiding other tribes was a way of survival. After Muhammad achieved the unification of the Arabs, war on wealthier neighbours was primarily a political and economic rather than a religious aim – a culture that was based on raiding one's neighbours was transferred to a wider stage. It is true that the early Muslim conquests had a religiously inspired ethic of liberation, and indeed most of the conquered peoples regarded their new overlords as a better lot than those they had replaced. But conversion was not an important priority, and Muhammad's attitude to the other religions he knew

about was one of mutual tolerance and respect: 'our God and your God is one and the same, and it is unto Him that we [all] surrender ourselves.'[23] Even within Islam, heterodox beliefs were always less of a problem than heteropraxy, behaviour thought to be un-Islamic. To take another example, his treatment of women seems to have been thoroughly even-handed: the universal veil and the subjugation of women in modern Islam is a later arrival. Indeed, even after his time, we have a woman such as **Rabi'ah al'Adawiyah** (717–801 CE), the first of the great Sufis. The unfavourable image of Islam developed in the West is partly a legacy of Christian propaganda beginning

The faithful being called to prayer.

from the time of the First Crusade, and partly a consequence of the increasingly anguished and defensive positions taken up in the Islamic world over the past century. Having said this, it is important to acknowledge that, as with Christianity, the world of Islam could and can be brutal and intolerant, whatever the original qualities of its founder. Islam has traditionally been more accepting of the heterodox views and beliefs of non-Muslims than those of its own people, and the brutal execution of the Sufi **al-Hallaj** in 922 CE was an example of what could happen if orthodoxy went too far.

Finally, a few comments about the general patterns of Islamic thought. The Hellenic influence was almost that of another religion, together with Judaism and Christianity. Just as both the Old and the New Testament were accepted as

he argued that every human being has access to reason and demonstrated that the prophets contradict each other. In this he was, of course, beyond the pale of Islam. The opposite argument was most strongly put by al-Ghazali (1058–1111 CE), author of *The Incoherence of the Philosophers*, who saw faith as weakened by the defense of reason. Moreover, he

The Badshahi Mosque in Lahore, Pakistan.

revelatory, so Aristotle and Plato came to be seen as another tributary of Islam. Muhammad's concerns were primarily social, ethical and theological; the relative lack of speculative thought in his work left a void in which it could flourish, with an early thinker such as **al-Ash'ari** (?874–?935 CE) arguing that although *falsafah* was not to be found in the Quran, there were also many other good things absent from it. A stronger line still was taken by his contemporary al-Razi (865–925 CE) who, as a Platonist, was naturally more inclined to assign primary importance to reason. Al-Razi believed in God, but not in religion, and attacked the whole principle of prophesy as flawed:

argued that descriptions of the nature of a prophet such as those given by Avicenna (980–1037 CE) came close to reducing the miraculous to mere psychology. Al-Ghazali's critique of *falsafah* is a powerful one, anticipating some of the arguments of Hume. After al-Ghazali, most Islamic philosophy found its way to the West, notably Averroës (1126–1198 CE), who made a powerful defence for discipline and stated that philosophers are higher than theologians for their ability to use scientific reasoning. In this he shows his Aristotelian influence.

The third aspect of Islam was, as we have seen, Sufism. From the beginning, it was seen as a second source of revelation, with apocryphal tales pitting the young girl **Rabi'ah** in debate against the aged and sombre Hassan (an early theologian), and always coming off better. The martyrdoms of both al-Hallaj and 'Ayn al-Qudat (1098–?1121 CE) were warnings that 'drunken' Sufism, in which the mystic is lost in the contemplation of God and liable to make controversial statements such as 'I am the Truth', was a dangerous game, at least when spoken openly to the populace. This point was reputedly made by al-Hallaj's master al-Junayd, founder of 'sober' Sufism, when he repudiated him not for heresy but for proclaiming a secret doctrine openly. Al-Ghazali, who had spent time as a Sufi mystic, did much to influence the development of 'sober' Sufism, which takes place after consideration, as it were the morning after, before the Sufi declares what she or he has seen in a state of mystical transport.

Whereas Hindu tradition, for example, is accretional and positively welcomes new unorthodoxy, Islamic tradition frequently yearns for a return to a pure, unadulterated form of Islam. This is naturally identified with the period during and immediately following the Prophet's life. Philosophically it generally means a clearing out of alien concepts, mainly those of Greece. Often this has had a revivifying effect on Islamic thought, clearing out the dead wood of intellectual constructs, as in the example of al-Ash'ari and Ibn Khaldun, but at other times the result has been stifling. The attack of al-Ghazali in *The Incoherence of the Philosophers* was perhaps a combination of both. Its attack on Greek-influenced philosophy effectively crushed it, at least in the Eastern end of the Muslim world, while the philosophy he proposes in its place has proved fruitful in its own right. Sufism, too, has suffered from this, accused both of setting up its mystics as rivals to the Quran's unique status and for the idolatry inherent in its reverence for saints and their tombs.

A Muslim raises his hands in prayer at Mecca, the holy shrine of Islam in Saudi Arabia. The city of pilgrims' tents at the foot of Mount Ararat can be seen in the background.

RABI'AH AL'ADAWIYAH

717–801 CE

A Prayer of Rabi'ah

O God, if I worship You for fear
of Hell, burn me in Hell,
And if I worship You in hope of Paradise,
Exclude me from Paradise.
But if I worship You for Your Own sake,
Grudge me not Your everlasting Beauty.

The first major mystic of Sufism and Islamic saint was a woman, Rabi'ah al'Adawiyah. She is best known for the compilations of her sayings collected by later biographers, notably Farid Ud-Din 'Attar (d. *c.* 1230 CE). Born into a poor family in Basra, Iraq, she was sold into slavery as a girl and reputedly freed by her master when he witnessed her maintain night-long vigils after a long day at work.

Sufism is analogous to medieval Christian mysticism. Its practitioners, named Sufis after the woollen robes they wear as a sign of solidarity with the poor (*tasawwuf* means 'to dress in wool'), are doctrinally part of the Sunni tradition of Islam. Their main practice, however, is a devotional form of mysticism that takes them beyond the Islam of the ordinary practitioner or scholar of the day. There is evidence that Sufism was present as a form of worship associated with the Ka'ba in Mecca before the time of Muhammad. The revelations of Sufi saints are regarded as authoritative, while the stories of their lives are accorded a respect and an importance similar to

the *Hadith*, the sayings of Muhammad. For this reason, Sufism has often been regarded with some suspicion by non-mystical Muslims. It does seem to have drawn some inspiration from Neoplatonic philosophy and early Christian mysticism. Its striking quality, however, is the overwhelming emphasis placed on the love of God. The accounts of Muhammad's own mystical transports have helped to validate the Sufi experience, but their emphasis is much more emotional and devotional. The favourite Sufi text from the Quran is 'the people whom He loves and who love Him'[24].

In this context, Rabi'ah was an important early exemplar of Sufism. She is popularly portrayed as the

---

The Two Loves

I love You with two loves – a selfish love
And a Love that You are worthy of.
As for the selfish love,
it is that I think of You,
To the exclusion of everything else.
And as for the Love that
You are worthy of,
Ah! That I no longer see any creature,
but I see only You!
There is no praise for me in either
of these loves,
But the praise in both is for You.

---

opponent of Hassan al-Basri (642–728 CE) in lively theological discussion about Islam, although these stories have more symbolic significance than historical accuracy. Hassan was an acquaintance of some of the companions of the Prophet and a rather severe early theologian. He is credited by some with the foundation of *kalam* (scholastic reflection on the Quran). He seems to have been a rather gloomy thinker, much occupied with thoughts of Hell. Rabi'ah, on the other hand, argued that fear of Hell should not be a reason for worshipping God. Neither should the hope of Heaven be a selfish motivation, but only the love of God. According to Rabi'ah, there are two aspects to this: the personal joy felt in the presence of God, and the love given without hope of reward. In the stories of the verbal duels between the two, it is Rabi'ah, the uneducated former slave girl, who invariably comes out best. Rabi'ah's devotionalism added to the other-worldly asceticism of Hassan could be said to have set the pattern for future Sufism.

Several principles important to Sufism are illustrated in Rabi'ah's life story. The pure love for God to the exclusion of all others is called by Rabi'ah *sidq* or sincerity. Rabi'ah was apparently asked by someone if she loved Muhammad and she replied that with the deepest respect to him, she had only one beloved. In this we see the beginnings of the Sufi tendency towards statements that could be wrongly interpreted by the unreflective faithful. *Tawakkul* is the principle of total trust in God, even to the point of not providing for oneself, akin to Christ's injunction 'take no thought for the morrow'. This leads to *rida,* a positive and active acceptance of the will of God. In her verbal jousts with Hassan, the concept of *ma'rifah* or gnosis is implicit: the mystical experiences of the untaught girl giving her access to a knowledge greater than that of the leading theologian. Perhaps the most

important Sufi concept is that of *fana'*, the extinction of the individual ego, or *nafs,* in union with God. As with Buddhist *shunyata* or emptiness, *fana'* indicates a realm of existence beyond thought and ordinary experience. It is in the attempt to communicate something about *fana'* that Sufism has developed its love of paradox.

In all of this it should not be forgotten that the real Rabi'ah was an uneducated woman. It is impossible at

Rabi'ah was...asked
by someone
if she loved Muhammad
and she replied that with
the deepest respect
to him, she had only
one beloved.

this remove to say how many of the stories about her have any basis in truth and how many of her sayings are authentic. Nevertheless, as in the example of Dame Julian of Norwich, her lack of formal education should not automatically lead to the assumption that she therefore lacked the ability to use deep and radical concepts in her explication of mystical experience. Her symbolic significance for later Islam was considerable.

He reputedly wrote some 270 works on a wide range of subjects, most of which are now lost, and some of which were translated in Europe, spreading his fame in the West. Al-Kindi was acclaimed by the Italian mathematician Cardano as one of the twelve greatest minds. His reputation and importance was even greater in the Islamic world.

His view of philosophy was that it consisted of three parts: physics, mathematics and theology, in ascending order of importance. By making theology a part of philosophy, albeit the highest part, al-Kindi naturally ran into opposition from theologians, the most extreme of whom went so far as to claim that the acquisition of knowledge was atheism. Nevertheless, it was his view that religion and philosophy were in harmony with each other. His philosophical work did not include a system of logic, which was introduced by **al-Farabi**. In *First Philosophy,* al-Kindi defines it as:

The knowledge of the true nature of things in so far as this is possible for man. The aim of the philosopher is, as regards his knowledge, to attain to the truth, and as regards his action, to act truthfully.

Al-Kindi's definition – true knowledge and true action – was to be influential on all subsequent Islamic philosophy because it connected philosophy to the central issue of how a Muslim ought to behave. He distinguishes 'divine science' (i.e. prophesy, from 'human science' including philosophy) and gives examples of philosophical problems resolved by the Quran, arguing that philosophy would not of itself have been able to arrive at such a solution. The effect of this made the Quran a subject

AL-KINDI
801–873 CE

Al-Kindi was the first true Islamic philosopher, although he is sometimes regarded as more of a theologian. He was learned in Greek and Arabic languages and translated a number of works, including those of Aristotle and Plotinus. Unfortunately, he was also responsible for mistakenly publishing the *Enneads* of the latter as *The Theology of Aristotle*, which caused much confusion in Islamic philosophy. He was descended from a man said to have been one of the companions of the Prophet and his father was governor of Kufah, with Basra then one of the two main centres of Islamic learning. His upbringing was privileged, and in adult life, he lived in famous luxury, possessing an enormous library. He seems to have incited jealousy in others and at one point was beaten and exiled, with his library confiscated.[25]

of philosophical examination for the first time. This is the nature of the harmony he established between philosophy and religion, paving the way for **al-Farabi**, **Avicenna** and **Averroës**.

The 'first philosophy' or the highest part of philosophy, according to al-Kindi, is the nature of God, and he found in the Greek thinkers a conception of God similar in some respects to that of Islam. The Aristotelians asserted that God was uncompound, immutable and the unmoved mover of all. According to the Quran, God was one, created the world from nothing and was the support for all living creatures. Unlike later philosophers, al-Kindi was orthodox in maintaining that the world was not eternal. He argued against the existence of infinity in space, time or in a chain of causality. This provides proof of God's existence (normally called the cosmological argument), because there must be a first cause that is not an effect.

His other main proof is the argument from design or teleological argument, in which he says that the order and harmony of the universe is evidence of a creator. Both these proofs were later refuted by **al-Ghazali**.

Al-Kindi's originality stems not so much from his ideas, many of which are borrowed from Hellenistic sources, but from his success in examining Islam through a philosophical lens. This was important for the development of early Islamic thought, because the Quran is much more concerned with conduct than with theosophical speculation. Al-Kindi's synthesis of Aristotle and Islam paved the way for the philosophers that followed him. And to those orthodox exponents that would condemn philosophy he showed that even they would have to acquire it: one cannot reasonably condemn that of which one is ignorant.

Muhammed and his followers. Reputedly Al-Kindi was a direct descendant of one of the Prophet's companions.

AL-HALLAJ
c. 858–922 CE

al-Hallaj this mystical ecstasy, in which it seemed anything might be said, became threatening to the authorities. Like **Rabi'ah**, al-Hallaj was not, strictly speaking, a philosopher. However, his *ma'rifah* or mystical insight led him to say things with profound philosophical and religious implications.

Al-Hallaj (also known as Mansur) was born in Iran and his father may have been a wool-carder. In his early youth, having learned the Quran by heart, al-Hallaj took up with a number of leading contemporary Sufis, completing his studies under the highly respected 'sober' Sufi al-Junayd in Baghdad. He completed three pilgrimages to Mecca before returning to Baghdad in around 908 CE. He had also led the first Islamic mission into India and Turkistan and gained a number of followers. Arriving in Baghdad, al-Hallaj attracted the

His most grievous
error, according to
the authorities,
was to say,
'Ana al-Haqq',
which means,
'I am the Real'
or 'I am the Truth'.

The development of early Sufism, beginning with its first saint **Rabi'ah,** finds its apotheosis in Al-Hallaj, its first martyr. A highly controversial figure, he was prone to utterances that the orthodox found unacceptable. A clash was inevitable given the tensions that existed between the dualistic worship of God essential to Islam and al-Hallaj's tendency towards monism, the doctrine of the identity of the Self with the divine. This may have been accentuated by Indian influences in early Sufism: al-Bistami (d. 874 CE), who was the chief proponent of a kind of monism, was taught by a master from Sind and may have been initiated in yogic practices. Al-Bistami's descriptions of his mystical experiences led to his being described as a 'drunken' Sufi, and with

suspicions of the civil authorities and was suspected of having played a part in instigating a rebellion of black slaves. His attempts to preach moral and political reform in Baghdad led to his arrest for rabble-rousing.

Al-Hallaj spent eight years in jail, in which time his case was closely debated. Although his political activities may have been the principal

SOME SAYINGS ATTRIBUTED TO AL-HALLAJ

I find it strange that the divine whole can be borne by my little human part,
Yet due to my little part's burden, the earth cannot sustain me.

(Akhbar al-Hallaj, 11)

I have seen my Lord with the eye of my heart, and I said: 'Who are You?' He
said: 'You.'

(Diwan al-Hallaj, M. 10)

I do not cease swimming in the seas of love, rising with the wave, then
descending; now the wave sustains me, and then I sink beneath it; love bears
me away where there is no longer any shore.

(Diwan al-Hallaj, M. 34)

reason for his imprisonment, the charge of heresy was more significant. Al-Hallaj loved to take up paradoxical positions, speaking of his admiration for the devil and rejecting Allah's injunction to bow down to Adam. His most grievous error, according to the authorities, was to say, 'Ana al-Haqq', which means, 'I am the Real' or 'I am the Truth'. Al-Haqq is one of the qualities attributed to Allah and this led to the allegation that Al-Hallaj had claimed to be God. Having upset the political leaders of his day as well as the religious orthodoxy, and even alienated Sufis like al-Junayd by putting aside the Sufi robe to preach to the masses, it is hardly surprising that in the end al-Hallaj was put to death. His execution was a thoroughly brutal affair involving public torture, mutilation, crucifixion, decapitation and burning. Al-Hallaj is said to have borne all of this stoically, forgiving his tormentors. In many ways, his life parallels that of Jesus, for whom he expressed admiration. Al-Hallaj's subsequent influence has been powerful; his life recalls not only Jesus but also the Islamic model of the true teacher who is killed by the worldly, as with the early imams. He also contributed to Sufism its tradition of paradoxical statements designed to unsettle the intellect and bring the devotee closer to a true understanding. However, al-Hallaj was a warning beacon rather than a rallying point for Sufis. The Sufi poet Hafiz said of al-Hallaj that his death was a punishment for having revealed the 'secret teaching'. Although many of the things al-Hallaj said would have been acceptable within the esoteric circle, it was untenable for Sufism to continue along a separate track from traditional Islam. There was a need for a synthesis between the two, which was not to be effected until the time of **al-Ghazali** (1058–1111 CE).

Al-Ghazali's solution, probably under the influence of the tradition of al-Junayd, was to say that it was wrong for Sufis to be held responsible for their mystical experiences, but that they should reflect on their validity before giving them utterance. The standard position of Sufism is not the absolute monism expressed by al-Hallaj, but a qualified monism in which the individual soul adores Allah while acknowledging that its whole existence is entirely dependent on Him. This position is in close proximity to that of the later Indian philosopher **Ramanuja**, whose thought explores all of its implications. Ramanuja's conclusion that absolute monism is merely a step on the way to the love of God is very close to that of Sufism. In this light, the 'secret teaching' of Hafiz is perhaps not meant to be understood as the ultimate teaching. The empirical experience of singularity of the soul is a secret because it seems at first to contradict Islam and could mislead the faithful. It is, however, only a step on the way to the experience of devotional union with Allah, which is unity without identity. The Sufi has no experience of his or her self as separate from the divine, but as a lover of the divine still has another who is the beloved.

Young Egyptian boys with wooden boards on which are painted the words of the Quran. The boys sing the words out loud to learn them off by heart.

AL-FARABI
c. 870–950 CE

Abu Nasr al-Farabi lived in a village near Farabi in Turkey until the age of 50. He then moved to Baghdad to further his studies, where he remained for twenty years before relocating to the court at Aleppo in old age. His works are all thought to have been written in the last thirty years of his life, making al-Farabi a remarkable example of late blooming. He became famous in Muslim philosophy as the 'Second Master' (Aristotle being the first). His funeral at Aleppo was attended by the Amir.

Although al-Farabi was a very learned man, it does not appear he understood any Greek. His comprehension of Greek philosophy, however, *was* good, and he was also talented at explaining it to an Islamic audience. His view of philosophy, as set out in *The*

Harmonization of the Opinions of Plato and Aristotle, for example, was that it was entirely unified. Thus, Plato and Aristotle propounded the same philosophy, as did the Stoics, Epicureans, Neoplatonists, and so on. Any divergence or disagreement is not due to the philosophers but to partisanship by their followers. By the same token, Islam and philosophy are

> *So let it be clear to you that, in what [Plato and Aristotle] presented, their purpose is the same, and that they intended to offer one and the same philosophy.*
>
> The Philosophy of Plato and Aristotle, p. 50

also at one, though externally different. In this, he goes further than the Neoplatonist Porphyry who reconciled Aristotle and Plato, and sets an example for **Avicenna** and **Averroës**. Al-Farabi was not the first of what might be called the 'perennial' philosophers, arguing that there is only one true philosophy, but he was the most comprehensive. He is similar in this enterprise to the Renaissance Christian humanist, Marsilio Ficino, although Ficino had the easier task of bringing together the already Platonized Christianity and Platonic philosophy.

Naturally, al-Farabi had to work hard to harmonize such a wide spectrum of thought and belief. The main issue at stake was the widespread belief that Aristotle had held several opinions that went against both Platonic thought and Islamic teaching. Al-Farabi was helped in arguing against this by **al-Kindi's** mistaken publication of the *Enneads* of Plotinus as *The Theology of Aristotle*, a misunderstanding that lasted for centuries. The question as to whether al-Farabi was really taken in, or was being disingenuous, is open to question. In a lesser-known work, *The Philosophy of Plato and Aristotle*, he makes no mention of *The Theology of Aristotle* in his exploration of Aristotle's ideas, and shows himself perfectly aware of the two philosophers' different theories (while indicating that he still regards them as reconcilable). Neither did **al-Ghazali** in his later attack on al-Farabi regard the latter's perennialist philosophy in his widely published *Harmonization* as worthy of serious debate. It may be, therefore, that al-Farabi held one set of

In al-Farabi's emanationism, the intellect can rise up through the spheres to become united with the primary intellect through reason and contemplation.

opinions privately and another publicly. In any case, his synthesis of systems of thought did not start from ignorance of their differences.

Al-Farabi's predecessor al-Kindi was the first Islamic philosopher but, despite his prodigious work, he did not put forward a system of logic. This was a major addition of al-Farabi's to the tradition. Part of this was his division of reasoning into five categories: the demonstrative, dialectical, rhetorical, sophistical and poetical. Only the demonstrative leads to certainty, and

this is the province of philosophers and scholars. The next best is the dialectic of theologians, such as his contemporary **al-Ash'ari**, while the rhetorical is merely persuasive; the sophistical is misleading; and poetical reasoning produces pleasant or unpleasant feelings. In al-Farabi's view, it is a mistake to address the common people with demonstrative reasoning. That is the function of religion, whereas philosophy should disguise itself in the clothes of mystification. This may seem élitist, but he was wiser than some of his successors who suffered persecution at the hands of the ignorant.

Al-Farabi's cosmology attempts to explain how the one God creates multiplicity through 'emanation'. It also tries to show how the immutable may create without changing itself. The concept of creation through emanation from God is taken from Plotinus, but the synthesis with Aristotle is al-Farabi's own. Intelligence, souls and matter (this triad he takes from Aristotle) are emanated from the first intelligence, God, who rules the first sphere, with the earth being presided over by the 'Active Intellect', identified by the Archangel Gabriel, ruler of the tenth, sublunary sphere. In al-Farabi's model of emanationism, the intellect can rise up through the spheres to become united with the primary intellect through reason and contemplation. This completes the Aristotelian picture, with earth at the centre and the cosmos rotating around it in crystalline spheres.

A criticism of the ten intelligences theory is that it does not really help with either the issue of how one becomes many, or of how the unchanging may create. The divine hierarchy could be regarded as a smoke-and-mirrors trick, disguising the problem of a logical gap with tiny steps. The problem is of course

Now these things are philosophy when they are in the soul of the legislator. They are religion when they are in the souls of the multitude. For when the legislator knows these things, they are evident to him by sure insight, whereas what is established in the souls of the multitude is through an image and a persuasive argument. Although it is the legislator who presents these things through images, neither the images nor the persuasive arguments are intended for himself. As far as he is concerned, they are certain. He is the one who invents the images and the persuasive arguments, but not for the sake of establishing these things in his own soul as a religion for himself. No, the images and the persuasive arguments are intended for others, whereas so far as he is concerned, these things are certain. They are a religion for others, whereas so far as he is concerned, they are philosophy. Such, then, is true philosophy and the true philosopher.

The Philosophy of Plato
and Aristotle, p. 47

merely academic today, but modern commentators would side with al-Ghazali in regarding it as logically fallacious. Nevertheless, al-Farabi's synthesis of different philosophies and Islam was persuasive both in Islamic and in later European culture. Avicenna is particularly indebted to it.

Another important idea of al-Farabi's was his theory of prophecy. This was an important issue because of the attacks of contemporary thinkers such as al-Razi (865–925 CE) who dismissed prophecy because it set up a special category of knowledge higher than reason. Developing Aristotle's thinking on dreams as an unfettered activity of the mind, al-Farabi elevates the dreaming state to one of reflection on ideas free of material distraction. A powerful and imaginative intellect (that is, of a true prophet) is able to rise in dreams to commune with the Active Intellect and receive spiritual truths from it. The Archangel Gabriel is thus identified with the Active Intellect, which becomes the messenger of God. This theory, as with al-Farabi's emanationism, was attacked by al-Ghazali in *The Incoherence of the Philosophers*.

Al-Farabi's theory of the intellect was derived from Aristotle, but he made important additions. The theory, simply put, is that there are three levels of the intellect in its upward-moving aspect. The *potential intellect* receives impressions passively; the *intellect in action* comprehends ideas within the impressions and can make use of them; and the *acquired intellect* is enlightened from above and moves among higher forms, akin to Platonic ideas that are beyond the world of matter. Although this third level of the intellect is essentially mystical in that it depends on the divine Active Intellect, al-Farabi insists

The Greek philosophers Plato and Aristotle. Al-Farabi argued that the seeming contradictions between their philosophies could be reconciled.

that the earlier stages must be gone through to prepare the intellect for revelation. It is easy to see why this theory should prove attractive in the West, as it joins together Aristotelian empiricism and Platonic gnosis. Within the Muslim framework, it also reconciles the three aspects of Greek philosophy, Islamic theology and Sufic mysticism. In the history of ideas, al-Farabi's remains one of the most balanced and pleasing theories of knowledge. It has been described as 'the most significant of all the theories of Muslim thinkers[26], and the most influential. Both Averroës and especially Avicenna were indebted to al-Farabi's theory and through them Christian Europe adopted it.

AL-ASH'ARI
c. 874–935 CE

Abu Al-Hasan al-Ash'ari was the chief formulator of the Sunni position in Islam. As is well known, the two main strands of Islam are the Sunni and the Shi'ite; however, as the main difference between the two is political rather than philosophical, we will not enter into it here. Suffice it to say that the Sunni have always been the more numerous and may be considered to be the mainstream of Islam. As a member of the Islamic aristocracy in Basra in Iraq, and a descendant of one of the Prophet's companions, al-Ash'ari was wealthy enough to be able to devote himself entirely to the study of theology. He was the beneficiary of the growth of learning under the Abbasid Caliphs, under whose autocratic rule Greek philosophy had first been translated. He founded an important theological school that counted among its later alumni **al-Ghazali** and **Ibn Khaldun.**

The rationalist theologians, the Mu'tazilah, of which al-Ash'ari was a prominent member, had established *kalam* or theological discussion and gained considerable prominence. By the time of al-Ash'ari, however, their thinking had become arid and far removed from real experience as well as from traditional Islam, and he broke with them at the age of 40. The Mu'tazilah and the orthodox positions had become polarized over the years, with the Mu'tazilah continuously questioning everything and the orthodox becoming increasingly anti-intellectual, for example asserting that all the dogmas of the faith had simply to be accepted without consideration. The orthodox position was clearly unsustainable and al-Ash'ari developed a new approach to *kalam* that suited orthodox convictions. Essentially, the Asharites maintain the primacy of revelation over reason in *kalam* (as **al-Kindi** did in *falsafah*), reversing the rationalist position. Another aspect of this is the question of good and evil. Al-Ash'ari maintains that good and evil are not intrinsic to an action, but are determined by the Quran and by Shari'ah law – there is no good or bad, but revelation makes it so.

Al-Ash'ari found a middle course that was generally acceptable to the majority. For example, there was a debate about whether the Quran was eternal or created. The orthodox claimed it was eternal and that to claim that it was created was an 'innovation'. Al-Ash'ari pointed out that as Muhammad had not given an answer either way, it was equally an innovation to claim that it was eternal. Having destroyed the arguments of his opponents, he offered his own solution: the Quran should be considered to be eternal with respect to its meaning, and created with

The tomb of the Abbasid Caliphs in Cairo.

respect to its words. Another important theological question of the time was whether the attributes of God (merciful, wise, vengeful, all-powerful) were the same as his essence or not. Again, while the rationalists held that they were the same, causing the attributes effectively to disappear or make God bulge with contradictions, the orthodox position that they were different tended to anthropomorphize and multiply God, as in Hinduism. Al-Ash'ari's argument was similar to that of the Indian proponents of *bhedabheda* (identity-in-difference)[27] – the attributes were both part of the essence and external to it. So, for example, God is not wise in his essence, but in practice, his words have the attribute of wisdom. Thus attribute and essence are neither entirely the same nor quite different.

On the question of free will, Asharism has to avoid deterministic fatalism and unfettered free will. Al-Ash'ari asserts that man can choose between right and wrong, ultimately leading him to Heaven or Hell. However, God is strongly present in this conception of will, being the active principle in making the choice available, in empowering the individual to choose, and in fulfilling the choice and realizing its consequences. This doctrine, which was similar to that later developed independently by Malebranche as *occasionalism* (in which God acts to carry thought into action), is an attempt to combine a strong conception of God as the doer and sustainer of all with the need for individual responsibility. In this instance, al-Ash'ari may be treading on dangerous ground, and some of his followers tended towards the old orthodox deterministic position.

A somewhat unwilling philosopher, al-Ash'ari evolved an original system of metaphysics from Aristotelian roots. According to his metaphysics (or, according to some scholars, that developed and completed by his follower al-Baqillani), the world consists of momentary atoms, brought into being by God and then disappearing again. There is no causality in the normal sense and no laws of nature; it is just that we can observe that God typically and regularly does things in this way. Fire does not cause wood to burn: God produces the fire, and when fire is close to wood, we may observe that he habitually burns the wood. A miracle is merely an exception, but no more special from God's point of view than any other occurrence. Macdonald describes Asharite metaphysics as 'the most daring metaphysical scheme, and almost certainly the most thorough theological scheme, ever thought out[28]. It has parallels, as we have already seen, with *occasionalism*, and also with the Buddhist arguments against causality and permanence with, of course, strikingly different aims. Al-Ash'ari's thinking was very influential in later times, particularly through al-Ghazali, who makes use of his ideas to attack the philosophers, notably **Avicenna** and **al-Farabi**. Al-Ghazali's influence was decisive in making Asharism the main theology of Islam from his time onwards.

The Mosque of Omar in Jerusalem, otherwise known as the Dome of the Rock. It is an ornate shrine built on the spot where Muhammed is believed to have ascended to heaven, and the site of the Temple of Solomon.

AVICENNA (IBN SINA)
980–1037 CE

Along with **Averroës** (Ibn Rushd), Avicenna was one of the Islamic philosophers best known in the West. He was also an influential physician and author of *The Book of Healing* and, most famously, the *Canon of Medicine*. His reputation in medicine in the Europe of the Middle Ages was equalled only by Hippocrates and Galen, while his philosophy was absorbed into the mainstream of Scholasticism. He was, like many Islamic thinkers, encyclopedic in his interests and, of all the Muslim philosophers perhaps the most prolific. His *Kitab al-Shifa* is a compendium of learning, encompassing logic, geometry, arithmetic, astronomy, music, natural science and metaphysics. It is said to be the largest work of its kind by any single man[29].

Avicenna was born in Persia and possessed a prodigious intellect. He had memorized the Quran by the age of 10 and had mastered all of the traditional branches of Islamic learning by 21, and was a respected physician as well. His successful cure of the Samanid emperor gave him access to a magnificent library that enabled him to further his studies. In later life, however, he was less fortunate in his circumstances as the death of his father and political upheavals in the region caused him to lead an unsettled existence. Whatever his circumstances, however, Avicenna continued to work prodigiously. A full day's work at court would be followed by sessions of discussion and composition with students, often lasting most of the night. For the last 14 years of his life, however, Avicenna lived in Isfahan, where he enjoyed uninterrupted peace in which to work.

Avicenna's philosophy built on the work of **al-Farabi** (870–950 CE), who argued that philosophy and religion are in harmony with each other. Al-Farabi was the founder of the doctrine of emanationism, which is a development from Plotinus. Intelligence, souls and matter (this triad he takes from Aristotle) are emanated from the first intelligence, God, who rules the first sphere, with the earth being presided over by the 'Active Intellect', identified with the Archangel Gabriel, ruler of the tenth, sublunary sphere. In emanationism, the intellect can rise up through the spheres to become united with the primary intellect through reasoning and contemplation, a similar process to that described by Plato in the approach to the Good.

Avicenna was an accomplished physician, scientist and philosopher.

Al-Farabi also had an original theory about the status of a prophet as a highly imaginative person who is able to connect in either sleep or trance with the Active Intellect and thereby receive spiritual truths.

Avicenna thought of God as the only absolutely uncompound, simple entity. This creates a problem as Avicenna follows Aristotle in holding that God would know only universals, being outside of time and space, which define particulars. The orthodox criticized this as being inconsistent with the Quran, which says, 'Not a particle remains hidden from God in the heavens or on the earth'. Avicenna's way around this was to argue that God could see the whole chain of cause and effect from outside time, and would therefore be aware of each particular event in its context. This explanation was never fully accepted. **Al-Ghazali**, in particular, criticized Avicenna's apparent limitation of what God could know. The rather remote and impersonal concept of God in Avicenna could be seen as one of the drawbacks in his philosophy.

His idea of a prophet is of someone with deep imaginative power, enabling identification with the Active Intellect. Along with this he must be charismatic, politically gifted, and possess the ability to express philosophy allegorically, allowing it to be widely understood in the form of religion.

Avicenna's own brand of psychology is interesting and, in some ways, original. Our five outer senses are mirrored inwardly by five inner faculties, including memory, imagination and our sense of value. Like Aristotle, Avicenna holds that the intellect is that in the individual that is god-like – indivisible, immaterial and imperishable. It is a mirror that reflects ideas from the Active Intellect (see p. 101) and which is capable of being, as it were, polished. Avicenna is Platonic rather than Aristotelian in his view that universals are learned from above rather than from experience. To take a classical Greek example, we do not intuit the universal idea of 'triangle' from seeing many triangles. Rather, the

of philosophic thinking that was not orthodox. His belief in the eternity of the creation, his idea of a prophet as a highly imaginative person and his (private) rejection of bodily resurrection all came to be considered heterodox. In addition to this, his conception of God is rather distant and cold, as is his view of the individual intellect. So although his influence on Europe was huge,

Avicenna being received by the Governor of Isfahan in Iran.

supersensuous idea 'triangle' is revealed to reason by the higher intelligence. The ideal triangle is free from the imperfections of any physical triangles, which only serve to prepare reason for revelation. According to Avicenna, thought is the faculty that brings about universality in forms.

After Avicenna's time, he was attacked not only by al-Ghazali but also by Averroës and, later, **Ibn Khaldun**, causing his influence to decline in the Islamic world. He became symbolic of a certain kind

Avicenna did not enjoy such a wide following within his own culture. This is perhaps unfortunate as, in addition to his status as the most important of the Aristotelians, he a lso made efforts to found an Oriental Philosophy, a mystical theosophy that seems to pre-figure later developments in Persia. Most of his works on this have sadly been lost.

AL-GHAZALI

1058–1111 CE

Abu Hamid Muhammad al-Ghazali inherited a rich tradition of theology and mysticism and went on to develop a system of thought that was to bring the two together. His life was fascinating, both to his contemporaries and in subsequent history, and has contributed, some say unduly, to his influence as a thinker. He is in some ways reminiscent of St Augustine, with whom he is often compared for his formidable intellect, his internal struggles, his energy and his faith. He is also a contradictory figure, as we will see.

As his father and brother were celebrated Sufi mystics, the young al-Ghazali underwent spiritual training, but failed to reach the mystical states he hoped for. His early bent was for scholarship and he swiftly progressed to be appointed professor of theology at Nizamihah University in Baghdad. This seems to have been equally unsatisfying, as al-Ghazali's relentlessly questioning mind exposed the inadequacy of both theology and philosophy as it was then practised. Al-Ghazali sets out his aims in terms reminiscent of Descartes:

The search after truth being the aim which I propose to myself, I ought in the first place to ascertain what are the bases of certitude. In the second place, I ought to recognize that certitude is the clear and complete knowledge of things, such knowledge as leaves no room for doubt, nor any possibility of error.[30]

At 36, the strain of being unable to find a solid foundation for truth became too much. Al-Ghazali suffered a severe nervous breakdown, resigned his post and left for Damascus to become a wandering Sufi. Having proved to himself that neither observation nor reason were adequate to the purpose of finding truth, he was instead to find a spiritual source, speaking of a light which God infused into his heart. Instead of reasoning our way to truth, it is the grace of Allah that is the key to knowledge. He spent eleven years in this way, practicing meditation and asceticism, after which he returned to teaching and writing. One reason for this return to active life was the tradition that Islam would be renewed by a true teacher every century: al-Ghazali was persuaded by others that he was the teacher for the century beginning (in the Christian calendar) in 1106 CE[31]. His *Revival of the Religious Sciences* is a vast work dedicated to this end, and is still the most read Islamic text after the Quran. Al-Ghazali is credited in addition with the authorship of hundreds of works, but many have been misattributed. Around 40 are now considered to be authentic.

Al-Ghazali was acutely aware of the divisions within Islam, and in an autobiographical work intended to justify his retirement from the university post he outlines four main strands in the faith. These are the al-Asharite theologians, the Sufi mystics, the *falsafyah* (philosophers) and the Shi'ite followers of the Imams. Al-Ghazali had criticisms of all of these groups, including theologians who tried to rely on philosophical proofs and those Sufis who held to unorthodox monist doctrines[32]. However, it was the philosophers and especially the Shi'ite theologians that were his real targets. To deal with the latter first: Islam as a religion has traditionally been divided into the Sunni and the Shi'ite strands. These each had their beginnings in the early politics of the succession to the Prophet. In essence, the Shi'ite belief was in the imams, the bloodline of Muhammad. For them, only a true Imam could teach Islam; while the Sunnis, on the other hand, took the pragmatic view that *Shari'ah* law should be allowed to develop as an interpretive tradition, augmenting the words of the Prophet. For al-Ghazali the authoritarianism of the Shia was a mystical blind alley: all of the true imams were dead and the bloodline had ended.

For our purposes here, however, al-Ghazali's attack on the philosophers is of more importance, as the first examination of Greek-influenced Islamic philosophy by a theologian. Al-Ghazali was the first theologian equipped to offer such a critique and did so, first in his *The Intentions of the Philosophers*, a book which was influential in Europe and which sets out the key ideas of thinkers like Avicenna (Ibn Sina) and al-Farabi, and finally in his masterpiece, the *Tahafut al-Falsafyah* (*The Incoherence of the Philosophers*). At the root of his

antipathy to the philosophers was his conviction that theology depended on faith and not on reason, which, in al-Ghazali's unhappy experience, had not succeeded in bringing him the answers he craved. Because reason cannot be relied upon to prove God or other truths, it should be relegated to a secondary position. His critique of the *falsafyah* is not that philosophy should not take place, but that its findings should start and end with the Quranic revelation. Al-Ash'ari and al-Ghazali after

> '*The imponderable decisions of God cannot be weighed by the scales of reason.*'

him both take an agnostic position towards the mysteries of God, as is seen in the example, cited twice by the latter, of a child who finds himself in heaven but in a lower place than a man. He asks God why he should be in a lower place, to which the reply is that the man did many good works. The child then asks why he had to die before he did good works, to which God replies that he ended the child's life because he knew he would have become a sinner. The cry goes up from the damned in hell as to why they were not caused to die before they sinned. Al-Ghazali comments that 'the imponderable decisions of God cannot be weighed by the scales of reason and Mu'tazilism [Islamic rationalism]'. He was, however, in favour of logic as a discipline and promoted its use in theological training.

Al-Ghazali attacked in particular three claims by *falsafyah* that, as **Avicenna** had, he found to be heretical. These were that the world is eternal, that

God cannot know particulars and that the resurrection of the body (mentioned in the Quran) was a myth. These ideas had grown up in the tradition of Islamic philosophy as successive thinkers built on an essentially Aristotelian set of assumptions. Al-Ghazali said, quite reasonably, that there is a vast difference between the Quran and Aristotle. His attack on the *falsafyah* in *The Incoherence* was all the more powerful because it made use of the Aristotelians' own methods of argument. The three heresies are today of merely historical importance, but al-Ghazali's arguments against them produce some fascinating philosophy all of their own.

One of the most pivotal arguments advanced by al-Ghazali is his critique of causality. The target here was the doctrine of Emanationism, which posits a vast hierarchy of cause and effect from God down to man based on Aristotelian cosmology[33]. Al-Ghazali objects to the idea of 'natural law': that is, the view that the universe is governed by physical laws of nature. In particular, the law of causality makes God subservient to his own creation, and to the laws that affect mankind. God may do as he wishes at all times. His argument against causality is that it is based on observation and not on natural law: we may observe that fire burns, but we cannot assert that it will do so in all cases. What we have observed is not a 'natural law' but one example of many that God has his habitual way of acting. This also serves to justify miracles, which are not violations of some natural law, but merely unusual acts of God. In this he is reminiscent of the occasionalism of **al-Ash'ari**, who is the major influence, but it is intriguing to note parallels in other traditions – with the eighteenth-century philosopher David Hume in the West, for example, and with the materialism of **Charvaka** in

India. Islamic theology, in its enthusiasm for sweeping out presumptuous philosophies, here uses similar arguments to those of the atheists and the materialists – an irony that a Sufi would appreciate.

Another important question, and here again the influence of al-Ash'ari was decisive, is that of free will. Al-Ghazali cannot accept a strong determinist argument because that would make heaven and hell meaningless. Instead, he posits a three-tier system: the world of matter is entirely without free will; man has a limited free will, allowing him to choose between right and wrong; and God has total free will.

The Scottish philosopher David Hume.

On the question of what God can know, al-Ghazali argued against the Emanationist argument that God knows only timeless universals and is above particular temporal details, asserting that this goes against Quranic statements of

God's omniscience. Al-Ghazali can be seen as a reactionary force against Hellenism, which as understood by Islam was more like a rival religion than a system of thought. Such was the influence of *al-Tahafut* that al-Ghazali is held responsible for almost shutting down philosophy as a separate discipline in Eastern Islam, making it entirely subsidiary to religious aims. The greatest response to it came nearly half a century later from the West when **Averroës** (Ibn Rushd), who was active in Spain and Africa, wrote *Tahafut al-Tahafut* (*The Incoherence of 'The Incoherence'*).

Such was the influence of al-Tahafut that al-Ghazali is held responsible for almost shutting down philosophy as a separate discipline in Eastern Islam.

Al-Ghazali's most constructive aspect was his integration of Sufism with the mainstream, a task to which he was uniquely suited. In *Revival of the Religious Sciences*, he set out the basis of Islamic spirituality, showing how it progressed to the higher mystical states of Sufism. Later in life, al-Ghazali came to see theology as merely subsidiary or preparatory to mysticism. In accordance with this, the prime virtue for al-Ghazali is love, which allows for a direct cognition of God by the soul. This strand of his thinking was very influential and culminated in the Persian school of Isfahan some three centuries later. In his *Mishkat al-Anwar* he explains, following al-Junayd, the father of 'sober' Sufism, 'the words of lovers when in a state of drunkenness must be hidden away and not broadcast'. A Sufi should not be held responsible for what he or she says in the 'drunken' state brought on by mystical experience, but should reflect on it in sobriety and modify his or her words according to reason and piety. He then quotes the famous utterances of **al-Hallaj** (I am the Truth), Abu Yazid (Glory be to me) and Abu Sa'id (Within my robe there is nothing but God), closing with the strange sentence, 'beyond these truths there are further mysteries, the penetration of which is not permissible'. Whether 'not permissible' means mysteries that should not be explored, or those that are heretical and should not be expressed remains ambiguous as al-Ghazali's never clarifies his meaning.

What is certain is that the 'sober' Sufism founded by al-Junayd and so successfully promulgated by al-Ghazali puts mystical experience – the direct perception of the divine – at the centre of Islamic practice. It provides a model within which the excesses of Sufic enthusiasm are tempered by reference to scriptural authority. The mysticism that emerges is not the absolute monism or identification of the self with God suggested by the three quotations above, but a qualified monism in which the individual self disappears in contemplation of the single reality of Allah.

AVERROËS
(IBN RUSHD)
1126–1198 CE

And Linus, Tully and moral Seneca,
Euclid and Ptolemy, Hippocrates,
Galenus, Avicen, and him who made
That commentary vast, Averroës.

Inferno, IV

Avicenna is the only other Muslim mentioned here by Dante. The followers of Averroës in Christian Europe were known as the Latin Averroists and they regarded him both as a faithful transmitter of Aristotle and as a great thinker in his own right. Others, notably Thomas Aquinas, objected to those aspects of his interpretation of Aristotle that were thought incompatible with Christian teaching, especially concerning the immortality of the individual soul. Bertrand Russell regards Averroës' version of Aristotle as being generally more authentic than that of Aquinas. His ideas on the intellect were especially influential. Averroës argues that the intellect of God and that of man are radically different: God's intellect is the cause of existent things, and existent things are the cause of man's intellect. Elsewhere he says, 'Intelligence is nothing but the perception of things with their causes[34]. The function of the intellect is to strip matter away from pure concepts, as for example when we look at a figure of a triangle and perceive its perfect mathematical form without the physical imperfections of its drawing. The concepts do not exist in a Realm of Pure Form, however, as Plato maintained, but only in the mind of man. Averroës takes the soundly scientific view that the world is well ordered and susceptible to reason. The world is created by the benevolence of God and the happiness of man rests in his ability to rise out of the corruption

Averroës is regarded by many as the most significant Islamic philosopher. He was born in Cordova, then a centre of learning to rival Damascus and Baghdad in the East. Raised in the traditions of *fiqh* (jurisprudence), he was a younger contemporary of the philosopher Ibn Tufail, whom he met at the court of Abu Ya'qub, then Amir in Cordova. The Amir requested that he write a commentary on Aristotle. This huge work became famous in Christian Europe, and accordingly it is with Averroës' name that Dante closes his list of pagan thinkers in the first circle of Hell:

of matter into the eternity of the higher spheres (his cosmology, like that of the other philosophers before him, is Greek). Latin Averroism was influential in Europe well into the fifteenth century.

The most significant of Averroës' works for the Muslim world is his refutation of **al-Ghazali's** *Tahafut al-Falasifah* (*The Incoherence of the Philosophers*), in the *Tahafut al-Tahafut* (*The Incoherence of 'The Incoherence'*). Unfortunately, its delightful title is not reflective of its contents, which are a thorough and systematic demolition of what was, in al-Ghazali, a rather rambling though comprehensive argument. Averroës suffered, like many Islamic philosophers, from the antagonism of the *Ulama*, the orthodox religious teachers, whose wide popular support enabled them to influence their political rulers. He was banished from Cordova to nearby Lucena and his books were publicly burned, although he was restored to favour after a short time and lived the remainder of his life in Marrakesh. Averroës' exile and disgrace give an indication of the political climate in which he lived. A central issue of the time was whether philosophy and religion were incompatible. According to al-Ghazali, the philosophers were *kufr* (heretical), which meant that they could be executed for maintaining their beliefs if this charge were upheld. Averroës sought to argue against this in his work. He asks whether philosophy is prohibited, permitted, recommended or ordained by Islam. His answer is that it is at least recommended, because of Muhammad's frequent exhortations that Muslims should reflect on the universe. Averroës' definition of philosophy is that it consists of a reflection on living beings in order to gain an understanding

Averroës

of their creator. His definition of theology is intentionally reminiscent of **al-Kindi's** definition of philosophy as true knowledge and true practice.

Averroës makes use of **al-Farabi's** conception that there are five forms of reason (the demonstrative, the dialectical, the rhetorical, the sophistical and the poetical). Again, the highest form is the demonstrative and is the preserve of philosophers, whereas the al-Asharite theologians are restricted to dialectic. Reason and revelation should go hand in hand, but where revelation conflicts with reason its meaning must be regarded as allegorical. The hidden (*batin*) significance should be discovered through philosophy.

The debate between al-Ghazali's position – theological and mystical – and that of Averroës – philosophical and scientific – is an important one not only for Islam but also for the

Averroës was forced to do penance for his intellectual temerity.

rise of Western Europe. Broadly speaking, Islam followed al-Ghazali and Europe Averroës, although it is too much to say, as some Islamic scholars do, that the rise of science in Europe is therefore an outgrowth of Islamic philosophy. Relatively speaking, Averroës' philosophy is scientific: he rejected astrology and doubted alchemy, of which even Newton was a practitioner. But scientists such as Galileo had to defeat Aristotelian ideas before their own ideas and methods could flourish. What is more accurate to say is that in his defence of causality against the theologians Averroës influenced modern Islam in a positive way. Al-Ghazali and **al-Ash'ari** both denied causation on the grounds that to compel God to follow natural laws was to lessen his power. Averroës argues against this viewpoint, which was partly

intended to establish the reality of miracles. God is the wise creator and accordingly his creation follows just laws, of which causation is an example. He does not deny the possibility of miracles, but objects to creating a system of thought based on such exceptional occurrences. Pointing to the instance in which Muhammad had refused to perform a miracle on the grounds that he was only a human being, he asserts that the true miracle of Islam is the Quran. This Averroist position is the one taken by most modern Islamic thinkers.

On the issue of predestination, Averroës maintains an original position, one which rejects both the notions of free will and predestination in favour of determinism. Actions are determined by causes that are either external (circumstance) or internal (individual disposition). God sees all and creates the appropriate circumstances for our dispositions. Averroës is an optimist and regards humanity as generally well intentioned.

With regard to his philosophical antecedents within Islam, Averroës sided more with al-Kindi and Aristotle than with al-Farabi and Plotinus. Al-Farabi held that philosophy and religion were one, a unicity that is itself Neoplatonic and mystical. Averroës has a more analytical approach and was the first to distinguish between Aristotelian and Neoplatonist ideas, which had become intermingled due to al-Kindi's mistake of crediting the *Enneads* to Aristotle. His importance is far greater to Western than to Islamic thought, however. The huge influence Averroës had on Europe in the Middle Ages and the Renaissance has no equivalent in Islam, which hardly remembers him.

Averroës' teachings were condemned by Muslim theologians who made him retract them on the Quran.

RUMI

1207-1273 CE

The Sufi poet Jalal al-Din Rumi was born in Afghanistan, but wrote in Persian. In early adulthood, he moved with his family to Anatolia, fleeing perhaps from the displeasure of the local ruler or from the Tartars. The name 'Rumi' means 'Roman', 'Rum' being the name of Anatolia that was part of the former Roman Empire. Rumi was born into a prominent family and received an excellent education. At 24, he took over his father's post, teaching religious science and mysticism. A meeting with the enigmatic mystic Shams of Tabriz transformed Rumi's life, inspiring him to become a Sufi and a poet. The closeness of Rumi's relationship with Shams seems to have caused discord within the circle of Rumi's disciples and Shams was forced to flee. He was later persuaded to return, but around 1247 CE, he again disappeared, possibly murdered by one of Rumi's circle or family.

Rumi was the author of a vast literature, mainly poetry. He is regarded as the greatest literary figure in the Islamic world. His poetry is now much admired in the West as well. Rumi's non-denominational, integrationist love of God is today a deeply appealing and widely acceptable form of religion. Although the literary qualities of his verse are hard to assess by a non-Persian speaker, and can seem quite bland in translation, the reader gets a strong sense of an overwhelming mystical love of God. An analogy in English is with the poetry of George Herbert, who similarly combined brilliance with devotionalism.

Like other Sufis discussed in this book, notably **al-Hallaj,** Rumi was given to unusual statements that were open to misunderstanding. He once

---

Art as Flirtation and Surrender

In your light, I learn how to love.
In your beauty, how to make poems.
You dance inside my chest, where
no one sees you, but sometimes I do,
and that sight becomes this art.

The Essential Rumi, translations by Coleman Barks
with John Moyne, 1995.

---

proclaimed, 'as to my creed I am neither a Jew, nor a Zoroastrian, not even a Muslim as this term is generally understood'. He claimed to support all 72 sects of Islam and when accused of being an atheist and heretic, he agreed. He was also known for his unusual practices, which included music, song and a whirling dance that accompanied the composition of his poetry. Rumi was the founder of the Mevlevi order of 'whirling' dervishes. Despite this he does not seem to have suffered persecution. He was quite critical of Greek-influenced theological dialectic, as practised by his father's old adversary, Razi: 'If dialectics alone could reveal the secrets of the spirit, Razi would have certainly reached them, but the feet of the dialectician are wooden and the wooden feet are the most shaky.'

> 'As to my creed,
> I am neither a Jew
> nor a Zoroastrian, not even a
> Muslim as the term is
> generally understood.'

Rumi is not a philosopher, but his training and education equipped him to understand its complexities. His thought is instinctual and experiential, but a coherent philosophy emerges. He is an Emanationist after Plotinus, in the tradition of **al-Farabi** and **Avicenna,** which is to say that the world is an emanation or overflow from God. Like Aristotle, he maintains that the motive force of the universe is the love of God. Unlike any of these, however, for Rumi love really is greater than reason. Existence has a purpose for every soul, and that purpose is to evolve towards God. In a remarkable passage in the *Mathnawi,* Rumi sets out his philosophy of evolution:

*For several epochs I was flying
about in space like atoms of dust
without a will,
after which I entered the
inorganic realm
of matter. Crossing over to the
vegetable kingdom I lost all
memory of my struggle
on the material plane. From there I
stepped into the animal kingdom,
forgetting all my life as a plant, feeling
only an instinctive and unconscious
urge towards the growth of plants and
flowers...rising in the scale of animality
I became a man pulled up by the
creative urge of the Creator whom
one knows. I continued advancing
from realm to realm developing my
reason and strengthening the organism.
There was ground for ever getting
above the previous types of reason.
Even my present rationality is not a
culmination of mental evolution. This,
too, has to be transcended, because it
is still contaminated with self-seeking,
egoistic biological urges. A thousand
other types of reason and
consciousness shall emerge during the
further course of my ascent;
a wonder of wonders!*[35]

Several things are worth noting here. First, Rumi believes that souls are eternal, all seeking to evolve. These

Leibniz believed that the physical world was simply the surface of reality; ultimate reality was composed of the mind-like entities that he named monads.

souls might be compared to the monads of Leibniz, with Allah as the greatest of all souls. Second, time and space do not exist in the spiritual realm. Although this intuition develops over 'several epochs', Rumi still reports this as an experience. In line with this, he also wrote, 'I existed when there were neither names nor the things that are named'. Third, he sets forth a version of evolutionary reincarnation. Fourth, despite his comment about 'self-seeking, egoistic biological urges', the overarching idea is positive. One does not reach Rumi's God through self-denial but through self-transcendence. The ego is not destroyed but purified again and again until it is fit for the company of the quality-less Supreme. In this, Rumi shows his Islamic heart, affirming the eternity and integrity of the individual self. Life is not an illusion, but an affirmation of physical reality. The illusion is death.

A group of whirling dervishes. Muslim devotees of the Sufi sect perform their ritual dance barefoot.

IBN KHALDUN
1332-1406 CE

diplomat, and if his thinking had something Machiavellian about it, it might be said that his behaviour did as well. Born in Tunis, Ibn Khaldun belonged to a distinguished Arab (or possibly Berber) family. As a boy, he learned the Quran by heart and studied theology, grammar,

*His parents
and all of his tutors
fell victim to the plague,
which, Ibn Khaldun
reflected sadly,
'folded the carpet with
everything on it'.*

Ibn Khaldun is a unique and exceptional figure within the tradition of Islamic thought. He saw himself as the creator of a new science, an assessment with which many scholars would agree. Today, his field of inquiry would fall within the social sciences and would be categorized as cultural history. Some of Ibn Khaldun's insights foreshadow Western developments that did not take place until the past few decades. For this reason, although he does not fit into any of the normal categories of Muslim thought, he deserves to be regarded as one of the greatest minds of Islam. In addition to the great originality of his new science, he is also responsible for an important critique of the theology and philosophy of his time.

This life of Ibn Khaldun is fascinating and there is no doubt that he was one of the greatest figures of the fourteenth century. He was a tremendously able politician and

rhetoric and jurisprudence. The peaceful progress of his life and education was shattered by the cataclysm of the plague of 1349 CE that decimated the populations of North Africa and Europe. His parents and all of his tutors fell victim to the plague, which, Ibn Khaldun reflected sadly, 'folded the carpet with everything on it'. He contemplated emigrating before being summoned to office at the age of 20 by the ruler of Tunis. This was the beginning of a colourful political life in which Ibn Khaldun demonstrated again and again over the next 25 years his willingness to pursue personal gain and fame at all cost. No sooner would a new political master be on the throne than Ibn Khaldun would be at his side. He travelled from court to court around North Africa and Andalucia and Ibn Khaldun wasted no opportunity for intrigue and adventure. Two years in prison and countless intrigues later, Ibn Khaldun seems finally to have lost his taste for politics with the torture and execution of his friend Ibn al-Khatib, who was to Andalucia what Ibn Khaldun was to Africa: its greatest scholar, poet and political intriguer. He settled down to write his great *History* and completed it in 1382 CE. His earlier life caught up with him, however, and he was forced to flee Tunis (where he had again settled) for Cairo, under the pretext of making a pilgrimage to Mecca. There he was feted by the local scholars and shortly appointed to one of the highest judicial posts in the city. Throwing

Modern pilgrims circle the Al Kaba at the centre of Mecca in Saudi Arabia.

himself into his new role, Ibn Khaldun displayed such passion for justice and impatience with the habitual corruption of the judiciary

that he lasted less than a year in the job. He was restored to the post five times more in his life, but he never lasted long in it due to political intrigue, into which he entered with his old enthusiasm. He travelled in the East, making the pilgrimage to Mecca and also travelling to Jerusalem. At Damascus he found himself besieged in the city by the great Mongol leader Timur (Tamburlaine). With typical élan, he had himself lowered down from the walls and went alone to the tyrant's tent where he successfully negotiated the surrender of Damascus. He spent his last years in Cairo, still embroiled in political struggles, though never again at the pinnacle of political life. He died in 1406 CE.

Ibn Khaldun's critique of philosophy and theology is set out in the *Prolegomena* to the *History*. He takes pains to distinguish his new science from both the political philosophy of the time and the science of rhetoric, which is his term for dialectical theology. He neither attempts to show how people *should* be governed, nor to persuade anyone that the Islamic systems are inevitable. Instead, he undertakes a scientific examination of the different types of government that have existed and their relation to human nature. Through this, he hopes to arrive at an understanding of how the concept of government naturally arises, of what its natural forms are, and of history based on the observation of demonstrable realities. He writes that 'water is not so like to water as the future to the past'. His critique of previous historians includes their tendency to interpret Islamic history as inevitable and natural. In this view, the ruler has authority from God, via the Prophet, and society needs to be ruled by divine law and by prophesy. Ibn Khaldun points out that most societies are neither Islamic nor 'People of the Book', by which term Muhammad referred to Jews, Christians and Zoroastrians, and yet they succeeded in organising themselves on rational lines. He concludes that there are natural propensities in man that enable society and rulership, both of which he assumes to be essential goods. He also attacks his predecessors for their failure to apply common sense: for example, in recognizing that many of the accounts in traditional chronicles of number of armies and amounts of money must be wrong.

> *'The intellect should not be used to weigh such matters as the oneness of God, the other world, the truth of prophecy, the real character of the divine attributes, or anything else that lies beyond the level of the intellect.'*

Ibn Khaldun is critical of the Greek tradition of Plato and **al-Farabi** for similar reasons. He distinguishes between natural science and divine science (a division he takes from **Avicenna**) and maintains that the former has never been perfectly carried out with respect to mankind. Divine science aims at the good and depends on metaphysical questions as to its nature, which may be resolved either by revelation or by philosophizing. Revelation is self-validating; philosophizing is rhetorical, because its truths are not demonstrable. Natural science aims at what is demonstrably true. Ibn Khaldun's critique is thus not of religion or scientific philosophy, but of those whom he classes as mere rhetoricians, being those who claim to offer reasonable proof of what is divine. He writes, 'the intellect should not be used to weigh such matters as the oneness of God, the other world, the truth of prophecy, the real character of the divine attributes, or anything else that lies beyond the level of the intellect' (*Prolegomena 3*, 38). Like **al-Ghazali**, he rejects proof of God; unlike him, he does support philosophy in its proper place. The one philosopher who escapes his attack is **Averroës**, another judge who distinguished between true religion and true philosophy. In philosophy Ibn Khaldun looks forward to modern thinking, but in religion he yearns for a time before the invention of *kalam* or dialectical theology. He might on this account be expected to oppose Sufism, but he does not adopt a position similar to al-Ghazali's. Indeed, his poetry is Sufi in style.

To turn from his view of philosophy to what Ibn Khaldun called *'ilm al-'umran*, the science of culture. *Umran*, meaning culture or civilization, is one of two key terms associated with Ibn Khaldun's thought. The other is *'asabiya* or social cohesion, a quality he associated with the nomadic Arabs. The two main social groups distinguished by him are the nomads and the townspeople. His view of history, like that of Thucydides, is cyclical. It is also, as might be expected from his biography, a rather pessimistic view, in which instability and corruption are inevitable. The nomads are hardy, courageous and have strong *'asabiya*. The townspeople are cultured and wealthy, but weak individually and as a group. Ibn Khaldun's theory of *Umran* is that the nomads conquer the townspeople and rule over them for about three generations or 120 years, in which time they acquire the vices of the town. The ruler is then forced to hire mercenaries to protect his authority, but his empire is ready to fall at the first attack.

Ibn Khaldun's ideas on culture, though limited in their application to the cultural epoch in which he found himself, are a successful analysis of the observed facts. Plato's theory of the decline of society from aristocracy to tyranny (to take a contrary example) is, despite some interesting observations, created to fit his metaphysics. Ibn Khaldun's originality lies in his radical methodology, his convictions about human nature and his conception of *'asabiya*.

Arab nomads with their livestock and livelihood.

Part Three

THE
FAR EAST

CHINA, KOREA
AND JAPAN

CHINESE PHILOSOPHY: INTRODUCTION

The course of Chinese philosophy is frequently seen as a dialectic, with Confucianism the thesis, Daoism and Buddhism the antithesis and Neo-Confucianism the synthesis.

The three great Chinese teachers of spiritual wisdom – Buddha, Laozi and Confucius.

China's long isolation from the rest of the world has given its philosophy a strong individuality. To the east and south there were vast oceans and to the north and west impassable mountains, deserts and wasteland. The first outside influence was that of Buddhism, arriving near the start of the first century CE. There were subsequently several waves of Buddhist influence, and some other Indian ideas filtered through, but until early modern times there were no other significant philosophical imports. This had its positive aspect: Chinese culture was allowed to maintain its integrity for millennia. On the negative side, the lack of challenge to Chinese thought meant that it developed less variety than elsewhere and became

somewhat insular. Nevertheless, there is no doubt that China takes equal place as one of the three great philosophical cultures of the world. Whereas the West emphasized the rational, and India the spiritual, China is home to the world's greatest tradition of ethical and social thought. China's philosophy does have its spiritual side, and to a lesser degree, rational aspects but its distinctive contribution is its exploration of how we ought to live with each other.

This tradition is that of Confucius, the great founding figure of Chinese philosophy and the inspiration for much of its culture, government and law. He is the main wellspring of Chinese thought and its debt to him is no less than that of Western philosophy to Socrates. The deficiencies in Chinese philosophy are, very broadly speaking, the areas on which Confucius preferred not to focus. These are enumerated by Fung Yu-Lan as its lack of philosophical methodology, logic and epistemology, as well as a relative weakness in metaphysics.

Daoism or Taoism, the other great Chinese contribution is, in some sense, the perfect balance to Confucianism. It characterizes itself as the weak, feminine, passive and dark *yin* to Confucianism's strong, masculine, active and bright *yang*. Thus it represents the contemplative aspect of life, while

Confucianism represents the active principle of it. Confucianism in some form or other was part of the Chinese state since the Han Dynasty (206 BCE–220 CE) while Daoism sustained itself at the edges, communing with nature and developing an ascetic way of life. It is often identified with an egalitarian counter-culture. It was founded by Laozi (Lao-Tzu), but an equally great figure in its early history is Zhuangzi. Its later history is patchier than that of establishment Confucianism. Daoism seemed to degenerate easily into superstition, divination and magic. A frequent concern of Daoists was the search for the elixir of life, a pursuit totally at odds with the essential philosophy of its founders.

Buddhism, as has already been said, was the first substantial outside influence. Nevertheless, the strength of Chinese culture was such that it developed its own forms of Buddhism, often derived from the Daoism with which it has much in common.

In China, Zen (originally Chan) Buddhism was an original form that developed from Daoist sources and is distinctively non-Indian. Another important Chinese form we consider in this book is Huayen Buddhism, as complex intellectually as Zen is anti-intellectual.

The course of Chinese philosophy is frequently seen as a dialectic, with Confucianism the thesis, Daoism and Buddhism the antithesis and Neo-Confucianism the synthesis. The great Neo-Confucian renaissance of the eleventh and twelfth centuries saw Daoist and Buddhist concepts renew Confucianism, which then became a more balanced and robust system. This is not to say that all that was good in Daoism and Buddhism was swallowed up by Confucianism. Indeed, the suggestion of a Darwinian struggle for hearts and minds is mistaken. The Chinese saying 'three religions, one religion' reflects the relatively peaceful co-existence of the traditions. Overall, however, it would be correct to say that in terms of

A Zen garden being tended by a monk in Kyoto, Japan.

philosophy, the Confucians are the most important, and that they also have been the most important influence on Chinese society. Daoism and Buddhism become tributaries to the Confucian philosophical stream, despite their continuing religious importance.

It is worth noting here that a term such as 'Confucian' or 'Confucianism' is more or less unknown in Chinese thought. The Confucians were simply the *ru* *(ju)*, a word meaning 'literati'. Just as Socrates thought of himself as a philosopher, the *ru* were the educated élite who pondered on philosophical issues. They spoke about the Way or *Dao* but distinguished themselves from unorthodox thinkers, known as Daoists, and from Buddhists. In some ways, it would be more accurate to think of them not as Confucian but as the mainstream Chinese philosophers.

The twentieth century was the most traumatic period in Chinese history in over 2,000 years. Disruptive influences from Europe and its growing dominance had gradually rendered the old ways untenable. The empire finally ended in 1912, being replaced first by a republic and later by the Communism of Mao Zedong, who took power in 1949. Philosophically, too, the old order suffered its heaviest blow, with Confucianism finally removed from the centre of government and education. The same period saw a rise in interest in Chinese-derived forms of Buddhism and Daoism in the West. Although Western responses are often somewhat shallow, ultimately these systems may be recognized for what they have to offer. Daoism seems to appeal strongly to the Western sensibility because of its connection

---

Transliteration of Chinese

There are two main systems of transliteration of Chinese characters into Latin script. The older and more familiar is the Wade-Giles system, but it is generally acknowledged to be inferior to the newer pinyin *method, which is also the official method recognized by China. Although some Chinese names like Lao-Tzu and Mao Tse-Tung are familiar to us in their Wade-Giles transliteration rather than the* pinyin Laozi and Mao Zedong, *the latter method has been used throughout, with Wade-Giles alternatives generally given in parentheses. Translations in Wade-Giles retain the original transliterations, however.*

---

with nature and its antagonism towards system building, technology and commerce, while Confucianism has been relatively neglected. The final effect of the upheavals of the last hundred years on Chinese philosophy remains to be seen, but if the old systems can adapt to new challenges, they may prove resilient.

CONFUCIUS
(KONGFUZI,
K'UNG FU-TZU)
551–479 BCE

Confucius is a Latinization of Kongfuzi, literally 'Master Kong'. His name was first known to the West through the publication of Confucian works by Jesuits who settled in Peking in 1583. 'Confucius' soon became almost a byword in the West for Chinese wisdom. We might imagine that this myth greatly exaggerates the importance of Confucius in China but this is not so. Although there is often little relation between Confucius' philosophy and its historical impact, there is no more influential figure in Chinese thought.

The documentary accounts of Confucius' life are relatively uncontroversial, unlike some other philosophers of the period. The *Analects*, where his teaching is to be found, was probably started long after his death and was being 'edited' for over a century or two. However, the reported 'life events' involve no supernatural or impossible claims. Leaving aside apocryphal material, the accepted sketch goes like this. He was born in the state of Lu, present-day Shandong Province. His family may have been aristocratic, but by the time of Confucius' birth, they had no income from land holdings. Confucius thought he lived in turbulent times, as hinted at by a story told of his father in which he held up a portcullis gate with his bare hands to help his companions escape. However, China's Warring States period had not begun. His father died when he was only three and he was raised by his mother. By Confucius' own account 'I was of humble station when I was young. That is why I am skilled in many menial things' (*Analects*, IX, 6)[36]. According to the *Mencius*, he was once employed as a 'minor official in charge of stores', and at another time 'in charge of sheep and cattle'. By the age of 27, he may have been employed at the court of Lu in some capacity. Later, he may have been involved in diplomacy and was at the court of Wei. His role ended when he refused or was unable to advise the duke on military matters. In his late forties, some accounts report that he was appointed to the post of police commissioner in Lu, but he resigned after a short time. There followed 'for more than a decade' a period of travel in other states to the southwest of Lu. Confucius was then in his fifties and seems to have lived under threat of assassination. He was back in Lu in 484 BCE and seems to have been employed at court as a counsellor of low rank. Despite this there are several conversations recorded with the duke and his prime minister from this period. Confucius died in 479 BCE.

More important than Confucius' political life, however, is his establishment of a school, perhaps in his thirties, after which he was a professional teacher, much like the Greek Sophists. His learning may have stemmed from some military training – he taught his students charioteering and archery. But his intellectual passion was traditional ceremony. His teaching and appealing personality had an enormous effect on his students. This gives us Confucius' own playful description of himself:

> *The governor of She asked TzuLu about Confucius. Tzu-Lu did not answer. The master [i.e. Confucius] said, 'Why did you not simply say something to this effect: he is the sort of man who forgets to eat when he tries to solve a problem that has been driving him to distraction, who is so full of joy that he forgets his worries, and who does not notice the onset of old age.'*

Analects, VII, 19.

The most extreme accounts credit Confucius with over 3,000 students. A significant number founded other Confucian schools with varying emphases. Confucius is also credited with editing (or perhaps writing) some of the books that are known today as the 'Confucian Classics', including *The Classic on Poetry, The Classic on History* and *The Book of Li.* Among the huge corpus of Confucian works, however, the only one that attributes most of its teachings to 'the master' is the *Analects* (that is, 'literary gleanings'). The *Analects* do not purport to be the writings of Confucius, but a later collection of sayings attributed to him and to some of his disciples.

As with other Eastern cultures described in this book, philosophy and religion are not rigidly delineated. Confucian philosophy, like Daoist thought, became a popular form of religion and in later times competed with the third major religion in China and East Asia, Buddhism. None of these three has a 'true church' mentality and they are often seen as non-competitive. Chinese popular practitioners say, 'three religions are one'. Confucianism was probably the first idea system to take shape in China and its impact has been greater than the other two.

Confucianism can be described as civic humanism, principally concerned with human social life as opposed to the divine. Accordingly, its main interests are in ethics and moral psychology: how may we cultivate the character that reliably acts rightly? Confucianism concerns itself with such questions at all levels, from mundane family relations to interstate diplomacy and rule. Daoism, by contrast, emphasizes the metaphysical, in particular meta-ethics – questions about the ultimate nature, reality and knowability of the moral *Dao*. This leads some Daoists to become moral sceptics or relativists who locate human morality as a small part of the *Dao* of nature. Confucius emphasizes his thoroughgoing humanism by contrast when he says, 'It is man who is capable of broadening the Way (*Dao*). It is not the Way that is capable of broadening man' (XV, 29). Other Daoists (sometimes called 'primitivists') become anti-moral and anti-social, withdrawing from social life in quietism and solitude. A primitivist who says Confucius should follow him and 'run away from the world altogether' prompts him to comment:

'One cannot associate with birds and beasts. Am I not a member of this human race? Who, then, is there for me to associate with? While the Way [Dao] is to be found in the empire, I will not change places with him.'

Analects, XVIII, 6.

Confucianism contrasts with Buddhism partly in its avoidance of discussions on eternal life, a subject on which Confucius refuses to comment. He seems to have been agnostic about the afterlife and pragmatically advised wariness with regard to higher beings:

Fan Ch'ih asked about wisdom. The master said, 'To work for the things the common people have a right to and to keep one's distance from the gods and spirits while showing them reverence can be called wisdom.'

Analects, VI, 22.

Confucius marked a change in Chinese thinking on divine matters, even though he rarely spoke of them. In the earlier dynasty, religion was concerned with God as *Shang Di* 'the emperor above'. As for Confucius, some

of his disciples complained that he rarely spoke of *Tian* (Heaven or Nature), and that he refused to speak, as others did, of the Way or Will of Tian. This verbal change marks an important break with the previous conception of a personal and active moral authority. For Confucius and his successors, moral authority is impersonal, and its

guidance is given in the constant ways enshrined in nature. It would be wrong to suppose Confucius an atheist, since he accepts the authority of Tian, but nonetheless his philosophy functions without a personal deity.

At this period, other similar developments were taking place elsewhere in the world. New belief systems were springing up, such as the Upanishads, Buddhism and Jainism in India; and in Greece there was the growth of rational philosophy. All these, in their own way, represent moves away from tribal and ritual religion, whether towards ethical and social concerns (as with Confucius and Socrates) or towards speculative forms of philosophy and religion (as with Laozi, the Upanishads and Buddhism). However, it should be noted that Confucius is by temperament conservative. In this his approach echoes that of Socrates or the Upanishads, rather than the more radical Buddhism, insisting on respect for the old religion while 'keep[ing] one's distance'.

Another factor that distinguishes Confucianism is its emphasis on traditional ritual or propriety (*li*). If people live properly, according to tradition, then their behaviour will be correctly regulated. *Li* includes filial piety, respect for your ancestors, rite observance and performing

one's duties properly. Confucius is convinced that if people follow *li* it will lead to the reformation of their character and that of the state. For example, Confucius maintains that a man loyal to both his father and older brother (the two most important traditional relationships) will also be loyal to the state. Ritual, too, is to be valued not for its religious significance, but simply because it gives people something refined to follow:

Tzu-Kung wanted to do away with the sacrificial sheep at the announcement of the new moon. The master said, 'Ssu, you are loath

Confucius consults the I-Ching, the divinational Book of Changes.

to part with the price of the sheep,
but I am loath to see the
disappearance of the rite.'

Analects, III, 17.

Confucius' views on the importance of *li* (ritual) throughout society could be compared with Plato's ideas of justice; not as a legal system, but in terms of each thing being in its proper place.

Another important concept for Confucius is that of *yi* which roughly means 'morality' or 'duty'. Confucius did not relate this concept specifically to *li*, but it supplies his system with a moral principle against which social rituals may be assessed:

The gentleman is not invariably
for or against anything. He is on
the side of what is moral (yi).

Analects, IV, 10.

Rounding out the picture of Confucian moral philosophy is the enigmatic term *ren* (humanity). *Ren* is also translated variously as 'benevolence', 'kindness', and 'human-heartedness'. When asked about the meaning of *ren*, Confucius responded, 'Love your fellow man'. In his use of the term, Confucius makes it clear that he regards it as the most fundamental: 'What can a man do with *li* (ritual) who is not *ren?*' Thus humanity or loving-kindness becomes the guiding light for social order. Although Confucius is not clear on what *ren* might be – perhaps it is a catch-all word for human virtue – his successors developed these hints so that the term became perhaps

the most important in Chinese philosophy. Han Dynasty (206 BCE–220 CE) thinkers understood it more or less to mean 'love', eventually becoming 'universal love'. With the Neo-Confucian thinkers, led by **Zhang Zai** (1020–1077 CE), *ren* grew to encompass the entire universe, a concept usually expressed as 'forming one body with all things'.

'At 70,
I followed my heart
and did not err.'

For Confucius, however, *ren* is best seen as the cardinal element in the make-up of the 'superior man', a term that more than any other forms the subject matter of the *Analects*. The superior man (or in Lau's translation, the 'gentleman') is moderate, serious, respectful, loyal and flexible: he is 'on the side of what is moral.'

Another term he uses often interchangeably with that of the gentleman is 'the benevolent man'. Propriety and goodness are intimately linked. Elsewhere he says that a gentleman possesses both native energy and refinement, another sentiment echoed by Plato. Confucius' aim in political reform centres not on legislation but on the moral leadership of society: that is, on the moral character of the leader. A ruler asks him about capital punishment and his response is highly instructive:

'In administering your government,
what need is there for you to kill?
Just desire the good yourself and the
common people will be good. The
virtue of the gentleman is like wind;
the virtue of the small man is like

grass. Let the wind blow over the grass and it is sure to bend.'

Analects, XII, 19.

Another primary aspect of Confucius' social theory is the 'Rectification of Names', which he called the 'first principle of government'. In a narrow sense, it means the conformity of behaviour to linguistic codes, such as *li* and penal codes. In a broader sense, it comes to refer to a mirroring between a person's role and his name (which also denotes rank or status), and later to refer to a general correspondence between appearance (outer) and actuality, (inner). The 'Rectification of Names' is a very important concept in later Chinese philosophy and is considered separately on pp. 130–132.

Perhaps the best illustration of the aim of Confucius' philosophy is given in one of the longest of the *Analects,* in which Confucius invites four of his disciples to speak about what they would do if they could. One would take responsibility for a small, embattled kingdom; another would take on the management of a district; the third would take on the role of a minor ceremonial official. The fourth, Tien, says:

'In late spring, after the spring clothes have been newly made, I should like, together with five or six adults and six or seven boys, to go bathing in the River Yi and enjoy the breeze on the Rain Altar, and then to go home chanting poetry.' The master sighed and said, 'I am all in favour of Tien'.

Analects, XI, 26.

The arresting quality of this dreamy passage is the stark contrast it presents to Confucius' general concern with constant study, the appropriate observation of ritual and the reform of society. Here we have the Confucius who describes his life as culminating in ease and propriety: 'at 70, I followed my heart and did not err'. The effort to acquire wisdom and to cultivate oneself is undertaken for its own sake because it is a joy, and as this passage shows, has joy as its aim.

Although Confucius was not politically successful during his own lifetime, his ideas gradually permeated the politics of the empire following the Han Dynasty, which displaced the Qin Dynasty that had unified China in 221 BCE. The Han adopted Confucianism as a state ideology in the second century CE, and although with the fall of the Han in 220 CE Confucianism lost some of its appeal, it was later revived under the Song Dynasty (960–1279 CE), in particular by the orthodox Neo-Confucian thinker, **Zhuxi** (1130–1200 CE). Zhuxi's work codified Confucian thought and his commentaries formed the basis for Chinese civil service examinations, set up in 1313 CE and unchanged for some 600 years. Interestingly, these exams are perhaps the most direct example of Confucius' influence in the West, as they served as the model for those established by the East India Company, which in turn later became the basis of the public examination system of the British Empire and thus of the Western world.

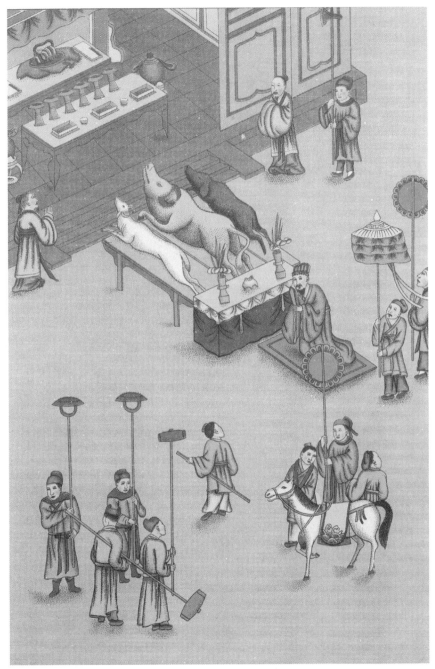

The Emperor Kao Tsu (personal name: Liu Pang), founder of the Han Dynasty, sacrifices a pig, a goat and a cow before the tomb of Confucius.

THE RECTIFICATION OF NAMES

The Rectification of Names was discussed first by **Confucius** *(551–479 BCE) and is, according to Wing-Tsit Chan, 'a perennial theme in the Confucian School, as well as in nearly all other schools' of Chinese philosophy. The topic came to divide those who maintained an interest in social and ideological forms and norms, and those that sought to question or break them down. The idea of 'rectification' arises from Confucius' view that names and actions had begun to change, corrupting everything. The process he describes is of a gradual drift of authority away from those who should exercise it – ideally the emperor – downwards to lesser figures. Power passes from the emperor to the nobles, from the nobles to the ministers and from the ministers to their officials. This leads ultimately to the downfall of the empire. For Confucius the solution is the Rectification of Names. This has two principal meanings: first, that the 'names' people have, that is, their job titles or roles such as minister, farmer, father, son, sister and so on, and their actual conduct should coincide; and second, that words and deeds should in general coincide.*

Confucius is asked what his first measure in government would be, and his reply is 'the Rectification of Names'. His account is as follows:

When names are not correct, what is said will not sound reasonable; when what is said does not sound reasonable, affairs will not culminate in success; when affairs do not culminate in success, rites and music will not flourish; when rites and music do not flourish, punishments will not fit the crimes; when punishments do not fit the crimes, the common people will not know where to put hand and foot. Thus when the gentleman names something, the name is sure to be useable in speech, and when he says something, this is sure to be practicable. The thing about the gentleman is that he is anything but casual where speech is concerned.

Analects, XIII, 3.

His other direct reference to the subject is when he says:

Let the ruler be a ruler, the subject a subject, the father a father and the son a son.

Analects, XII, 11.

Confucius' main concern here is ethical. If the 'gentleman' or 'superior man' is careful, accurate, clear and practical in his speech, then others will have a good lead to follow. If he is casual, unclear or unrealistic in what he says, then others will be confused. Furthermore there is the implication that those in authority must be responsible.

Confucius' discussion of the Rectification of Names is one of the more difficult areas in his philosophy. Insofar as the Rectification of Names is a principle of government, it is easy to follow. Its other aspect, the correspondence between word and deed, knowledge and action, and name and actuality, is more complex. The difficulty is not so much in what he says as in what he does not say or merely hints at. As with the question of human nature, which he refused to discuss, the topic became one of the fundamental questions for his successors. We will now look at some of these and their divergent views.

Hanfeizi *(280–233 BCE) makes the Rectification of Names into a matter for legislation. Everyone must do their duty and only their duty. Doing more than one's duty is as bad as doing less; exaggerating one's achievements and downplaying them are equally wrong. This extreme view leads to tyranny and is hardly in the Confucian spirit.*

*The Confucian **Xunzi** (298–238 BCE), Hanfeizi's teacher, examines the subject more closely. He relates it to our sense perceptions. If we see something with the eyes but fail to name it properly, 'there is no knowledge' and we are unable to make use of it. Thus, naming is part of the process of thinking. For Xunzi, names are conventional rather than fundamental: ordering things is not in any way natural, though it is necessary. In this, he diverges from the mainstream view, which is that there is something fundamental about names: the sage is someone who sees how things are and so divines the correct names for them. Typical of this approach is another Confucian, Tung Chungshu (c. 179–104 BCE), who is fascinated by etymology. For example, the word for people (min) is derived from the word for sleep (ming); therefore the people need to be awakened by education. Confucius did not discuss whether names are conventional or fundamental, and so he supports neither view.*

*The Rectification of Names was attacked by the socially radical followers of **Mozi** (c. 470–391 BCE) on the grounds that one-name-one-thing was unsustainable. A similar line was taken by the 'School of Names' thinkers, such as the paradox maker Gongsun Long. In the chapter on Xunzi we examine how he tackles these challenges to the concept. Social order is essential to Xunzi and, for him, the growth of linguistic logic provides a way for the social order to be questioned. His development of a more subtle version of the Rectification of Names is itself an excellent and rare example of Chinese logic.*

In the Neo-Confucian movement of the twelfth century onwards, the theme continued to be an important one. **Wang Yangming** (1472–1529 CE) took the idea further than anyone had before in arguing that name (or knowledge) and actuality (action) were the same thing. Knowing about something without acting on it, or acting without knowledge, was a mistake, and to divide the two was a logical error. Again, the name, or the knowledge one possesses, is a moral injunction to do what is right and fitting.

Daoist thinkers take an opposite view. **Laozi** (Lao-Tzu), for example, opens his Daode Jing with the enigmatic words:

> The Way (Dao) that can be told of is not the eternal Way;
> The name that can be named is not the eternal name.
> The Nameless is the origin of Heaven and Earth;
> The Named is the mother of all things.
> Therefore let there always be non-being so we may see their subtlety.

While Confucius argues for external clarity and order, Laozi emphasizes the underlying mystery of life. The true teacher 'spreads doctrines without words'. Names have their power – 'the named is the mother of all things', but the fundamental reality is precisely that which is unnameable.

Zhuangzi argues in a similar way that the Confucian view lacks subtlety and substance: 'Words are not just wind. Words have something to say. But if what they have to say is not fixed, then do they really say something?'

MOZI (MO TZU)

c. 470–391 BCE

Mohism, the philosophy founded by Mozi, was with Confucianism one of the two most important early schools of thought in China during the Warring States period (403–222 BCE). It was destroyed by the Qin unification and oppression of rival thinkers and, because of its fierce opposition to Confucianism, became anathema when the Han Dynasty made Confucianism the state orthodoxy. Confucians criticized it as being too idealistic in its universalism while the Daoists viewed it as being too severe and demanding with its utilitarian morality. Within 300 years of his death, Mozi's school had disappeared. Mohism was never to recover its former importance, although its utilitarianism and anti-Confucianism led to a revival of interest in China in the twentieth century.

Like many Chinese thinkers from the pre-imperial age, Mozi's life is not well documented. He was born in either Lu or Song province (present-day Shandong). Various accounts of his life suggest that he was an artisan, a follower of Confucius and a kind of mercenary or, as the first-century BCE chronicle *Shi Ji* has it, that he was a powerful Song government official. In any case, Mozi eventually gave up his former pursuits and became a wandering teacher, attempting like **Confucius** to convince various rulers to adopt his ideas. At least three schools of disciples promulgated Mozi's ideas, while others worked to end offensive warfare and some developed semantic and proto-scientific thought. In the *Mozi*, the book that sets out Mohist thought, the schools present their rival interpretations, with three different essays on each topic. Some parts of the *Mozi* are later additions and it is doubtful that Mozi actually wrote any of the book, but it is generally accepted to be representative of his thought.

> '*When I do what Tian wants, Tian does what I want.*'

The central value in Mozi's philosophy is *li* (benefit or utility) which he develops into altruistic utilitarianism. The important virtue is universal love (*jianai*) which Mohists contrast with Confucians' emphasis on filial relations and 'graded' concern for others. Mozi's reasoning here is that if everyone followed a doctrine of partiality to their kin, it would be worse for everyone. In this view, the well-being of one's family comes to depend on the well-being of all. This virtuous concern for the social welfare is commended not because it is natural or good in itself, but because it produces good utilitarian consequences. However, in other places he appeals to *Tian* ('Heaven' or 'Nature') to justify his valuing of utility. As he observes characteristically, 'when I do what *Tian* wants, *Tian* does what I want'[37]. *Tian* approves of moral action and naturally rewards it, while punishing immorality. Although Mohism has attracted interest in recent times for its similarity to Christian teachings on love, its appeal to universal utilitarianism is in reality very different.

In contrast to Confucianism with its emphasis on family piety, Mozi taught that people should do what would result in universal good for all people. Doing good (*li* or 'benefit' or 'utility') is explained mainly in material terms. We 'love' our neighbours by supplying their physical needs for food, clothing and shelter – not by showering them with some emotion. Our concern for those farther afield, even those in foreign states, should motivate us to accept peaceful policies. Mozi bitterly condemned all 'offensive' warfare. Curiously, he did not think of war as motivated by selfishness, but by moral disagreements. But the result is the opposite of what anyone would call moral. So he urges us to abide by a common, unambiguous and measurable standard of morality – general utility. According to Mozi, the main evil in society is selfishness or partiality towards those that are close to us. Partial love is no love at all. Other Chinese thinkers did not dismiss this idea, but its failure to acknowledge the particular ties of family and hierarchy were felt to be its weakness. As the Confucian **Xunzi** wrote two centuries later: 'Mozi has insight about equality (universal love) but not about inequality (distinction in human relations)'.

Mohism was opposed to anything that did not directly contribute to people's well-being. Thus he criticized the Confucian preoccupation with showy rituals and ceremonies – particularly those associated with China's lavish funeral practices and the elaborate concerts and musical performances for the rulers. Mozi thus goes much further than Confucius, who loved all these things while expressing coolness towards the primitive beliefs that had done much to put them in place. Confucius' conversation with Tzu-Kung (quoted in the previous chapter) on the subject of an animal sacrifice draws up the battle lines between Confucianism and Mohism: 'you are loath to part with the price of the sheep, but I am loath to see the disappearance of the rite'. On the other hand, Mozi does maintain a commitment to Tian and argues for the utility of maintaining public discourse about spirits and ghosts. Mozi is equally critical of elaborate funerary and mourning ritual because they lead mourners to waste fortunes and to throw away years of productivity. He even goes so far as to criticize the tradition of celibacy during the mourning period on the grounds that people should carry on with the duty of reproduction.

Mozi's critique of music is that it is wasteful and extravagant – the term used for music also translates as 'pleasure' or 'entertainment' and Confucius often pairs it with his *li* (ritual). In ancient China, the term probably referred to lavish royal concerts, complete with acrobats. In Mozi's view, the musicians could better employ their keen senses in tilling the fields or making cloth, the rulers should not waste their time attending recitals, and the state should not spend its resources on maintaining

Mozi viewed music as a wasteful extravagance.

expensive troupes of performers. Nothing in Mozi's formulation suggests he is opposed to casual or unprofessional music-making, but nowhere does he express any aesthetic sense. Confucius, by contrast, is recorded as having been so overwhelmed by a beautiful musical performance that he did not notice the taste of his food for three months afterwards. In contrast, Mozi's philosophy is reminiscent of the caricatured utilitarianism of Dickens' *Hard Times*, where Gradgrind judges the value of every activity by its productivity alone.

An interesting feature of Mozi's rejection of music and other cultural 'entertainment' is the absence of any conception of subjectivity. His formulation of utilitarianism does not appeal to pleasure and pain, nor to happiness and unhappiness. His objection to music simply skips over the pleasure it may bring. This lack of subjectivity and aesthetic sensibility is a surprising feature of early Chinese thought which has no theory of 'experience' or 'consciousness', nor any idea of an 'inner life' or mind-body dualism. While many of the early thinkers seem to have been naturalists, there were exceptions, such as **Zhuangzi** (pp. 141–145), whose utilitarianism nevertheless hinged

on an objective, numerical standard of measurement. For Mozi, the standard is numerical as well, and the 'greatest good for the greatest number' is the unproblematic 'greatest good'.

Despite its narrow utilitarian focus, there are undeniably attractive elements to Mohism. Although we may think that, even from a practical point of view, Mohism might defeat itself through sheer joylessness, there is little to object to in its emphasis on practical charity and good governance. The universal concern for others is unprecedented and foreshadows modern liberal humanism. Mozi's emphasis on the *xiaoren* or 'inferior person' as opposed to the Confucian ideal of the *zhunzi* or 'superior gentleman' is refreshingly egalitarian. While Confucius does appeal to all levels of society, his aim is to raise people to the level of *zhunzi*; Mozi's philosophy represents no such ambition.

As to the divine, Mozi appeals to the Will of *Tian*, which corresponds to the Daoist idea of a constant *Dao* or Way, against which judgements of good may reliably be made. We learn the Will of *Tian* by looking at the natural harmony designed for our benefit. We then harmonize our morality as a state by reporting what policies are beneficial and getting approval from the ruler who promulgates the policy for everyone. In common with most thinkers of his era, Mozi idealizes an earlier period (in his case, the Xia Dynasty of 2183–1752 BCE) when good governance and universal love predominated. Unlike others, he also speaks of 'an earlier state of nature' in which anarchy and violence predominated. We should note here that Mozi does not believe that good is innate. Rather, he finds that while man has a natural tendecy to want to be moral, there is no common standard to guide him. Therefore, some sort of naturally given value must be found in order for a social morality to be formulated that accords human actions with the production of the greatest possible good for all. Mohism and Confucianism are in fundamental disagreement on this point, as we shall see in particular with the later Confucian, **Mencius**.

From here we arrive at Mozi's conception of the role of the ruler or Son of Heaven (*Tian*). Because of the disagreement over values that exists, people are led to choose the wisest among them as the arbiter of moral judgment and to set him up as the Son of Heaven. This allows a society to have a standard bearer for their moral judgments, who, for his part, accords his ethical norm with that of *Tian*, which, as we already know, is universal utility. The ruler chooses his ministers, the nobility, and finally the village leaders who organize the system of harmonized moral judgments all on the basis of moral merit and wisdom. In this way, the multiplicity of value systems is removed, and the consequent impulse to war. According to Mozi, this process necessitates reforms in the very language we use to express judgments, since speech itself needs to

reflect utilitarian morality if people are to understand how they must act in order to arrive at universal well-being – *Tian*'s goal and the natural good.

As a socially-concerned thinker, Mozi rejects fatalism. His critique of Confucianism on this score is probably unjust, but it is plain that any doctrine of fate or divine preordination would be destructive of Mohism. Mozi argues that the public guiding discourse should include phrases such as 'there is no fate' and 'there are spirits.' Including these, rather than their opposites, in the public discourse results in better behaviour and thus more benefit for people in general. Our words and actions have direct bearing upon the good of humanity. This is not a matter of material cause and effect, nor is it a spiritually-based causality such as the Indian law of *karma*. Mozi believes not only that our actions have consequences in the world, but also that Heaven actively intervenes to answer just prayers, reward good actions and punish the unjust.

Mozi's philosophy includes elements that we naturally associate with early modern Western thought: utilitarianism, state-of-nature arguments in favour of morality and authority, as well as pragmatic theories about language and equality. His analytic terms, however, also undoubtedly set the stage for the development of a more sophisticated Daoism. Some critics have argued that Mozi's critique of Daoism was crucial in stimulating the refinement of Confucian thought in the work of Mencius and Xunzi. Some scholars argue that his impact may rival that of Confucius himself, despite its lack of recognition.

One of the controversies surrounding Daoism is its claim to be the primeval 'Way'. Most of the Chinese philosophers idealize some earlier golden age in which, they assert, the principles of their philosophy were practised naturally. The emperors and teachers of these golden ages are generally thought to be mythical. It is particularly important to Daoism to establish itself as the embodiment of the natural order, as opposed to the unnatural civilization they believe is represented by the 'Confucian' virtues such as *ren* and *yi*:

LAOZI (LAO-TZU)
Flourished 4th century BCE?

When the great Dao *declined,*
*the doctrines of humanity (*ren*)*
*and righteousness (*yi*) arose.*
When knowledge and
wisdom appeared,
there emerged great hypocrisy.
When the six family relationships
are not in harmony,
there will be the advocacy of filial
piety and deep love to the children.
When a country is in disorder,
there will be praise of loyal ministers[38].

Laozi is acknowledged, with **Zhuangzi**, as the founder of Daoism (Taoism). It is questioned whether he really existed as an individual or whether his work is by the hands of many. Perhaps, like several of the other early classical works of China, the *Laozi* or, as is better known, the *Daode Jing (Tao Te Ching)* represents Laozi's thought but is the creation of his followers. The *Daode Jing*, literally *The Classic of The Way (Dao) and Its Power (De),* is a short work in poetic form that has inspired more commentary and more translation than any other work in Chinese. Its influence on virtually all aspects of Chinese life from government to cookery is immeasurable.

The Daoist critique is that if virtue really existed, there would be no need to keep talking about it. Confucius' key virtue is *ren*, 'benevolence' or 'human-heartedness'. Laozi writes dramatically:

Heaven and Earth are not
*humane [*ren*]*
They regard all things as straw dogs.
The sage is not humane
He regards all people as straw dogs.

Neither the sage nor the universe is *ren* because they are impartial. Daoism promises to restore us to the Garden of Eden, while, according to this view, Confucianism struggles in a fallen

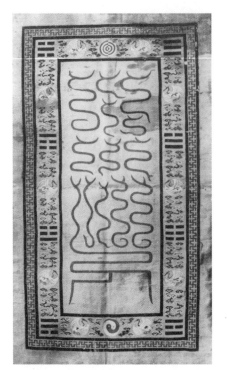

Taoist sacred diagrams on a wall hanging from the Ming period (1368–1644 CE).

Daoist sources tend to place Laozi around the sixth century BCE, perhaps as an older contemporary of Confucius. Others date Laozi to as late as the fourth century BCE. Fung Yu-Lan in *A History of Chinese Philosophy* points to the account of Daoism in the *Shi Ji* chronicle:

> *The Daoist School urged men to unity of spirit, teaching that all activities should be in harmony with the unseen, with abundant liberality towards all things of nature. As to practice, they accept the orderly sequence of things from the Yin-Yang School, gather the good points of the Confucians and Mohists, and combine with these the important points of the (School of) Names and Law. In accordance with the changes of the seasons, they respond to the development of natural objects.*
> *Their achievements fit everywhere.*
> *Their ideas are simple*
> *and easily carried out.*
> *They perform but little,*
> *but their achievements are numerous.*

world. Traditional accounts of Laozi's life vary. According to one he was born in Juren in the state of Chu. He worked as an archivist for the state of Zhou before deciding to retreat from the world and leave China. Travelling westward on a water buffalo, Laozi was recognized by a border guard who refused to let him pass until he had written down his wisdom. Over two to three weeks, he composed the 81 short chapters of the *Daode Jing*, which satisfied the guard. He was apparently never seen or heard from again. Other highly improbable legends that find Laozi instructing Confucius in ritual and enlightening the Buddha merely serve to confirm how important to Daoism its claim to be the first teaching is.

If this is correct, Laozi came after not only Confucius (551–479 BCE) but also **Mozi** (founder of the Mohist School), who died around 391 BCE. However, he would be earlier than **Zhuangzi** (369–286 BCE) and **Mencius** (371–289 BCE), both of whom are familiar with the *Daode Jing*.

The summary of the Daoist School given in the *Shi Ji* seems completely believable. The *Daode Jing* is a reaction to an existing orthodoxy rather than (or perhaps as well as) being the ancient, timeless Way its adherents claim. The strength of Laozi's criticism

Laozi riding a water-buffalo.

proves the point that in his time, at least, the *Dao* was not the single, natural Way of yore but a radical alternative to a much more prevalent philosophy. It derives much of its strength from its ethic of opposition.

The symbolism of *yin* and *yang*, the two contrasting but complementary principles, in Chinese philosophy are another way in which Daoism positions itself in relation to Confucian values. From the Daoist perspective, Confucianism is *yang* in its concern with masculinity, structure, growth, externality and enlightenment, while Daoism is *yin* in its femininity, flexibility, quietism, internality and passivity. In its positive view of femininity, Daoism is unique in ancient philosophy. Even the most progressive tendencies in Greek and Indian thought of roughly the same time do not come close. The three most common analogies for the *Dao* in Laozi are those of woman, infant and water. All have the *yin* qualities of passivity, weakness and potentiality. Fittingly, although Daoism has never attained the status of Confucianism in Chinese public life, it has exerted its influence in a more covert fashion. Many of the most important characteristics of Chinese Buddhism can be traced back to Daoism and Laozi, in particular Chan (Zen) Buddhism, as well as of Neo-Confucianism.

Laozi's key principle is of course that of the *Dao* or Way. There are two main aspects to this: the *Dao* is the way to be and behave; and it is the way things are. It is something like the idea of natural law in Western philosophy – a single principle underlying both moral conduct and physical reality. By according with the *Dao* rather than selfish desire, a human being is fulfilled. The *Dao* is an important principle in all of the early Chinese philosophers, but the emphasis thinkers such as Laozi and Zhuangzi placed on the idea was such that they became known as the Daoists.

The sheer variety of translations and interpretations of the *Daode Jing* attest to its brevity and difficulty. From its very opening words, the *Daode Jing* sets out a view radically different from rival Chinese philosophies:

*The Way (Dao) that can be told of is
not the eternal Way;
the name that can be named
is not the eternal name.
The Nameless is the origin of
Heaven and Earth;
the Named is the mother
of all things.
Therefore let there always be non-
being so we may see their subtlety.*

The 'Rectification of Names'
(see pp. 130–132) is a key theme in
many of the other thinkers that we
consider in this book, going back
to Confucius. It means a correlation
between word and deed, classification
and reality. Philosophers as diverse
as the idealistic **Mencius** and the
tyrannical **Hanfeizi** agree that the
reform of society depends on a clear
agreement between names (titles) and
roles. Laozi, on the contrary, maintains
that what can be named passes away.
The eternal *Dao* or Way is beyond name.

Another perspective Laozi gives on
this is that:

*The sage manages affairs without
action (wuwei)
and spreads doctrines without words.*

The principle of *wuwei* is, after the
Dao, the most important in Laozi.
It is not to be understood as inaction,
but as doing nothing contrary to
nature, going with the flow of the Way.

Another Daoist term that
challenges Confucianism is *xu (hsu)*
or emptiness: '*Dao* is empty'. Again,
the emptiness of *Dao* is not that of
something that has no substance or
reality, but the emptiness of a bowl of
infinite capacity, an infinite womb. It is

easy to see how Daoism prepared the
way for the arrival of Buddhism in
China, in around the second century
CE. *Xu* is close to the *shunyata* or
emptiness of Madhyamika Buddhism,
although it would be a mistake to
equate the two. Perhaps the key
difference is that Daoism consistently
affirms the world while Buddhism
reaches beyond it. Although Daoism
is associated with hermitage and
withdrawal, neverthelss withdrawal is
regarded as productive of life in the
world and consistent with wordly
ends: 'because he has no personal
interests...His personal interests are
fulfilled'. Tranquillity is important to
Laozi but it does not imply a retreat
from the activity of the world.
Rather, the retreat is from belief in
the efficacy of activity. Confucius, on
the other hand, speaks frequently of
his indefatigability.

Another important difference
between Laozi and Buddhism is the
degree to which he affirms spiritual
reality: 'the essence is very real; in it are
evidences'. If Buddhism as a philosophy
tends to say 'no' to everything, Daoism
says 'yes'.

*...the great man dwells in the thick
(substantial), and does not rest with
the thin (superficial).
He dwells in the fruit (reality)
and does not rest with the
flower (appearance).*

To Laozi, reality of the *Dao* is not
achieved through the superficial
constructs of learning. Living in reality
differs from thinking about its
appearance. This theme is developed
further in the next chapter on Laozi's
fascinating successor, Zhuangzi.

ZHUANGZI
(CHUANG TZU)
369–286 BCE

Zhuangzi, along with **Laozi** (Lao-Tzu), is regarded as the co-founder of what came to be known later as Daoism (Taoism). As with Laozi, there are many who question whether he really was an individual, or whether his works, the *Zhuangzi*, are an anthology of works of many individuals who later were called Daoist sages. There is even a tradition that refers to the two sages as one, but this only began several centuries after the *Zhuangzi* and the *Daode Jing*. As it stands, there are several key differences between the two, and if they were not real individuals, nevertheless they represent real and distinct schools of thought. We will assume here that there was a historical Zhuangzi, although not all of the *Zhuangzi* was written by him. The current version of the *Zhuangzi*

was compiled by Guo Xiang around 300 CE. Guo Xiang is important both for his arrangement of the *Zhuangzi* and for his editing out of what he regarded to be inauthentic material. An earlier recension of the *Zhuangzi* is known to have comprised 51 chapters, but the extant one by Guo Xiang only has 33. For some reason – perhaps judicious editing – the 33-chapter version entirely replaced the older one which is now lost. The *Shi Ji* chronicle seems to refer to an earlier version of 100,000 words which was impractical due to the variety of doctrines it seemed to propound.

Only the first seven chapters, the 'Inner Chapters', are regarded by most scholars as the work of Zhuangzi. Chapters 8–22 are traditionally known as the 'Outer Chapters', while Chapters 23–33 are the 'Miscellaneous Chapters'. Some scholars divide the *Zhuangzi* even further, detecting at least five different authors. It is beyond the scope of this book to distinguish between these, and we will therefore treat the entire work as a repository of Zhuangist thinking, with special reference to the Inner Chapters. The Inner Chapters do not mention Laozi, but the authors of the Outer Chapters evidently knew and drew upon the *Daode Jing*.

What we know of the life of Zhuangzi is drawn from sources centuries later. These accounts tell us that he was a civil servant in the Meng (present-day Henan) province. He apparently gained a great reputation for wisdom and turned down King Wei's request that he become his prime minister. A version of this story is in chapter 17 of the *Zhuangzi*:

*Once, when Chuang Tzu [Zhuangzi]
was fishing in the P'u River, the king*

of Ch'u sent two officials to go and announce to him: 'I would like to trouble you with the administration of my realm.'

Chuang Tzu held on to the fishing pole and, without turning his head, said, 'I have heard that there is a sacred tortoise in Ch'u that has been dead for three thousand years. The king keeps it wrapped in cloth and boxed, and stores it in the ancestral temple. Now would this tortoise rather be dead and have its bones left behind and honored? Or would it rather be alive and dragging its tail in the mud?'

'It would rather be alive and dragging its tail in the mud,' said the two officials.

Chuang Tzu said, 'Go away! I'll drag my tail in the mud!'[39]

Whether or not there is any literal truth to this story, Zhuangzi still serves to symbolize several of the priorities of the 'primitivist' strand of Daoism. He prefers nature to civilization; lived life, though unrespectable, to the living death of venerated formality; and simplicity to sophistication. That said, even in translation it is clear that the *Zhuangzi* is a work of considerable poise and sophistication. Its literary style is delightful and represents an advance on the *Daode Jing*.

The *Zhuangzi* and *Daode Jing* share common conceptions of the terms *Dao* (the mystical and transcendent Way) and *De* (the Virtue or Power of the Way in manifestation). Zhuangzi develops from this a far more explicit mysticism, including the meditative techniques described in the Inner Chapters. He attributes this instruction to Confucius, who is playfully transformed in the *Zhuangzi* to a Daoist:

Unify your attention. Do not listen with the ears, listen with the mind. Do not listen with the mind but listen with the vital breath (qi). The ears only listen to sounds. The mind is only aware of its objects. But to focus on the vital breath is to be empty and await the arising of objects. It is only the Way that settles in emptiness. Emptiness is the fasting of the mind.[40]

What this hints at is a Daoism rooted in transcendental meditative experience, paralleling the Indian Vedic concept of meditation on *prana* (breath). Meditation allows the adept to 'merge with the Great Pervader', to become one, as it were, with the *Dao*. Like many Daoists, however, Zhuangzi is not content with this inner experience: he makes 'Confucius' say, 'to stop making footprints is easy but it is difficult to walk without touching the ground.' In other words, sitting in meditation (where one makes no footprints) is the easy part; much harder and more important is the living, participating meditation of ordinary, everyday life. As we noted in the chapter on Laozi, this outward-looking mysticism is important in distinguishing Daoism from Buddhism, although later it will influence the development of the distinctively Chinese form of Chan or Zen Buddhism.

Whether inward or outward, it is clear that Zhuangzi's reliance on mystical experience is key to both the sceptical and primitivist tendencies in his thought. His faith in a monistic *Dao* gives Zhuangzi the absolute security to dismiss both the intellectual and the social constructs of those who are less flexible. One of his most important passages (in Chapter 2) questions whether we can know anything to be real:

Once Chuang Chou dreamt he was a butterfly, a butterfly flitting and fluttering around, happy with himself and doing as he pleased. He didn't know he was Chuang Chou. Suddenly he woke up and there he was, solid and unmistakable Chuang Chou. But he didn't know if he was Chuang Chou who had dreamt he was a butterfly, or a butterfly dreaming he was Chuang Chou. Between Chuang Chou and a butterfly there must be some distinction! This is called the Transformation of Things.

Zhuangzi questions the reality of both waking and dream states by indicating their inconstancy, just as would the Indian Vedantin thinker **Gaudapada** some centuries later. Another passage from the same chapter examines whether we have a consistent self:

Joy, anger, grief, delight, worry, regret, fickleness, inflexibility, modesty, wilfulness, candour, insolence – music from empty holes, mushrooms springing up in dampness, day and night replacing

each other before us, and no one knows where they sprout from. Let it be! Let it be! [It is enough that] morning and evening we have them, and they are the means by which we live. Without them, we would not exist; without us, they would have nothing to take hold of. This comes close to the matter. But I do not know what makes them the way they are. It would seem as though they have some true master, and yet I find no trace of him. He can act – that is certain. Yet I cannot see his form. He has identity but no form.

In *A Sourcebook of Chinese Philosophy*, Wing Tsit-Chan points out that this passage has 'fortified the long tradition of agnosticism' in China. Confucius is also agnostic on regions beyond common experience, suggesting that we stick to what we can know; Zhuangzi is very different in hinting that we should consider such questions and dwell in their mystery. Compared to other thinkers from the classical period of Chinese thought, Zhuangzi is unusually concerned with subjective, inner experience.

Zhuangzi's agnosticism extends to the very language he uses:

Words are not just wind. Words have something to say. But if what they have to say is not fixed, then do they really say something? Or do they say nothing? People suppose that words are different from the peeps of baby birds, but is there any difference, or isn't there?

This could be wrongly taken as a purely destructive scepticism, but Zhuangzi here attacks the grounds for certainty of the Confucian and Mohist thinkers who argue back and forth about terminology:

When the Way relies on
little accomplishments
and words rely on vain show,
then we have the rights and wrongs
of the Confucians and the Moists.
What one calls right, the other calls
wrong; what one calls wrong,
the other calls right.
But if we want to right their wrongs
and wrong their rights,
then the best thing to use is clarity.

Zhuangzi seems to argue here that the concern, for example, of the Confucians with ritual misses the point. Such 'little accomplishments' are not enough, they are not the Way. In the same vein, it is most important to dwell on the meaning, the 'something to say', even if that something changes from moment to moment, than to hang on to words that are constantly being undermined by the constantly changing nature of their subject-matter. Elsewhere Zhuangzi says that words are like a net for catching fish. The meaning is the main thing (i.e. the fish), and when we have caught it, the words are set aside. It is not possible to determine the meaning of words in themselves, any more than it is to catch a fish in the street. Meaning is always dependent on context. There is another well-known story which illuminates Zhuangzi's view on knowledge:

Chuang Tzu [Zhuangzi] and Hui
Tzu [Huishi] were strolling along
the dam of the Hao River when
Chuang Tzu said, 'See how the
minnows come out and dart
around where they please!
That's what fish really enjoy!'
Hui Tzu said, 'You're not a fish –
how do you know what fish enjoy?'

Chuang Tzu said, 'You're not I,
so how do you know I don't know
what fish enjoy?'

Hui Tzu said, 'I'm not you, so I
certainly don't know what you know.
On the other hand, you're certainly
not a fish – so that still proves you
don't know what fish enjoy!'

Chuang Tzu said, 'Let's go back to
your original question, please. You
asked me how I know what fish enjoy
– so you already knew I knew it
when you asked the question. I know
it by standing here beside the Hao.'

Although we may sympathize with Huishi's suspicion, the point being made comes across strongly. Zhuangzi maintains that reality can only be known through immediate experience and not through speculation. Huishi then speculates about what Zhuangzi knows or does not know and comes to the conclusion that Zhuangzi does *know* the happiness of fish. Hence the critique is not directed at having knowledge about something, but at the tendency to express it in a rigid and objective way. At around the same time, similar discussions were taking place within Indian philosophy: 'that which is not uttered by speech, but that by which speech is revealed, know that alone to be Brahman,

A Chinese Taoist monk.

and not what people worship as an object[41]. Compared with the East, Western philosophy has had far less subtle preoccupations with knowledge and with language.

Zhuangzi's politics, like those of **Laozi**, are guided by the principle of *wuwei* (action through inaction) A government should do as little as possible, not just in the sense that it should render itself unnecessary through good governance but in the more radical sense that it is better for the government to rule through passivity:

There has been such a thing as letting mankind alone and tolerance; there has never been such a thing as governing mankind. Letting alone springs from the fear lest men's natural dispositions be perverted and tolerance springs from the fear lest their character be corrupted. But if their natural dispositions be not perverted, nor their character corrupted, what need is there left for government? …From the Three Dynasties downwards, the world has lived in a helter-skelter of promotions and punishments. What chance have the people left for living the even tenor of their lives?[42]

the teachings of Confucius. His own work, the *Mencius*, was also highly regarded, being one of the Four Books to constitute the Confucian education system that was formalized after 1313 CE.

Mencius was born in Zou province (present-day Shandong). His father, like that of Confucius, died when he was only a child and he was raised by a mother who went to extraordinary lengths to secure an ideal education for her son. First employed as a teacher and then as a government official in Qi, he eventually took to the roads, like Confucius and Mozi before him, in order to promote his ideas to a succession of rulers, with a similar lack of success. He seems to have ended up living in seclusion with a group of his students and it is believed he perhaps composed the *Mencius* around this time, although at least some of it dates from after his death.

MENCIUS
(MENGZI, MENGE K'E)
371–289 BCE

Mencius is traditionally considered to be the 'Second Sage' of Confucianism. He stands in relation to **Confucius** the way Plato does to Socrates. Just as Plato was responsible for turning Socrates into a key figure within Western thought, it is unlikely that Confucianism would have had anything like the impact it did without the contributions made to it by Mencius. He added a metaphysical dimension to Confucius' ethical teachings, much as Plato's ideas were enhanced by those of Socrates. Although not a direct pupil of Confucius himself, Mencius was taught for a time by the sage's grandson and remains one of the few reliable authorities we have for

*'Moral principles
please our minds
as beef and mutton
and pork please
our mouths.'*

Mencius may have been an exact contemporary of **Zhuangzi** but neither mentions the other in their writings. Fung Yu-lan speculates that this may have been because Mencius regarded Zhuangzi as a mere follower of the notorious Yang Zhu[43], while Zhuangzi saw Mencius as just another Confucian scholar. If these suppositions are indeed true, neither could be said to have studied the other's philosophy closely.

A fundamental factor to understanding Mencius' work is his relation to the other philosophers of the time – a very prolific period for Chinese thought. Just as the critique of Brahmanism in India expressed by figures such as **Charvaka** and the **Buddha** led to the rise and refinement of Indian philosophy, so we see Confucianism defining itself through Mencius in response to its detractors. One of the principal oppositions that we see is to Legalism (see **Hanfeizi**), an influential philosophy that maintained man was self-centred and untrustworthy. Against this Mencius argued the exact opposite. He gave the example of a toddler heading towards an open well and argued that anyone would naturally help to prevent a calamity. This idea harks back to the Confucian notion of *ren* ('benevolence' or 'human-heartedness'). In Mencius, the latter translation seems more appropriate. Even though it would perhaps be naive to suppose people are naturally benevolent, Mencius is subtle when referring to unconditioned human response. He clarifies that the natural response of the heart can be either corrupted or refined: 'slight is the difference between man and brutes. The common man loses this distinguishing feature, while the gentleman retains it'[44]. In his conviction about the germ of goodness residing in mankind, Mencius is challenged by **Xunzi**, a Confucian philosopher who held the opposite belief.

A further important dispute occurs between Mencius and the Mohists, the followers of **Mozi**. The latter was a utilitarian thinker who opposed Confucius' regard for tradition and ritual. Mencius again bases his defence on the natural responses of the human heart. In response to the Mohist critique of elaborate funerary rites, he harks back to an imagined natural state

(making use of Mozi's own methods) and to the origins of burial practices. He quotes the example of primitive man, who pained at the sight of a loved one being eaten by scavengers, would naturally have developed a consolatory reaction designed to honour the departed and console the living. Mencius argues that burial rites come from such a response. It is difficult not to feel that Mencius' argument is psychologically convincing and his view of the innate goodness of human nature eventually prevailed in Chinese thought, persisting to the present day. Mencius teaches the doctrine of the Four Beginnings to illustrate how virtue emerges from instinctual response:

The feeling of commiseration is the feeling of humanity; the feeling of shame and dislike is the beginning of righteousness; the feeling of deference and compliance is the beginning of propriety; and the feeling of right and wrong is the beginning of wisdom.
Men have these Four Beginnings just as they have their four limbs.[45]

Accordingly, the sage or wise person teaches men about what they innately have inside. Mencius uses the analogy of a renowned chef who is establishing the principles of good flavour. Just as the chef does not invent good flavour yet he understands what it is that people enjoy about food, 'the sage is the first to possess what is common in our minds. Therefore moral principles please our minds as beef and mutton and pork please our mouths.' Confucian ethics were considerably refined by Mencius. In particular, he developed the idea of *yi*, which he defined as 'the path a man ought to follow'. A minor element in Confucius, it becomes a categorical imperative in Mencius' teaching like that of Kant, a command that must be followed even to the point of death: 'I like life and I also like righteousness. If I cannot have both of them, I shall give up life and choose righteousness.'

Politically, Mencius is the most democratic of Confucian thinkers (the Mohists' justification of the state hints at democratic choice and Mohist groups apparently chose their leaders democratically – then followed them to the death). Confucius followed the traditional doctrine of the Mandate of Heaven, which stipulated that the natural authority of kings would be withdrawn when the king lost his virtue. Mencius, probably again influenced by Mohism, interpreted this to be judged by people 'voting with their feet.' If a king is benevolent, people will flood to his kingdom, filling his coffers and his army. Mencius calls this 'winning the people's heart-minds':

If a ruler regards his ministers as his hands and feet, then his ministers will regard him as their heart and mind. If a ruler regards his ministers as dogs and horses, his ministers will regard him as any other man. If a ruler regards his ministers as dirt and grass, his ministers will regard him as a bandit and an enemy.

As has already been mentioned, Mencius added a metaphysical dimension to the existing core of Confucian teaching. The traditional belief in Chinese philosophy that the universe consists of *qi (chi)*, a substance graded from coarse to fine, from the heaviness of the earth to the lightness of the heavens, had its roots in folk religion. According to Mencius, a human being is made up of a mixture of coarse and fine *qi* and his spiritual path is a matter of 'cultivating his own *qi*':

Nourish it with integrity and place no obstacle in its path and it will fill the space between Heaven and Earth. It is a qi *which unites rightness and the Way…it is born of accumulated rightness and cannot be appropriated by anyone through a sporadic show of rightness…whenever one acts in a way that falls below the standard set in one's heart, it will collapse… you must work at it and never let it out of your mind. At the same time, while you must never let it out of your mind, you must not forcibly help it grow either.*[46]

The Confucian tradition before Mencius emphasizes the active and public life in a way that somewhat alienates the act of contemplation. While Daoism and later Buddhism emphasize 'being', the Confucians emphasize 'doing'. By uniting morality with metaphysics, Mencius hints at the beginnings of a kind of Confucian mysticism. His example would be crucial to the new direction taken by future Neo-Confucian thinkers from the eleventh century onwards, who incorporated Daoist and Buddhist ideas in order to strengthen and renew Confucianism.

XUNZI (HSUN TZU)
c. 320–230 BCE

Confucius had two important successors during the Warring States period (403–222 BCE). The first was **Mencius**, who promoted Confucius' ideas on *ren* (human-heartedness), adding a metaphysical dimension and teaching that human nature was essentially good. The second was Xunzi, who focused on *li* (ritual) and the agency of society in forming an individual's character. He dramatically emphasized the importance of social convention by maintaining that 'man's nature is evil; goodness is the result of conscious activity'. It is not surprising therefore that the debate on 'nature versus nurture' should have become so central. Confucius' emphasis was on outward, 'demonstrable' behaviour, such as ritual, government and culture. He seems to have deliberately kept silent on the subject of human nature, but the question was taken up by both of his main successors. Xunzi was the more influential figure during the Qin and Han dynasties (ending 220 CE). Centuries of Buddhist domination of Chinese thought followed, after which Mencius emerged as the model for a system capable of fuelling a veritable Confucian renaissance. It was his version of Confucianism that came to dominate China's imperial system for the remainder of the eleventh to twentieth centuries. Xunzi, on the other hand, was a neglected figure in Chinese philosophy until the nineteenth century when he enjoyed a revival of interest. Xunzi is the most important critic of early Chinese philosophy and delivered attacks on Mencian Confucianism, Mohism, Daoism and on a range of other less well-known systems of thought.

> *'Man's nature is evil;*
> *goodness is the result of*
> *conscious activity.'*

According to the *Shi Ji* chronicle, Xunzi was born in Zhao (present-day Shanshi and Henan). At the age of 50, he was attracted to the court of Ji on the east coast, along with many other intellectuals, where he was acknowledged to be a most brilliant scholar. Eventual jealousies from rivals at court led to Xunzi's flight to Chu in the south, where he became magistrate of the city of Lanling before a coup against the local ruler led to his removal from office. Not much is known with any accuracy about the actual dates when Xunzi lived, but he was certainly active between 298 and

Li Si

'The superior man is serious about what lies in himself and does not desire what comes from Heaven. The inferior man neglects what is in himself and desires what comes from Heaven.'

238 BCE. He also kept a school, including among his pupils the Legalist philosopher, **Hanfeizi**, and Li Si, who was first the prime minister of Qin then, after its final victory, of the empire as a whole. It was Li Si who recommended that all books in the empire be burnt, to defeat all non-Legalist thinking, especially Confucianism. It is impossible to decide how far Xunzi can be held responsible for the authoritarian attitudes of his two disciples. As the teacher of these undeniably influential figures, his own authoritarianism was clearly of substantial influence on them. Xunzi did maintain that the ultimate authority rested with the *zhunzi* or 'cultured gentleman'. His pessimism regarding human nature has affinities with Hanfeizi's cynical 'class interest' analysis. He also advocated a positive effort to manipulate human nature which Legalism took to the extreme. However, compared to the radical anti-traditionalism and anti-moralism of both his students, Xunzi's reflective philosophy was fairly moralistic and constituted a sophisticated argument in favour of tradition. Their ideas and practices represent a continuation of his dogmatic assertiveness but are also a radical break with his sometimes very cautious reflective argumentation.

Xunzi's philosophy is based on the fundamental conviction that man needs socialization in order to be good. Hanfeizi's cynicism about role interests led to his acute paranoia when dealing with court ministers and high officials. Xunzi sought to promote education and clarity of thought: 'the superior man is serious about what lies in himself and does not desire what comes from Heaven. The inferior man neglects what is in himself and desires what comes from Heaven[47].' The word *Tien*, normally translated as 'Heaven', is a useful barometer for Chinese philosophy from this period. For **Mozi**, it means a God who responds to the prayers and the actions of men. For Confucius and Mencius, it represents the abstract will of God: how things should be. For the Daoists, it is more like 'Nature': how things are under natural law. Xunzi's critique of the view of the 'inferior man' is that he looks for an outside, possibly supernatural agency to come to his aid. In this he develops Confucius' emphasis on self-reliance: 'it is man who is capable of broadening the Way; it is not the Way that is capable of broadening man.' Xunzi writes as a pragmatic naturalist: 'if the foundations of living [i.e. agriculture] are strengthened and economically used, then Nature [*Tien*] cannot bring [about] impoverishment.'

As with its pupil Hanfei, Daoist thinking proves a useful source for a philosophy that is in many ways alien to it. Xunzi is not in the least mystical, but uses Daoism as the starting point for a naturalistic and scientific approach. On the subject of fortune, he writes, 'it is good fortune to regard [rites and sacrifices] as ornamental but it is evil fortune to regard them as supernatural'. In other words, good fortune is about having the right attitude and education. This extrapolation is from Confucius, but while the latter refuses to speculate on the supernatural, Xunzi disregards it in its entirety.

Xunzi's view of the physical universe is as a natural continuation of Confucianism. It is a triadic system such as that found in *The Doctrine of the Mean of Heaven, Earth and Man*. Xunzi writes, 'Heaven has its seasons, earth has its wealth and man has his government'. The first two we have no control over; the third is our only proper area of concern. Perhaps Xunzi's most original contribution to Chinese thought is his view of man as an agent operating within the confines of nature:

*Instead of regarding Heaven
[or Nature] as great and
admiring it, why not foster it
as a thing and regulate it?
Instead of obeying Heaven and
singing praise to it, why not control
the Mandate of Heaven and use it?
Instead of looking on the seasons
and waiting for them,
why not respond to them
and make use of them?
Instead of letting things multiply
by themselves,
why not exercise your ability
to transform them?
Instead of thinking of things
as things, why not attend to them
so that you don't lose them?
Instead of admiring how things
come into being,
why not do something to bring
them to full development?*

Such a view was far too radical to have a profound influence on Chinese

thought, but it may well have been the beginning of the world's first scientific tradition. Its enthusiasm for utilizing nature is reminiscent of Western eighteenth- and nineteenth-century Enlightenment ideas. Today, we would have reservations about the lack of respect for nature shown in Xunzi and perhaps more enthusiasm for the enjoyment of 'thinking of things as things' rather than merely as the means to an end. In this our instincts are closer to the traditional Chinese view of the harmony between man and nature, even if our economics are not. If the Daoist term *wuwei* is translated as 'taking no action [that is] contrary to nature', then it will be seen that Xunzi is no Daoist.

Another important contribution made by Xunzi was his consideration of the traditional question of 'the Rectification of Names' (see box pp. 130–132). This was Confucius' solution to the problem of a breakdown within the social order and implies that first, each will play his allotted part in society, and second, that the 'superior men' will set the example for others through understandable and sincere speech. Xunzi is aware of two attacks on Confucius' principle. The first was that of later Mohists who had rejected the Rectification of Names on the grounds that a given thing could properly be called several things – thing, living thing, animal, mammal, primate, human, male, father, and so on. The second critique came from the linguistic paradoxes created by the so-called School of Names. The most notorious is Gongsun Long's 'a white horse is not a horse'. Gongsun Long argued that if one specified a white horse, but was given a yellow horse, one would naturally reject it.

Therefore a 'horse' is not a 'white horse' by definition. This raises the point that the process of rectifying names entails the principle of one-name-one-thing and thus leads to a paradoxical impasse.

Xunzi has to accept that the Confucian system will not work on a one-name-one-thing basis, and so makes use of the Mohist theory to re-develop it. The word 'horse' is a 'simple name' while 'white horse' is a 'compound name'; 'knowing that different actualities have different names, [he concludes that] one should let different actualities always have different names'. Xunzi is, however, an unwilling logician at best. Having established that the logical paradox does not destroy Confucian thinking, he quickly moves to assert that semantic theorizing should be forbidden because it uses names to confuse what is being named and thereby sows disorder. Xunzi suggests the ruler prohibit such activities as they will sow the seeds of disorder. Like most Confucians, he sees this chaos in the form of the entire kingdom accepting the same discourse. The judgement of the superior man or sage, rather than logic, is sufficient to decide the way in which a name ought to be used. It is this attitude, or one close to it, that Li Si called on when he chose to burn books and bury scholars.

Xunzi's view of the unreliability of human nature is essential to his thinking, because from this, he demonstrates the importance of education, training and social propriety. In the writings of Mencius they were merely ways of training the heart in its existing humanity, but in the *Xunzi* the ritual becomes an external system of social control within which it is appropriate to pursue desires in an ordered society. Only if society is carefully structured so that different ranks have their own appropriate values can one allocate scarce natural resources in a way that will satisfy everyone concerned. The difference between Confucius' two successors is brought forth in their views regarding the attainability of ultimate wisdom. Both argue that anyone has the potential to become a sage, but while Mencius holds this out as a real possibility, Xunzi is characteristically sceptical: 'it is possible for a man with feet to walk all over the world and yet so far there has not been any who is actually able to do so.' The reason why we do not walk all over the world, or become sages, is that the motivation is lacking. Xunzi's awareness of the natural context in which man exists is, in the final analysis, his greatest strength and weakness. By the standards of his time, Xunzi is without parallel as a scientific mind and as a critic of philosophy but his safety-first pragmatism always wins out over philosophical daring. There is much in the *Xunzi* to admire but little to delight in. For Confucius, as for Mencius, social controls and rituals finally bear their fruit in the form of tranquillity, easy action and joy: 'at 70, I followed my heart's desire, without overstepping the line'. But for Xunzi, social control will always be with us.

HANFEIZI
(HAN FEI TZU)
c. 280–233 BCE

Hanfeizi, or Master Hanfei, was a unique and pivotal figure in the history of Chinese philosophy. A pupil of **Xunzi**, the leading Confucian scholar of his day, Hanfei nevertheless rejected a rigid commitment to conventionalism. Although an aristocrat, Hanfei's philosophy justified the emperor's treatment of the aristocracy in accordance with the same objective standards applied to everyone else – except to the emperor's person, of course. Like the early Daoists, he is regarded as a member of a group known as the Legalists that existed only as a projection of later historians. Neither Daoism nor Legalism was an actual association in the classical period.

Living during the violent and unsteady Warring States period, Hanfei put forward a practical solution to the problem of how to achieve and retain power. He credited Lord Shang, prime minister of the state that finally unified China (who almost certainly was not the author of *The Book of Lord Shang*), as well as Shenzi (350–275 BCE) and Shen Pu-hai (d. 337 BCE), with the three core concepts of his theory. The most important of these were objective standards of reward and punishment, promotion and dismissal. Its underlying motivation, at least in Hanfei, is self-interest. Hanfei recognized that the main threat to a ruler comes from his ministers. By holding them to measurement-like standards of performance, a ruler or king can keep his cabinet of advisors from controlling him by 'persuasion.'

At the same time, it would protect the general population, giving them clear guidelines for avoiding punishment and preventing officials from using punishment to reward loyalty. Hanfei developed the ideas behind Legalism to their logical and extreme conclusion: that no one is above the Law, and that the Law never shows mercy. The Confucian doctrine of the 'Rectification of Names', which **Confucius** uses as a corrective measure to restore natural order – 'let the ruler be a ruler, the subject a subject, the father a father...the son a son' (*Analects*, XII, 11), becomes in Legalism a measure for governing (and threatening) high officials by preventing them from acting outside of their job description. Confucians tell numerous stories about the injustices they perceived implicit in this idea. An officer who spontaneously undertook a daring and successful raid on the enemy was executed for insubordination. A tavern keeper who covered the king with his coat as he slept met the same fate. Hanfei writes of ministers who present their achievements modestly:

It is not that the ruler is not pleased with the big accomplishments [of his minister], but he considers the failure of the big accomplishments to correspond to the words worse than the big accomplishments themselves. Therefore he is to be punished.[48]

Hanfei's writing is energetic and full of hard-headed pragmatism. He rejects both the backward-looking Confucians and the moralizing Mohists, taking instead the approach that any way of achieving total order is as good as any other. Although it would be wrong to overemphasize the influence of his master Xunzi, Hanfei draws heavily on his arguments for preventing people from disagreeing with the way of the empire. This became the adequate justification for killing philosophers and burning books. Furthermore, he follows Xunzi's theory that human nature is inherently evil. Xunzi observed that goodness is not innate in man, any more than straightness is innate in wood. For Xunzi this supports the argument for education and training by a wise master. Hanfei uses the same illustration but to different purpose:

> *Although there is a naturally straight arrow or a naturally round piece of wood[49] [once in a hundred generations]...the skilled worker does not value it. Why? Because it is not just one person who wishes to ride and not just one shot that the archer wishes to shoot. Similarly, the enlightened ruler does not value people who are naturally good and do not depend on reward and punishment. Why? Because the laws of the state must not be neglected and government is not for only one man.*

Not only is it not possible to rely on people being naturally good, Hanfei argues that the naturally good person is of no particular social worth. Precisely because Hanfei's 'two handles' of punishment and kindness cannot manipulate him, the naturally good person should be removed from the equation. The entire system of Legalism operates around an ethic of manipulation. Do not trust people, says

Hanfei, rather trust your own ability to force them to obey you.

The *Hanfei* contains a commentary on Laozi who advocates small, passive forms of government. Hanfei argues that when objective standards are in place and working well, there is no need for a ruler to do anything. His people are already acting according to common standards. The *wuwei* (action through inaction) of the Daoists arises from the conception of a transcendent *Dao* as well as scepticism about moral doctrines working reliably. The *wuwei* of the Legalists comes about because the state consists of self-enacting standards of behaviour and a total acceptance of ruler-instituted ways of measuring, judging and acting: 'like water flowing and like a boat floating, the ruler follows the course of Nature and enforces an infinite number of commands.'[50] Hanfei also followed Xunzi's advocacy for brutal punishment, arguing that the more brutal the measure, the less it will need to be used. Needless to say, this did not work out in practice and the Legalist dynasty has few equals in history in terms of the frequency and the severity of the punishments it meted out. Neither Macchiavelli nor the Islamic social theorist **Ibn Khaldun** approach Hanfei's cold-bloodedness and perhaps only in the writings of George Orwell and Franz Kafka do we find something that exceeds it. It hardly needs to be said that despite the appropriation of *wuwei* by Hanfei, he is totally at odds with the spirit of **Laozi** and **Zhuangzi**. Nevertheless, Hanfei's interpretation of Laozi reminds us that the text was widely read and used by many besides the students of Zhuangzi. In effect, Hanfei created an artificial *Dao* in order to engineer a man-made paradise. Hanfei had a slightly different view of human nature than Xunzi. Rather than thinking of people as motivated by selfish desires, Hanfei characterized them as adopting the values of their status or rank. Thus he believed that no one could be trusted to impart judgement objectively, for example writing that 'consorts and concubines long for the early death of the ruler'. This insight into the communitarian formulation of our self-identity flows neatly out of the social conception of man, also shared by Confucianism

Qin Shih-Huang-di

and Mohism, given Hanfei's inherent pessimism. Its truth was borne out in his own life. He lived in the state of Han and petitioned King An with an outline of his ideas. They were rejected, but a rival king, Qin Shih-Huang-di, was impressed. One of

Hanfei's fellow students at the school of Xunzi was Li Si, who went on to become the Qin ruler's prime minister. When Hanfei attempted to enlist as an advisor of the Qin, Li Si argued he could not be trusted and imprisoned him. Li Si then sent Hanfei a phial of poison which he took, realising he was in an impossible position.

Li Si put many of Hanfei's ideas into practice. The rigorous discipline introduced into the state of Qin helped it to conquer all other states and China was unified for the first time in 221 BCE. This achieved, Shih-Huang-di set about establishing his fledgling empire on Legalist grounds. The scale of the ambition and single-mindedness displayed by Shih-Huang-di and Li Si was truly remarkable. The problem of Mongol invaders attacking from the north was effectively dealt with by the construction of the Great Wall begun in 214 BCE. The problem of rival, non-Legalist philosophies was addressed by ordering that all books be burnt to 'make the people ignorant'. Li Si wrote:

In the past, the empire was divided. Because there was no emperor, the feudal lords were active and in order to confuse the people they harped on antiquity...Now your majesty rules a unified empire in which distinctions of right and wrong are as clear as your own unapproachable authority. Yet there are those who unofficially propagate teachings directed against imperial decrees and orders. When they hear of new instructions, they criticize them in the light of their own teachings...the people are thus encouraged to be disrespectful

Qin Emperor Shih-Huang-di burns those books in his kingdom which oppose his views.

Your servant therefore requests that all persons possessing works of literature and discussions of the philosophers should destroy them. Those who have not destroyed them within thirty days after the issuing of the order are to be branded and work as convicts.[51]

As a result of this edict, much of the literature of the early Qin period was lost. The only remaining copies of many works were held in the imperial library, but this was torched by a rebel army in 206 BCE. Hanfei directly influenced Li Si in this, who wrote that 'in the state of the enlightened ruler, there is no literature of books and records but the laws serve as the teaching.'

The reign of Emperor Shih-Huang-di demonstrated with breathtaking strength of purpose the value of unity in law, philosophy, politics, economics and the military. The Argentinian writer Louis Borges admiringly remarked on the emperor's unique quality: a mind that could conceive both the destruction of all human knowledge and the erection of a wall around an empire that size. His success was in large part due to the influence of Legalist thinking. However, the rapid decline of the Qin Empire soon after Shih-Huang-di's death was the perfect illustration of the inherent weaknesses in extreme forms of Legalism. Hanfei was correct in thinking that it was possible to rule an empire with the iron fist of law but wrong in assuming that the population would accept 'an infinite number of commands' and punishments. In retrospect, the Confucian concept that the emperor rules owing to the Mandate of Heaven (which was in itself dependent on justice and righteousness) was more sustainable and humane.

HUINENG
638–713 CE

The earliest record of Buddhism in China dates back as early as 2 BCE. The first Chinese translations of Buddhist texts were produced about 150 years later, and by the third century CE, two main schools were active, distinguished by the Sanskrit names of *prajna*, meaning 'knowledge' and *dhyana*, meaning 'meditation'. The School of *Dhyana* was later to develop into the most distinctively Chinese form of Buddhism. *Dhyana* was being transformed into Chan or, as it is now more commonly known, Zen.

Meditation in China was not very similar to its Indian equivalent. In India, meditation is typically associated with sitting still and concentrating one's mind inwardly using a variety of methods, including breath control and the silent mental chanting of *mantras*. In China, it was understood through Daoism and associated more with outward-looking states. By the time of Zen, however, it had come to simply mean 'enlightenment'. This religious practice is frequently associated with the 'sudden enlightenment' (*satori*) method, as distinguished from the 'gradual enlightenment' method, although in reality both methods persisted within the Zen tradition.

Traditionally, the first Zen patriarch is Bodhidharma (460–534 CE). More is known, however, about a later figure called Hongren (601–674 CE), the Fifth Patriarch. He was the first to advance the *Diamond Sutra* in China, subsequently regarded as China's key Buddhist text. The *Diamond Sutra* is part of the 'Perfection of Wisdom' tradition that emphasizes the mind (see **Nagarjuna)**.

Huineng's story is recorded in the *Platform Sutra* of the Sixth Patriarch, a collection of stories about his life, assembled by his followers. He was born into a poor family in the Guangdong province, something of a backwater state. Although allegedly an illiterate wood peddler, Huineng seems to have read the *Diamond Sutra* in his twenties and then set off to study under Hongren, the Fifth Patriarch. The scriptures tell how he successfully reasons with Hongren about being allowed to stay in spite of his 'barbarian' origins, although he is given only a menial position pounding rice in the kitchens. Hongren then makes the announcement that he will give the title of Sixth Patriarch to whoever can write a verse expressing 'the basic idea' of Buddhist teaching. The leading disciple, Shenxiu, attempts it is as follows:

The body is the tree of perfect wisdom
the mind is the stand of a bright mirror
at all times diligently wipe it
do not allow it to become dusty.

Hongren declares that while this is the best of the entries, it is not enough. Then Huineng writes his verse:

Fundamentally perfect wisdom
has no tree
nor has the bright mirror any stand
Buddha-nature is forever
clear and pure
where is there any dust?

Needless to say, Hongren goes on to acclaim the verse as evidence of Huineng's superior wisdom. Hongren does not, however, openly declare Huineng's achievement. Instead he gives him secret instructions within the *Diamond Sutra* through which Huineng achieves immediate enlightenment. Hongren then advises him to leave in stealth in order to avoid the jealousy of the other pupils.

The story should be understood in light of the political struggles which followed. Huineng's disciple, Shenhui, engaged in a bitter fight with the Northern School of Shenxiu after Huineng's death over who was the true Sixth Patriarch. It seems possible from the story of the *Platform Sutra* that Shenxiu was accorded the title but that Hongren never accepted Huineng. Hongren's compliments to Huineng are made privately, while publicly he is seen to be hostile to the 'barbarian'. On the other hand, it may be, as the tradition of the Southern School holds, that Huineng was indeed proclaimed to be the Sixth Patriarch in 661 CE. Shenhui's apparent possession of the relics belonging to Hongren eventually seemed to settle the matter. The *Platform Sutra* is now regarded as the original classic of Zen Buddhism.

There is no evidence that Huineng ever tried to promote his own claims. Judging from his words, he seems to have been an extraordinary genius, possessing a rare mind akin to that of the Indian Madhyamika Buddhist, Nagarjuna. The two verses we have just discussed encapsulate the differences between Shenxiu and Huineng's new approach. The traditional way to enlightenment involves constant purification of the mind in preparation for this attainment. Huineng denies even the possibility that Buddha-nature can be defiled. In a fundamental sense, we already are Buddhas. This is why enlightenment can be so sudden. Rather than adhering to the traditional path of formal meditation, Huineng argued for a freer form of meditation, with the aim of achieving *samadhi*, which in the Chinese tradition means 'calmness'. In the words of the *Platform Sutra*:

Good and learned friends, calmness (samadhi) and wisdom (prajna) are the foundations of my method. First of all, do not be deceived into thinking that the two are different. They are one substance and not two. Calmness is the substance of wisdom and wisdom is the function of calmness. Whenever wisdom is at work, calmness is within it. Whenever calmness is at work, wisdom is within it...do not say that wisdom follows calmness, or vice versa, or that the two are different.

'Our nature is originally pure.'

If Nagarjuna is Huineng's spiritual forefather within Buddhism, perhaps more important for our consideration here is the influence of Daoism. Huineng, like the Daoists, insists on a monistic view. The knowledge and the effect of enlightenment are simply different ways of looking at the same thing. Another Daoist idea, the 'absence-of-thought, 'means not to be defiled by external objects.' The idea expressed here is not that the mind is unconscious, but that it is free from attachment. Huineng criticized the Northern School claiming that it emphasized inactivity to the point of stupefaction, which he said was inconsistent with the Way (*Dao*). The Southern Zen master, on the other hand, would be able to go about his business normally, dwelling constantly within his Buddha-mind and remaining unattached to any object, either external or within the mind. The Daoist ethic of activity through inactivity is thus given a distinctly Buddhist angle. Another concept that was alien to Indian Buddhism, but which is reminiscent of Daoism, is the idea of 'becoming a Buddha in this very body'. Whereas Buddhism traditionally regarded the body as an obstruction, Zen follows the Daoist path of acceptance of all things as they are. Huineng's frequent refrain that 'our nature is originally pure' means that to reject anything is to create a false duality. It should be said that although the enlightenment of the Northern School may be characterized as gradual and that of the Southern School as sudden, both acknowledge the two methods of achieving enlightenment. As Huineng comments, 'those who are deluded understand gradually, while the enlightened achieve understanding suddenly. But when they know their own minds, then they see their own nature, and there is no difference in their enlightenment.' The fundamental difference between the two is not the speed with which enlightenment is attained but, as we have seen, in their conception of the mind. The Northern School emphasizes the constant effort behind mental purification, while the Southern School teaches that the real effort is in seeing the mind's original purity.

Huineng's Zen became known as the Zen of the Patriarchs, while the older tradition, which traces its ancestry back to Bodhidharma, is known as the Zen of the Perfected One. The two co-existed amicably, although Huineng's *satori* Zen grew in popularity before a revival of Confucianism caused its decline in the eleventh and twelfth centuries. At this point, Zen became popular in Japan, where it developed into its modern form. Huineng's Southern School corresponds to the Rinzai Zen of Eisai and Shenxiu's Northern School to Dogen's Soto Zen. In the twentieth century, Zen captured the imagination of the West with its sophisticated understanding of the mind, coupled with its ethos which advocates an enjoyment for simple living.

FAZANG
(FA TSANG)
643–712 CE

Descended from an Uzbekistani grandfather, Fazang was born in Zhangan (present-day Sian, central China). He was a Buddhist who attempted to synthesize previous forms of Chinese Buddhism. His own tradition can best be described as a form of Mahayanist Buddhism based on the *Avatamsaka* (Garland) *Sutra*. A translation of this *sutra* was first brought over to China in the sixth century, where it produced a school of adherents called the Huayen, normally translated as the 'Flowery Garland' School. Its popularity proved to be far greater in China than anywhere else. The school is known as Kegon in Korea and also has followers in Japan.

Fazang became a monk and at 28 was a follower of the two Huayen founders, Dushun and Chihyan. Like other Buddhists of the time (see **Huineng**), he was invited to the court of Empress Wu, where he lectured on Buddhist philosophy using the statue of a golden lion as an illustrative device. His summary of Buddhist philosophy is illuminating, although one can easily see why the empress found Fazang hard going. He distinguishes five classifications within Buddhism. The first is Hinayana (Theravada), the earliest teaching of the Buddha, which claims that because the lion is dependent on its cause, it can have no real character or nature. The second is Mahayana, which states that the lion not only has no character, but also no substance or existence: it is empty. The third is the Chinese branch known as Tiantai, which states that although the lion has neither character nor existence, even so it still possesses a qualified reality. The fourth is Zen (see the previous chapter on Fazang's contemporary, Huineng), which declares that on attaining enlightenment, the consciousness goes beyond both emptiness and its own existence in order to find tranquillity. Finally, the Huayen School declares that final enlightenment or 'Perfect Reality' is a vision of the universe as an undifferentiated and interfused mass. Everything is seen clearly as unreal, a vision that unifies all with one and one with all. The aim of Huayen is to reach the state known as *Bodhisattva* (Buddha-to-be). Fully enlightened, the *Bodhisattva* nevertheless retains his physical form yet delays a state of full Buddhahood out of compassion for his fellow sentient beings.

A young Buddhist monk.

Fazang uses a number of other images in his work to illustrate the difficult concepts of Huayen. Most importantly there is the jewel-studded net of the Hindu god Indra. Each jewel reflects every other gem and the net itself, so that the whole is reflected in every part, just as every part is contained within the whole. By knowing any one 'fact', all may be known at once. In addition to this, every fact is interlinked and cannot exist in isolation. Beneath the reality of a 'factual' world, resides a further reality, that of 'Principle', which corresponds somewhat to the noumenal realm of Kant or the World of Ideas of Plato. The Realm of Fact is produced by the Realm of Principle, which is that of the mind. Thus Fazang is an idealist philosopher, asserting the primacy of the mind above all else. Like Plato, he maintains that the world of Principle is eternal and unchanging, although Fazang believes that it has no reality after enlightenment.

Fazang's ideas were to exercise a profound influence on Neo-Confucianism. Just as was happening in India at around the same time, Buddhist concepts were beginning to seep into non-Buddhist philosophy.

The exterior of a Buddhist temple complex at Tatung in China.

ZHANG ZAI
1020–1077 CE

Zhang Zai was a pivotal figure in Neo-Confucian philosophy and taught both the Cheng brothers, as well as strongly influencing **Zhuxi**, the greatest figure of the period. A key concept for Zhang Zai, which was also massively influential for Neo-Confucianism, is that of the universe as one entity with many different manifestations. The Great Ultimate, a term underlying the fundamental reality in the *Book of Changes* (*Yi Jing* or *I Ching*), is said by Zhang to be the same as *qi*, the material force and binding substance of the physical world. Even more important is the idea of humanity (*ren*) 'forming one body with all things'. This has been described as the most significant Neo-Confucian concept of all and is worth considering in more detail.

Although this idea was implicit in early Confucian thinkers, especially **Mencius**, Zhang's formulation still managed to inspire Neo-Confucianism. The 'Western Inscription', engraved on the West window of Zhang's lecture hall, is his most important text. Here is part of it:

Heaven is my father and Earth is my mother, and even such a small creature as I finds an intimate place in their midst.
Therefore that which fills the universe I regard as my body and that which directs the universe I consider as my nature. All people are my brothers and sisters, and all things are my companions.

Cheng Yi, who accurately predicted that nothing like it had been written since Mencius, acclaimed this revolutionary and moving text. However, it goes beyond Mencius in its extension of *ren* to the entire universe. Zhang seems to have been influenced by the Buddhist ethic of universal compassion, and it certainly inspired Neo-Confucianists for centuries to come. Zhang differs from the Buddhists, however, in his insistence on traditional Confucian relationships and hierarchies, which he emphasizes in a series of examples on ideal conduct. Love for all is manifested through, though not limited by, particular relationships.

What 'forming one body' means here is that our humanity cannot help but respond compassionately to the suffering of another. The classic example given by Mencius (371–289 BCE) is that of someone who witnesses a small child about to fall into a well. According to **Wang Yangming's** (1472–1529 CE) insightful analysis, 'this shows that his humanity (*ren*) forms one body with the child'. The argument continues, taking in the suffering of animals, broken plants and even damaged objects: 'even when he sees tiles and stones shattered and crushed, he cannot help a feeling of regret. This shows that his humanity forms one body with tiles and stones.' It is as if harm to an apparently separate person, animal or thing were tantamount to harming ourselves. Our own body is plainly not harmed but our humanity (*ren*) is conceived as a universal body: 'that which fills the universe I regard as my body.'

Even a petty or mean person, a 'small man', feels this same impulse. Wang Yangming continues: 'although the mind of the small man is divided and narrow, yet his humanity that forms one body can remain free of darkness.' Problems arise when the small man's mind is 'aroused by desire and obscured by selfishness…compelled by greed for gain and fear of harm, and stirred by anger, he will destroy things, kill members of his own species and will do everything. In extreme cases, he will even slaughter his own brothers, and the humanity that forms one body will disappear completely'.

The mausoleum of Confucius in Qufu, China.

ZHUXI (CHU HSI)
1130–1200 CE

Zhuxi is the most influential philosopher in Chinese history since **Mencius**. As a Neo-Confucian, he re-shaped Confucian thought and further formalized it at the heart of Chinese culture. In particular, he established an important canon of Confucian works, primarily the Four Books (the *Analects* of **Confucius**, the *Mencius, The Great Learning* and *The Doctrine of the Mean*). In 1313, these four works became the basis for the examination system of entry into the civil service, a system that survived until 1905 and which provided the model for Western public examinations. As well as establishing the Confucian canon, Zhuxi's view of the true Confucian bloodline became the norm. According to Zhuxi, this lineage began with the authors of the Confucian classics and continued with his predecessors,

Zhou Dun Yi, **Zhang Zai** and the Cheng brothers, who revived it in the eleventh century.

Zhuxi edited Confucian thought, pruning out any ideas he felt were alien to the tradition. His philosophy brings together Confucius, Mencius, the ancient metaphysics of *yin* and *yang*, the Five Elements or Agents, and Daoist and Buddhist ideas. An equivalent figure would have to be the Indian **Shankara**, who had a decisive influence in reviving and editing the philosophical classics contained in the Vedanta. Zhuxi saw himself as a transmitter rather than an originator but his 'great synthesis', in the phrase of Wing-Tsit Chan, proved to be a major development in Confucian thought and Chinese culture alike.

Confucianism underwent a period of stagnation during which it was neither advancing nor developing. Although it was often the most important philosophy from an official perspective, Daoism and Buddhism had greater vitality during this time and continued to advance. Its rebirth as Neo-Confucianism began a couple of centuries before Zhuxi and flourished through the figures of five eleventh-century philosophers who all knew each other.

Zhou Dun Yi (Chou Tun-I) (1017–1073) was an unusual character. He gave the impression of being a kind of Zen monk but in actuality was much more influenced by Daoism. He introduced many of the ideas that were to become important to Neo-Confucianism. One of Zhou's statements gives a flavour of his approach: 'having no desire, one is vacuous while tranquil and straightforward while in action'. Confucianism had always been more concerned with activity than with tranquillity. This was not surprising, given Confucius' concern with the ethical and social side of living and his refusal to entertain metaphysical speculations. In practice, however, the contemplative side of life had been effectively ceded to Daoism and Buddhism. Zhou's vision in a sense reclaimed this important aspect for Confucianism. The short sentence above is full of challenges to the orthodoxy: desirelessness, vacuity and tranquillity all sit uncomfortably alongside traditional Confucianism. In so doing, he sets the scene for the thinkers that followed.

Zhang Zai (1020–1077) had two particularly influential ideas. The first was his conception that the universe is one but its manifestations are many. The second, and most defining, is his idea of *ren* (human-heartedness or love) 'forming one body with the universe'. This is perhaps the key concept in Neo-Confucianism and is treated separately in the chapter on Zhang. As we will see below, Zhuxi adopted Zhang's ideas on the subject. As with Zhou Dun Yi, we can see Zhang developing a more holistic and unitive philosophy.

Cheng Hao (1032–1085) and Cheng Yi (1033–1107) are perhaps the only well-documented example of blood brothers who were also major philosophers, although the sixth-century Indian Buddhist Vasubandhu, and his brother, Asonga, are perhaps another. They were students of both Zhou Dun Yi and Zhang Zai and were friendly with the fifth great thinker of the time, Shao Yong (1011–1077) (as Zhuxi rejected most of his ideas, they will not be considered here). Remarkably, the ideas of the Cheng brothers are widely different from each other, with Cheng

Yi being the founder of rationalism in Neo-Confucian thought, and Cheng Hao the first of the idealists. Commonly, however, they based their philosophies around Principle or *li*.[52] Principle is the uniting factor in the universe, unchanging everywhere. Their concept of *Tien Li* (The Principle of Heaven) encompasses both moral and natural law – how we should behave and how things are. Cheng Hao emphasized the former aspect, while Cheng Yi explored the latter.

'Fundamentally there is only one Great Ultimate, yet each of the myriad things has been endowed with it and each in itself possesses the Great Ultimate in its entirety.'

Of these five philosophers, Cheng Yi is the real forefather of Zhuxi and it was his rationalism which really influenced later Neo-Confucianism. Their tradition was known in later times as the Cheng-Zhu (Ch'eng-Chu) School. Cheng Yi's ideas, though influential, were by no means universally accepted and he suffered from official censorship. The fact that when he died only four people were brave enough to attend his funeral serves as an indication of the climate of the times. Zhuxi, too, was often falling foul of the authorities. Zhuxi's genius brought him many appointments, but generally, he was too radical to hold a job down for long. For example, in 1179 he was appointed prefect, but in 1182, he was demoted to a lowly position for the offence of having written to the emperor denouncing official corruption. Similar appointments in 1190 and 1194 ended unfavourably, and he was finally threatened with execution. The only job Zhuxi was apparently able to hold down was that of temple guardian, which suited his studious temperament very well. However, over a thousand mourners attended his funeral.

Perhaps the most important idea within Zhuxi's philosophy is that of the Great Ultimate. This he borrowed from Zhou Dun Yi and is akin to the idea of the Brahman or Absolute in Indian philosophy or the Good in Greek. Zhuxi says, 'the Great Ultimate is nothing other than Principle'. In this way, he unites Zhou's Great Ultimate with the idea of Principle that, as we have seen, he derived from the Cheng brothers. 'Fundamentally there is only one Great Ultimate, yet each of the myriad things has been endowed with it and each in itself possesses the Great Ultimate in its entirety.' Zhuxi uses the image of moonlight falling on rivers and lakes to illustrate how the Great Ultimate manifests in many places and forms. The Indian Vedanta tradition uses a very similar illustration with sunlight reflecting in pots of water. It is interesting to note, however, that Zhuxi's image emphasizes the unity of light even in its manifestation as reflection, whereas the Indian one emphasizes the separate individuality of the pots. Perhaps this expresses Chinese sentiment for people as part of society or a corresponding lack of feeling for the individual soul. It more closely recalls **Fazang's** image of the universe as a bejewelled net, with each gem reflecting each other and the whole. Wing-Tsit Chan traces the Neo-Confucian idea of Principle back to Fazang's Huayen Buddhism which

has a world of 'Principle' underlying the ordinary mundaness of 'fact'.

The final question that arises now is one of how the world manifests itself. Zhuxi characterizes manifestation as a meeting between principle (*li*) and material force (*qi*). As we saw in the chapter on Mencius, *qi* (or *chi*) is the ancient Chinese concept of an energy or life force flowing through the universe. Good and evil are not contained within the Great Ultimate, but come into existence in its manifestation. Like all Confucians, apart from **Xunzi**, Zhuxi believes good to be essential and natural and evil to be incidental and unnatural.

A further passage explains more about the Great Ultimate and its relationship to the duality of *yin* and *yang* and to the Five Agents:

The Great Ultimate is similar to the top of the house or the zenith of the sky, beyond which point there is no more. It is the ultimate of principle. Yang is active and yin is tranquil. In these it is not the Great Ultimate that acts or remains tranquil. It is simply that there are the principles of activity and tranquillity. Principle is not visible; it becomes visible through yin and yang. Principle attaches itself to yin and yang as a man sits astride a horse. As soon as yin and yang produce the Five Agents, they are confined and fixed by physical nature and are thus differentiated into individual things, each with its own nature. But the Great Ultimate is in all of them.

Zhuxi's view of *ren* is an interesting one and derives from

Zhang Zai: '*ren* is the Principle of love, and impartiality is the Principle of *ren*. Therefore 'if there is impartiality, there is *ren*, and if there is *ren*, there is love.' We saw in **Mozi** the earliest appearance of impartial love, and how the Confucians criticized his lack of respect for loving relationships. In Zhuxi, impartiality is the Principle underlying love, and just as the Great Ultimate is fully embodied in each individual, so universal love is fully embodied in filial, fraternal or matrimonial love. So universal love is realized in Zhuxi as the source of loving relationships.

Zhuxi considers human nature to be at one with Principle. The Way or Principle is the nature of the universe as a whole, and in individual people or things, it becomes their nature.

Zhuxi inherited Cheng Yi's rationalism. His brother Cheng Hao's idealism was taken up by Zhuxi's contemporary, Lu Xiangshan (Lu Hsiang-Shan) (1139–1193), who emphasized the primacy of the mind. For Zhuxi, the old Confucian injunction to undertake 'the investigation of things' meant rational exploration. For the idealists, everything is contained within the mind and therefore its exploration is all that is necessary. Zhuxi was far more influential than Lu Xiangshan on the subsequent course of Chinese thought and cultural life but it was not until **Wang Yangming** (1472–1559) that idealism found its way to a wider audience once more.

A pictorial representation of the cosmic duality of yin *and* yang.

WANG YANGMING
1472–1529 CE

Wang was an energetic and effective thinker, better known in his time for his abilities as an administrator and military leader than as a philosopher. Struggling against the tide of corruption and nepotism that was crippling Chinese society at the time, Wang suffered frequent setbacks. In 1506, he was exiled to a semi-barbarous region for two years for having offended a eunuch. Between 1510 and 1521, however, he was finally able to enjoy a glorious and remarkable career that included administering justice and economic reform, fighting rebellions and establishing schools. From 1521 to 1527, he was again sidelined, this time in his native state, before being recalled on one last, successful military campaign to quell a rebellion. He died in 1529.

On his wedding day, Wang became so absorbed in a discussion with a Daoist priest that he did not return home until the following day.

The most influential Chinese philosopher of the last thousand years is undoubtedly **Zhuxi**. His rational form of Neo-Confucianism became the norm, and after 1313, his selection of the Confucian classics formed the basis for civil service examinations. In his time, opposition came from the Neo-Confucian idealist Lu Xiangshan (1139–1193), but it was to be three centuries before another philosopher could launch a veritable challenge on Zhuxi's ideas. This attack came from Wang Yangming, who was an idealist like Lu, and held the mind to be *the* fundamental reality. The school of philosophers that followed Wang is known as the Wang-Lu School, and was founded to oppose the one founded by Zhuxi on the basis of Cheng Yi's philosophy (known as the Cheng-Zhu School).

Wang Yangming's philosophy was very influential for its time and for a further 150 years after his death. Although he resisted the prevailing orthodoxy, Wang did not have a serious philosophical opponent. The political situation in the Ming Dynasty was very difficult and scholarship was at a low ebb. When he was young, Wang tried out most of the various options available for intellectual endeavour, including Zhuxi's Confucianism (then in decline), literary composition, the science of war and the Daoist search for

The Drum Tower, built during the Ming Dynasty, on Beijing's northern boundary.

the elixir of life. Wang's energy was evident right from the beginning. He and a companion, for example, are said to have sat down before a bamboo grove for seven days in a Zhuxian attempt to 'investigate the principles' in it. Eventually, he tired of this and gave up. Like Confucius, he had a reputation for forgetting what he was doing when engaged in learning: on his wedding day, Wang became so absorbed in a discussion with a Daoist priest that he did not return home until the following day. Progressively, Wang developed his own brand of philosophy. His first major breakthrough came while in exile in 1508 and he continued to refine it until 1521, when he completed the essentials of his philosophy at the age of 50.

Wang argued against Zhuxi's identification of Principle with things, maintaining that principles resided in the mind instead. A demonstration of this (which may seem self-evident to us) is that filial piety continues well after the parents are dead and buried. Principle is not to be found in things themselves (i.e. the parents) but in the mind of the individual. In Wang's opinion, Zhuxi's rationalism had a negative effect as it fragmented and disturbed the mind:

People fail to realize that the highest good is in their minds and seek it outside. As they believe that everything or every event has its own definite principle, they search for the highest good in individual things. Consequently, the mind becomes fragmentary, isolated, broken into pieces; mixed and confused, it has no definite direction.

Conversely, Wang's idealism would have the opposite effect:

Once it is realized that the highest good is in the mind and does not depend on any search outside, then the mind will have definite direction and there will be no danger of its becoming fragmentary, isolated, broken into pieces, mixed or confused. When there is no such danger, the mind will not be erroneously perturbed, but will be tranquil.

Wang's solution to the philosophical impasse resulting from an overemphasis on 'the investigation of things' and the philology in Zhuxi's followers was what he called 'the extension of the innate knowledge of the good'. Instead of working from the outside in (from observation and study towards inherent Principle), he declares that the basis for this should be 'the innate knowledge of the good', identifiable with the Principle of Nature. Wang's philosophy reconnects with that of **Mencius** (371–289 BCE) and his concern with demonstrating that man's nature is good.

Wang, like nearly all Confucian thinkers, focuses his attention on ethics. This concern works well for Wang because ethical concepts (for example,

filial piety) are, in a certain sense, largely mental. His exposition of 'forming one body with all things', for example, is a pleasing and clear account of the topic (see **Zhang Zai**) and demonstrates the strength of his approach. In terms of his concern with a decline in morality, the fragmentation of philosophy and the loss of connection with the Confucian tradition, Wang's idealism was a success.

Compared to Western idealism, however, Wang's philosophy of mind is very undeveloped. Metaphysically, Wang struggles to account for phenomena. His claim that 'there is nothing under Heaven external to the mind' was challenged by someone who pointed at some blossoming trees on a cliff and asked what they had to do with the mind. His reply, that the colours show up when one looks at them is, at best, inadequate. Although Wang is a philosopher of the mind, he is not really interested in intellectual matters but in moral reform. His philosophy argues that knowledge and action are the same thing, and his life illustrated this. Therefore Wang could be said to be an exemplary philosopher in every sense.

Wang's view of the practicality of knowledge in action was an important theme in subsequent philosophy. It could even be said to have been carried to its logical conclusion during the twentieth century through the ideas of **Mao Zedong** (Mao Tse-Tung). Despite Mao's materialistic philosophy, his theory of mind echoes that of Wang.

DAI ZHEN (TAI CHEN)
1723–1777 CE

The two main Neo-Confucian schools of thought were the rationalism of **Zhuxi** (1130–1200) and the idealism of **Wang Yangming** (1472–1529). Zhuxi used the faculty of reason to investigate Principle within things, while Wang looked within the mind. Although by comparison to Wang, Zhuxi was relatively interested in 'the investigation of things', he did so in order to uncover Principle and thus the Great Ultimate. A direct Western parallel would be to Plato: that 'things' were of importance only insofar as they pointed the way to the truth, which was determined by pure reason.

A second challenge to Zhuxi came from Dai Zhen. He criticized Zhuxians for treating Principle (*li*) as a 'thing'. Dai Zhen was part of a tradition known as Han Learning, going back to the thinkers of the Han Dynasty (206 BCE–220 CE), the first scholars to have explored the Confucian classics, such as the *Analects*, the *Mencius*, *The Doctrine of the Mean*, and so on. Followers of Dai Zhen were also known as the School of 'Investigations Based on Evidence', that is to say they were empiricists. The School of Han Learning liked to devote itself to objective and critical reasoning on subjects such as philology, history and mathematics. Dai Zhen stood out because he regarded such study as only a means to an end, which, as a good Confucian, meant moral philosophy and its practice.

Ching-Hai, the first entrance gate to the temple of Confucius.

DESIRE

One of the most interesting questions within Chinese philosophy is that of desire. It is not a major issue for the early thinkers. **Confucius** *does not condemn it, but seems to regard it as in need of management: the final step of his learning is, 'at 70, I followed my heart's desire and did not err'.* **Mencius** *advised a king who confessed to having a weakness for sex thus: 'if your majesty loves sex, let your people enjoy the same, and what difficulty will there be for you to become the true king of the empire?' Mencius speaks about desire a great deal and makes it a central tenet of his philosophy. For example, our desire for honour is the seed of propriety. The 'superior man' neither insists on fulfilling his desires nor on suppressing them. They are natural and therefore good on the whole, although 'for nourishing the mind there is nothing better than to have few desires.'* **Xunzi** *has an interesting point to make about a philosopher who he said understood having a few desires 'but not having many'. The importance of the latter is that it helps a king to rule by giving him an understanding of what the people want.*

Daoism, on the other hand, is more censorious. **Laozi**, *who speaks a great deal about desire, says 'do not display the objects of desire, so that people's hearts shall not be disturbed' and that 'the sage desires to have no desire'. The Daoists saw the ideal of vacuity as being a desireless, empty state. Nevertheless, there is a strong and surprising tendency in later Daoism towards hedonism and self-preservation at all costs, as in the notorious words attributed to Yang Chu (440–360 BCE). This also emerged in the Neo-Daoist 'Light Conversation' School of the third century CE, whose iconoclasm extended to moral conventions.*

Of all Chinese philosophies and religions, Buddhism is the one most opposed to desire, as would be expected. It was a core belief of the **Buddha** *that desire or thirst* (tanha) *was the principal cause of suffering.*

Desire became a hotly debated topic in Neo-Confucian thought when Zhou Dun Yi (1017–1073 CE), influenced by Buddhist and especially Daoist thought, became the first orthodox Chinese thinker to speak of desireless vacuity as a virtue. **Zhang Zai** *(1022–1077 CE) was the first to oppose principle and desire: 'those who understand higher things, return to the Principle of Nature, while those who understand lower things, follow human desires'. He related* yang *to the moral nature and* yin *to material desire.* **Zhuxi** *(1130–1200 CE) crystallized Neo-Confucian thinking on the subject, writing about it extensively to establish the polarity between desire and principle. Even* **Wang Yangming** *(1472–1529 CE), who opposed Zhuxi* *on many issues, was at one with him on this question. Neo-Confucianism did not espouse an ascetic retreat from all desire: the real enemy was selfish, partial desire.*

Wang Fuzhi (1619–1692 CE) was the first thinker to take a different tack, returning once more to the original teachings. He wrote, 'Mencius continued the teaching of Confucius, which is that wherever human desires are found, the Principle of Nature is found'. His influence was slight, however, and it was only with **Dai Zhen** *(1723–1777 CE) that Zhuxian orthodoxy came under serious scrutiny. Dai Zhen was perhaps too ahead of his time to be popular, but he had his followers even before a revival of his ideas took place in the early twentieth century.*

As a ten-year-old child, Dai Zhen was supposed to have challenged his teachers on the authenticity of Confucian writings: 'how do we know that this is what Confucius said?' He later came to question not what Confucius had said so much as the interpretations that were foisted upon Confucianism by Neo-Confucians.

Dai Zhen rejected much of the Neo-Confucian tradition, reinstating desire as an acceptable and natural part of life, much as did his Scottish contemporary, David Hume. He argued against the polarity of desire and Principle, stating instead that 'Principle consists of feelings that do not err'. This is an important restatement of Confucius' 'at 70, I followed my heart's desire and did not err'. Dai Zhen's rejection of Neo-Confucian Principle is also Humean in flavour: he says that the Neo-Confucians wrongly speak of Principle when they regard it as a real thing or single essence pervading all things. Principle does not exist in a transcendental realm but is to be found in the disciplined human heart: in other words, it may be identified with *ren* (human-heartedness). He wrote with perspicacity that 'the ancient sages did not seek benevolence, righteousness, propriety and wisdom outside the realm of desires, and did not consider these in isolation from blood, breath, mind and spirit.' Dai Zhen goes against Daoist- or Buddhist-influenced ideas of withdrawing from the world: 'to let others live but not to live oneself is against nature'. He maintains that 'all activities in the world should consist of nothing more than encouraging this fulfilment of desire and the expression of feelings.' Dai Zhen is not promoting hedonism here but a sincere and disciplined way of life in which the individual plays a full part in society and lives squarely and honestly with himself.

MAO ZEDONG
(MAO TSE-TUNG)
1893–1976

Born into a fairly prosperous peasant family in Shaoshan (Hunan province), Mao's early childhood was not particularly hard by the standards of the day. Although the family prospered further, Mao's peasant roots remained deeply ingrained in his character. His primary school education included a grounding in the Confucian classics, but at the age of 13, his father took him away to work on the farm. Determined to gain a full-blown scholarly education, Mao rebelled and pursued his studies in a nearby town. In 1905 the Confucian-based civil service examinations were abolished and Western learning began to find its way into the scholastic curricula, marking the beginning of a period of great intellectual uncertainty for China.

In 1911 Mao was involved in the rebellion launched against the decadent Qin Dynasty. It was his first experience of war. By 1912 the empire that had existed more or less intact since 220 BCE had fallen and been replaced by a republic. Mao continued his studies, drifting from one subject to the next, learned about Western traditions, and eventually graduated in 1918, going on to Beijing University, where he became involved with the founding members of the Chinese Communist Party (CCP) which was officially formed in 1921 and where Mao gradually gained prominence. Its central figure from 1934–1935, he led the Red Army on the Long March and was instrumental in fighting off the Japanese invasion of 1937. The civil war ended in 1949 with his declaration of the People's Democratic Dictatorship (later the People's Republic of China). Mao was Chairman of the Party Secretariat and Political Bureau from 1943 but effectively controlled the party and all of China until his death in 1976. His rule did not have the grinding brutality of Stalin's regime, but his capricious and ruthless policies often led to great destruction and suffering.

In terms of philosophy, Mao was not a particularly original thinker. His ideas were largely derived from the Communist figures that preceded him: Marx, Engels, Lenin and Stalin. He did, however, ponder deeply the philosophy of dialectical materialism that underlies Communism, and his practical application of its ideas is original. Through his political eminence, he became without a doubt the most influential twentieth-century thinker within China.

The most important concept in Mao's philosophy is that of contradiction. He wrote, 'contradiction is universal and

Mao wrote many essays and papers. His Little Red Book *has been translated into many different languages.*

absolute, it is present in the process of development of all things and permeates every process from beginning to end.' Marx's model of history is built on the principle of contradiction or conflict: the ruling class and the subject class, or capital and labour, are in perpetual conflict. One day this conflict will result in a crisis where the working class will triumph. Eventually this new situation will give rise to a further crisis, but in Marx the whole emphasis is on the logical end to the present conflict and the happy situation that will then prevail, whereas in Mao the principle of contradiction becomes 'universal and absolute'. Contradiction in Mao has something of the *yin-yang* philosophy about it (see p. 165). It seems almost an article of faith with him, as is seen in this passage from *On Contradiction:*

The sciences are differentiated precisely on the basis of the particular contradictions inherent in their respective objects of study. Thus the contradiction peculiar to a certain field of phenomena constitutes the object of study for a specific branch of science. For example, positive and negative numbers in mathematics; action and reaction in mechanics; positive and negative electricity in physics; dissociation and combination in chemistry; forces of production and relations of production, classes and class struggle in social science; offence and defence in military science; idealism and materialism, the metaphysical outlook and the dialectical outlook in philosophy; and so on – all these are the objects of study of different branches of

*science precisely because each
branch has its own particular
contradiction and particular essence.*[53]

Mao's examples of contradiction in different fields are drawn from Lenin. Some are good analogies, some less so. Positive and negative numbers are a poor analogy for Marxist dialectic because their opposition is not dynamic: the result is just another positive or negative number. Mao is on even shakier ground when he declares these contradictions represent the 'essence' of their respective fields. Positive and negative numbers are not the 'essence' of mathematics, any more than positive and negative electricity are the essence of physics, or the metaphysical and the dialectical the essence of philosophy. Mao was well-educated and his misconception here can only be due to infatuation with the idea of contradiction itself.

Mao's second important idea is his theory of knowledge, which is again directly derived from Marxism. In his essay *On Practice*, Mao holds that knowledge proceeds from experience of the material world, and that experience equals involvement:

*If you want knowledge,
you must take part in the practice
of changing reality.
If you want to know the taste
of a pear, you must change the pear
by eating it yourself.
If you want to know the structure
and properties of the atom,
you must make physical
and chemical experiments to
change the state of the atom.
If you want to know the theory
and methods of revolution,
you must take part in revolution.*

*All genuine knowledge originates
in direct experience.*

Only after having 'experienced' the experience (so to speak) can one make the 'leap' and conceptualize perceptions as knowledge. Knowledge is then put into practice once more and further perception takes place. Mao displays affinities here not only with Marxism but also with Neo-Confucian thought going back to **Wang Yangming** (1472–1529). Being an idealist, Wang maintained a position opposite to that of Mao: the world was entirely contained within the mind. Nevertheless, his theory of knowledge, like Mao's, sustained that knowledge and action were the same thing. This influenced later thinkers, such as Kang Youwei (1858–1927), whose utopianism was an important non-Marxist influence on Mao.

We will now also look at how Mao's ideas were put into practice. His theory of contradiction distinguishes between contradictions that are 'antagonistic' and 'non-antagonistic', another Leninist concept. The antagonistic contradiction will need a struggle before it can be resolved, whereas a non-antagonistic contradiction can be dealt with through pure discussion. The contradictions between the proletariat and the ruling class were antagonistic, while Mao believed those between the CCP and the people were not. In 1956, Mao announced a new policy of intellectual freedom in response to a growing desire by Chinese Communists to avoid the tyranny of Stalinist Russia. He spoke of 'letting a hundred flowers blossom and a hundred schools of thought contend'. The policy was a failure, however, and resulted in a crescendo of criticism and complaint. Mao, believing all Chinese intellectuals had failed him, began to pursue a ruthless policy of suppression. Within a year, some 700,000 'rightist' intellectuals had been sent to work the land as peasants in order to re-educate them.

Despite this experience, Mao used the politics of contradiction to maintain his stranglehold on power, and the principle of contradiction to pursue his vision of 'continual revolution'. He believed that in any revolution counter-revolutionary elements would inevitably emerge within the new power structure. He frequently declared purges against those whom he saw or declared to be enemies of the revolution. The most dramatic example of this was the

Mao as a young Communist.

Cultural Revolution of 1966. All over the world, students were rising up against the political establishment of the 1960s. Only in China did its leaders positively encourage these groups to voice their protest. Hundreds of thousands of students and lecturers spontaneously formed Red Guard units from universities all over China and carried out savage attacks on the supposedly counter-revolutionary bureaucracy. Within months, China was in a state of virtual anarchy and Mao was forced to call out the army to snatch back control from the Red Guards. The Cultural Revolution had spiralled out of control and China descended into a civil war that involved the Red Guards, the army and other factions. It ended only in 1968.

The other major disaster of Mao's career was the Great Leap Forward of 1958, which involved organizing the peasant population into communes. This was the third major re-organization of China's labour force in as many years – Mao's passion for revolution being the main reason for this – and was economically disastrous. The people's communes proved cumbersome and unmanageably large units. An estimated 19 million died from famine and disease.

It is interesting to ask whether Mao represents a total break with the past or whether, despite his repudiation of Chinese philosophy, he was in fact influenced by it. Confucianism could be seen as paving the way for Maoism in several respects. First, both philosophies have an ethical and social focus in which the needs and desires of the individual are subsumed into those of the group. Second, there is an emphasis on activity as opposed to reflection, which is broadly Confucian. As we saw in his essay *On Practice,* Mao argues that the only way to learn anything is through practice, principally the practice of economic activity. Third, the Confucian Doctrine of the Mean was an influence on Mao's political practice: typically, he would follow a period of turbulent change with one of calm and peace, even at times reversing some parts of the earlier revolution, in preparation for the next wave of upheaval. Fourth,

Mao, accompanied by his second-in-command, Liu Shaoqi, passing along the ranks of revolutionaries during a rally in Beijing (Peking).

Confucianism does not depend on the agency of God. Overall, however, the differences far outnumber any similarities. It would be more accurate to say Mao recognized that the best way of making Communism function within China was to work with an awareness of the existing ideas in its culture. In this light, Confucian elements can be seen as expedient additions rather than as fundamental to Mao's philosophy.

In many ways, however, Maoism has more affinities to Daoism and to the traditional philosophies of *yin-yang* and the Five Elements or Agents. By identifying with the underdog and with women's rights, and by opposing the establishment, the educated classes and their technical expertise, Mao aligns himself with the Daoist *yin* ethic of **Laozi**. Continual revolution, too, could be seen as an echo of the Principle of revolution that characterizes the Five Agents theory, with each element taking centre stage in turn. We saw in the chapter on **Hanfeizi** how the ideas of Daoism could be misused to support tyranny, when the Way or *Dao* becomes identified with the Way set down by the emperor. Mao could almost be seen as a

mystical sage-king, whose perception of the Way alone defined what it was. He was certainly revered as a national obsession, particularly in later years, but this was largely due to widespread fear among the population of his frequent purges. In this context of mass hysteria, Mao's capriciousness was elevated to a national virtue: only *he* was able to keep the sacred flame alight, while others allowed themselves to be seduced by capitalist ideology. Often this would lead to death, but in the practice of self-denunciation and re-education can be seen the twisted remnants of a mystical path, in which Mao and Communism come to replace the Way of Heaven.

A quarter of a century after Mao's death, China seems to have come through a difficult period of transition rather well: far better, for example, than Russia. The lot of the average Chinese citizen has improved dramatically, both socially and economically. However, critics are still undecided as to whether Mao should be more praised for his role in raising up the peasants and changing the face of China or branded a mass criminal, along the lines of Stalin.

KOREAN PHILOSOPHY

*The key figures in Korean Zen are those
that attempted to show that its anti-intellectual
and anti-scholastic tendencies could be
reconciled with a highly complex system such as Huayen.*

*Monks pray before a shrine in Bomunsa
Temple on Songmo Island, Korea.*

As China's smaller neighbour, Korea
has always resided in its shadow.
In the history of global thought and
religion, it certainly has suffered from
the prejudice that sees it as a mere
bridge in the transmission of influence
eastwards to Japan, and believes it
to have contributed nothing of its
own. Korea's recent history has not
helped either. Annexed by Japan
in 1910, and later divided into the

hermetically sealed Communist North
and democratic South Korea, the
twentieth century saw Korea fall victim
to external forces, which led to an
inevitable neglect of its culture. In
recent times, a cultural re-evaluation
is beginning to offer a more balanced
view of Korea's contribution to the
world stage. Its importance lies
principally as a contributor to the
Chinese tradition of Confucianism and
to Chinese-flavoured Buddhism.

Let's consider Buddhism first. The
two most important Chinese forms of
Buddhism, both in terms of their
influence and their distinctive Chinese
identity, were the Chan (Zen) School
and the Huayen (Flowery Garland)
School. The latter was a refinement of
orthodox Mahayanist Buddhism and
regarded itself as the pinnacle of one
thousand years of Buddhist thought,
subsuming and surpassing the earlier
forms. Based on the *Avatamsaka*
(Garland) *Sutra*, Korean Buddhists
were important from almost the very
beginning. The central Huayen figure
is **Fazang**, and the influence of
Korean thinkers, especially Wanhyo
(617–686), was important to this
tradition. Wanhyo was pivotal in other
ways, too, particularly in showing a
talent for synthesis and unification
which characterizes many Korean
thinkers. He hoped that Buddhism
would become the state religion and

proselytized about it tirelessly, founding the Popsong or Dharma Nature School as a result. Wanhyo sought to understand the divisions that existed between different schools of Buddhism, such as the Yogacara and Madhyamika (known in China as Tiantai), by envisaging in their varying approaches a kind of *via positiva* and *via negativa* to the same problem. Wanhyo saw the former as being an attempt to climb towards a higher consciousness and the latter as an attempt to explode the false thinking that gets in the way of this attainment. He also promoted an esoteric brand of Buddhism, with some doctrines revealed only to the initiated.

Zen was much more problematic for the Koreans, and the key figures in Korean Zen are those who attempted to show that its anti-intellectual and anti-scholastic tendencies could be reconciled within a complex system such as Huayen. Uich'on (1055–1101) was ordained as a Tiantai teacher in China and attempted to set up a monastery which would bring together Tiantai (Ch'on'tae in Korea) and Zen (Sen in Korea). In the end, he was unsuccessful but the Zen Buddhist Chinul (1158–1210) achieved his very aim about a century later. He pioneered the use of the pithy verse paradoxes known as *kungan* in Korea or *koan* in Japan. Chinul also demonstrated that Zen's experiential approach could be combined with a more gradual, study-based, scriptural version of Buddhism, much as the Japanese Zen master **Dogen** would a generation later. As founder of the Chogye School of Zen, he did as much as anyone to ensure the continual dominance of Zen in Korean Buddhism.

However, Confucianism steadily gained ground during this period and in the Choson Dynasty of 1392–1910 was quickly established as the state religion. During this time, Korea was even more strongly Confucian than China, because the competition from rival traditions was far less. The great period of Korean Confucianism arrived during the sixteenth century with Yi T'oegye (1501–1570) and Yi Yulgok (1536–1584). The dominant Neo-Confucian thinker was **Zhuxi**, whose school in China received a major challenge from the idealism of **Wang Yangming**, who died in 1529. Yi T'oegye and Yi Yulgok, both of whom are closer to Zhuxi, worked to illuminate some of the most important points in Zhuxi's thinking, in some ways more successfully than many of their Chinese contemporaries.

JAPANESE PHILOSOPHY

Of all the Eastern traditions considered in this book,
there are very few distinctive responses to the challenges of
Western modernity and the ideologies of capitalism
and Communism...Only in Japan is the Western challenge
creatively met and accepted.

Buddhist monks in the snow at the
Shingon monastery in Koyasan, Japan.

Japanese, like Korean philosophy, is largely based on Chinese systems. For Japan, the most important of these is Buddhism, followed by Confucianism. Although Daoism is far less significant in itself, it was nevertheless an influence on the development of Zen. The native Shinto religion will not be dealt with here.

Although there have been a great many Japanese thinkers, this book will look in detail at only a few of the most original ones. For this reason, we gloss over the early period and look first at Buddhism in the twelfth and thirteenth centuries. It was during this period that most of the distinctively Japanese forms were developed. An important concept was the idea of the 'degenerate age' or

mappo, the period in which it was thought that a decline in culture meant that a practice of the **Buddha's** doctrines was almost impossible to follow. This idea had special significance for the Japanese. First, it led to the creation of various 'easy' methods of Buddhist practice; second, it eroded élitist concepts of who was an acceptable Buddhist aspirant; and third, it inspired a kind of Buddhism in ordinary life that fed into Zen practices such as painting, gardening and the tea ceremony.

Among the most important 'easy' methods were those of the Pure Land School. An ancient strand of Buddhism, it has roots in early Chinese and Indian traditions, emphasizing the power of the Buddha over the efforts of the individual. The Pure Land is a kind of Heaven presided over by the Amida Buddha, a transcendental being of whom the historical Buddha was said to be a mere *avatar* or incarnation. The aim of Pure Land Buddhism is to be reborn where the Amida Buddha will impart the teachings that guarantee Enlightenment. **Honen** and **Shinran** were highly innovative in their interpretation of this teaching. In reaction to them, **Nichiren** created his own form of 'easy' Tendai Buddhism based on the *Lotus Sutra*.

The other important development of this period, relating not so much to the 'easy way' as to the drive towards anti-intellectualism and anti-élitism, was the first successful introduction of Zen. The Rinzai Zen School of 'sudden enlightenment' was founded by **Eisai** and the gradualist Soto Zen School by his disciple, **Dogen**, one of the most important thinkers in any Eastern tradition. Notwithstanding this, Rinzai Zen is perhaps most influential today, largely through the efforts of the eighteenth-century monk Hakuin. He revived Rinzai as a practical doctrine among the poor and composed many Zen *koans* including the world-famous, 'when both hands are clapped, a sound is produced; listen to the sound of one hand clapping.' He also pioneered ink drawing and calligraphy as Zen activities. Although originally Chinese, the modern version of Zen, as well as its name, originated in Japan, where it became thoroughly embedded in many aspects of art, culture and daily life.

Perhaps the most interesting aspect of Japanese philosophy, however, is its development in the twentieth century. Of all the Eastern traditions considered in this book, there are very few distinctive responses to the challenges of Western modernity and the ideologies of capitalism and Communism. By comparison, modern Islamic, Hindu and Confucian philosophies seem like restatements of old ideas. Only in Japan is the Western challenge creatively met and accepted by figures like **Nishida** and others within the Kyoto School.

The next section takes a look at the twelfth and thirteenth centuries, during which distinctive Buddhist forms evolved, as well as at the twentieth century for which the philosophy of Nishida is the paramount example.

Japanese children practise calligraphy using a 'fude' Japanese pen.

HONEN

1113–1212 CE

Japanese Buddhism was in decline during the twelfth century. Some monasteries were rumoured to be decadent and lax, while others became fortresses and hired mercenaries for protection. Honen, the first great Buddhist reformer, believed that this decline in Japanese culture simply meant that a more simple, direct and easy form of Buddhism was needed. His idea was centred on the concept of *mappo*, a theory of historical decline from the time of the Buddha. Honen believed that he was living in the third and last stage.

Honen was the founder of Pure Land Buddhism as a separate school of thought – so far, it had always featured in Japan as an aspect of either Tendai or Shingon Buddhism. Classically trained as a Tendai monk at Mount Hiei, he came to the conclusion around 1175 that the best and most effective form of Buddhist practice was the repetition of the chant 'all praise to the Amida Buddha', known as the *nembutsu*. The Amida Buddha is the central deity of Pure Land Buddhism, a sect that originated in India and held the

belief that if enough merit was accrued in life, one could be reincarnated not on earth but in the Pure Land, a version of Heaven in which the aspirant could continue practising until full Buddhahood was achieved. This rebirth marks the point of no return as there is no doubt of having attained enlightenment once the Pure Land is reached.

Honen recognized that his reduction of Buddhist practice to the *nembutsu* was radical and he sought to keep it a secret from all but his closest followers. He wrote down his teachings and left strict instructions that they could only be released after his death. Nevertheless, word got out and Honen and some of his followers (including **Shinran**) were exiled for a short time. Although later pardoned, they continued to have a difficult relationship with the more orthodox schools.

The comparison has been made between Honen and his disciple, Shinran, and Martin Luther, the Protestant reformer of Christianity. Instead of focusing effort on attaining merit that would then bear the aspirant to the Pure Land, Honen instead emphasized the agency of the Amida Buddha, who was said to have taken a vow that anyone who uttered his name would be guaranteed to reach the Pure Land. Thus it was not necessary to undertake any other practice or to meditate, or even to know the meaning of the *nembutsu*: mere repetition was enough. Even the desire for enlightenment – hitherto the first essential step in Buddhism – was to be abandoned. The 'easy way' of the *nembutsu* was contrasted with the difficult way of those who tried to reach enlightenment through their own efforts. Honen's way is about faith, not works; about grace rather than human endeavour or virtue.

SHINRAN
1173–1263 CE

Founded by **Honen**, Pure Land Buddhism teaches that the 'easy way' of repetition of the *nembutsu* formula is the route to enlightenment. Honen's reticence about his teachings meant that his followers were left in some doubt as to his legacy. Shinran, the most important of these, eventually founded his own True Pure Land School which is regarded as the apotheosis of all Pure Land Buddhism. The Amida Buddha, the core figure of worship for Pure Land Buddhists, is understood to be the transcendental being of the historical **Buddha** (Siddhartha Gautama or Shakyamuni, 'the sage of the Shakya [clan]'). He is not thought to be an ordinary human being – as is claimed in the Theravada – but an incarnation of the Amida.

Shinran was among those monks shamed and exiled to Echigo on the coast along with Honen in 1207. There, he adopted the nickname Gutoku, meaning 'foolish' or 'stubble-haired', and married. Moving to the Kanto region, he lived among lay people for twenty years and built up a considerable following. In his sixties, he returned to Kyoto, where he wrote down his philosophy. Like Honen, Shinran embodies a novel and refreshing approach to Buddhism that is self-effacing, grounded and based on trust in the grace of the Amida Buddha. Shinran took the 'easy way' still further than had Honen. The Amida Buddha had made a vow that anyone who repeated his name would naturally be reborn in the Pure Land; Shinran asserted that even one repetition of the *nembutsu* formula was enough for this to happen.

This did not mean of course that the faithful should regard their salvation as assured. Coupled with the comfort of total faith in Amida was Shinran's rejection of personal pride in all its forms. Honen had rejected the traditional Buddhist belief in the aspirant's desire for enlightenment. Shinran rejected the egotistical self in all its manifestations. *Eko* or 'transferring merit' is normally understood to mean merit accrued by the individual and dedicated to the enlightenment of all without discrimination. Shinran's unique interpretation was that *eko* should be regarded not as individual merit but the merit of the Amida's own practice.

The principal aim of this practice is to achieve rebirth in the Pure Land of the Amida Buddha. At this stage, the individual reaches the point of non-retrogression and enlightenment is certain but Shinran emphasizes the attainment of *shinjin* or the state of 'Buddha-mind' instead. This is understood to be a state of non-duality in which there is no difference between true reality and the cycle of rebirth (*samsara*). Shinran taught that non-retrogression was the same as the attainment of *shinjin*. This leads on to the idea that the Pure Land is not the place to achieve enlightenment but simply the final step or aspect of the *Nirvana* that has already been achieved. The enlightened being then returns to earth to pursue the task of bringing every soul into full Buddhahood.

True Pure Land represents an extreme end of the Japanese Buddhist spectrum, in which the Buddha's emphasis on good works and intentions is almost entirely absent.

Nevertheless, Shinran's compassion, humility and practical application of Buddhist principles are yet another example of how the Buddha's real ideals could be realized by an apparently unlikely path. Like Christ, Shinran warned against the would-be holy person and taught that the sinner could be saved just as easily as the saint. His approach to Buddhism is characteristic of the Japanese love of piety. It is also a spirituality for ordinary life, a tendency that emerges in a very different way in Zen, the opposite pole of Japanese Buddhism.

A colossal bronze image of the Amida Buddha near Yokohama in Japan.

EISAI
1141–1215 CE

The decline in Tendai Buddhism and the sense that the last days of the world were fast approaching led to various reform movements in Japan. At one extreme was the True Pure Land Buddhism of **Shinran**, which emphasized the divine agency of the Amida Buddha in everything. At the other was Eisai's Rinzai Zen School, which emphasized human agency and self-reliance.

Trained in the orthodox Tendai tradition, Eisai visited China at the age of 28 to gather manuscripts. Some 20 years later, he made a second journey, this time meeting a Chan (Zen) master, who instructed him and declared Eisai to have achieved enlightenment. Although Eisai claimed that the great Buddhist monk Saicho (764–822), founder of the Tendai School, had already known about Zen and approved of it, Eisai should certainly be regarded as its founder in Japan. Not only did he introduce meditation and *satori* or 'sudden' enlightenment to Japan, he gave Zen its distinctively Japanese character.

Like Pure Land Buddhism, Rinzai Zen had a strong flavour for the ordinary, which led it to sacralize secular activities such as tea drinking. Eisai introduced tea to Japan from China and originated its ceremonial features. Not only was tea useful in helping monks to stay awake but the activity of making and serving it became a form of meditation in itself. It represents the origin of a number of Zen activities, such as archery, gardening, flower arrangement, calligraphy and painting, which all have become characteristic features of Japanese culture.

Japanese tea-ceremony utensils.

DOGEN
1200–1253 CE

Born into an aristocratic family, Dogen's father died when he was two, and his mother when he was seven. He described the sight of the incense rising and disappearing at her funeral as a direct insight into the impermanence of all things. Turning away from a career at the court, Dogen chose to follow Buddhism instead and was ordained a monk at the age of 13. Dissatisfied with the decadence of the Japanese Tendai sect, he left Mount Hiei shortly thereafter and went to study with the aged **Eisai**, founder of Rinzai Zen in Japan. Deeply impressed by Eisai, who died in 1215, the 14-year-old Dogen travelled for the next three years, after which he returned to study with Eisai's chief disciple, Myozen. At the age of 23, he suggested to Myozen that they travel to China to study Zen (see **Huineng**). There, Dogen found Rinzai Zen, as it was practised in China, to be

ultimately unsatisfactory but a meeting with the abbot Rujing of the Caodong (Tsao-tung) Zen sect changed his life. Rujing recognized Dogen's qualities, and at the age of 25, Dogen was recognised as his official successor. He returned to Japan where Caodong is known as Soto Zen.

The problem that had troubled Dogen from his earliest days as a monk was the Tendai conception of two levels of enlightenment: *hongaku* (original enlightenment) and *shikaku* (acquired enlightenment). If everyone was supposed to possess *hongaku*, why were good works then necessary? Dogen wondered why it should be that even already enlightened Buddhas should have to practise to achieve wisdom. Dogen saw how Buddhism had become lax through a failure to either penetrate the theoretical side fully or to properly practise. The prevailing view was fatalistic: the truths of Buddhism were understood in an earlier age but had now become impossible to sustain. One response to this was to aim for an 'easy way'. Dogen rejected fatalism: 'if you do not seek enlightenment [in the] here-and-now on the pretext of the Age of Degenerate Law or wretchedness, in what birth are you to attain it?'

From Dogen's stubborn refusal to accept mediocrity in any aspect of Buddhism came the remarkable rebirth of Soto. While Rinzai emphasized 'sudden enlightenment' based around study of the *koan* paradoxes, Soto monks followed a gradual path of constant meditation or *zazen*. Dogen's distinctively Japanese form of Soto Zen employs both *zazen* and *koan*. Dogen applied a new methodology to the *koan*, allowing for more subtle interpretations. Whereas the Rinzai use of *koan* is intended to defeat ordinary thought and so provoke a sudden realization, Dogen held

A typical Japanese Buddhist shrine.

that they could be expressions of the essential emptiness (*shunyata*) in everything.

Rinzai Zen corresponds to the Indian Yogacara 'Consciousness-Only' School and seeks to defeat ordinary consciousness by the mind-bending *koan* technique. It causes the collapse of ordinary perception and gives birth to true consciousness. On the other hand, Soto Zen, as practised by Dogen, corresponds to the Madhyamika 'Middle Way' School of **Nagarjuna**. The 'middle way' is that of a refusal to absolutely deny or affirm the reality of anything. Rinzai denies ordinary awareness; Soto puts both ordinary and higher awareness on an equal footing.

This explains the ancient paradox that *Nirvana* and *samsara* are the same thing. Neither is absolutely real, neither is absolutely unreal. Buddha-consciousness is not a true consciousness that invalidates a false consciousness, but the constant awareness that ultimately all states of consciousness are impermanent.

Dogen pushes beyond even Nagarjuna in his assertion that the Buddha-nature is itself in constant flux and subject to time. Nagarjuna's concept of emptiness serves to create a new foundation for reality. Stripped of its Buddhist doctrinal trappings, this is not very different from Hinduism. For Nagarjuna, emptiness itself, being the only constant, is the only resting place. But Dogen, like the Son of Man, has no place to rest his head. His perspective is not easy to comprehend, but it combines inner vigilance and constant practice with an unfailing attention to the things of the world. A lay person cannot deny the need for practice, and a monk cannot deny the needs of the world. This does not mean a mediocre combination of the two. Dogen welcomed anyone to his monasteries, regardless of talent, sex or background. His criterion for entry was sincerity. He declared the way of the *Boddhisattva* or 'Buddha-to-be' as 'I am Thus-ness; you are Thus-ness'. Nagarjuna proclaimed the emptiness of all, whilst Dogen advocates the fullness of all. This is what is meant when he writes:

When the self comes forward and confirms the myriad things, it is delusion; when the myriad things come forth and confirm the self, it is enlightenment.

Our problem is not outside of us, it is our belief that there is an outside, our desire to ring-fence a part of reality as 'me' rather than aiming at a total perception of one reality.

The Soto Zen emphasis on meditation is reminiscent of the ancient Buddhist teachings of the Theravada, but without the turning away from the world. Dogen is also a profound poet, and his insights into the natural world are reminiscent of Daoism. In his insistence on practice, Dogen went against the grain and made it difficult for Soto to thrive against the easier paths offered elsewhere, which seemed less élitist. Nevertheless, Dogen is regarded

as perhaps Japan's greatest philosopher as well as a great Buddhist teacher. His penetrating insights are still debated today and fuelled the remarkable modern revival of Zen as perhaps the only Eastern philosophy to engage fully with the West on its own terms.

Dogen

NICHIREN
1222–1282 CE

The great reforms of Pure Land and Zen Buddhism in twelfth-century Japan were inspired by the idea of the *mappo*, the third and final era of Buddhism in which the decline of the human race was inevitable. Their response was to look for an 'easy way', a simplification that would help those living in a time of anarchy and worldliness to find salvation. The third great movement to come out of this was that of Nichiren, a combative and strident monk who railed against the political rulers of his time.

Educated within the dominant Tendai tradition, Nichiren was taught that the essence of Buddhism was contained in the *Lotus Sutra*. Untypically for a Buddhist, he attacked all the other sects of his time as heretical and petitioned to have them outlawed. Pure Land and Zen were particularly singled out. He pointed to natural disasters and the threat of invasion by Kublai Khan's Mongols as indications that Japan was under threat because of its failure to follow the true path of the *Lotus Sutra*. He was exiled twice for his pains and, on being rebuffed a third time, retired with his followers to Mount Minobu late in life. Nichiren's direct involvement with politics sets him apart from most other Buddhist teachers. He was an influential figure in later times with his heartfelt nationalism and his desire to be 'the pillar of Japan, the eyes of Japan, the great ship of Japan'. Several new movements and religions were to be inspired by Nichiren's unusual Buddhism which still thrives today.

Like the Pure Land Buddhists, **Honen** and **Shinran**, Nichiren reduced the essentials of his Buddhism to the bare minimum. To him, a single recitation of the sacred formula, *Namu Myohorengekyo* (Adoration to the Lotus of the True Law) was enough to guarantee salvation. Like his predecessors, he claimed it was not necessary to understand the *Lotus Sutra*: the mere utterance of the sacred words was enough. Even if someone paused while reciting the *nembutsu*, the heretical Pure Land formula, this would be enough to reach enlightenment. Nichiren was the only major figure of his time who taught that women could reach enlightenment (a point of considerable debate at the time) without first being reincarnated as men.

A written example of the Lotus Sutra.

NISHIDA KITARO
1870–1945

The two most important figures in modern Japanese philosophy are D.T. Suzuki and Nishida Kitaro. Both were influenced by Zen Buddhism but have a profound engagement with Western philosophy. Suzuki and Nishida were friends from high school and remained in close contact throughout their lives. The former was one of the representatives at the World Parliament of Religions in 1893 (see the chapter on **Vivekananda**) and was influential in the comparative study of Western and Eastern modes of thought. Nishida, on the other hand, created a genuine synthesis of the two that is neither forced nor artificial. He and others in the Kyoto School represent the most interesting Eastern response to modern Western challenges.

Nishida spent his whole life studying and teaching, leading a life as apparently bland as that of Kant, who greatly influenced him. He once characterized his life as being split in two halves: the first half was spent looking at a blackboard; the second half was spent teaching in front of a blackboard. 'With regard to a blackboard, I have made only one complete turn – with this, my biography is exhausted.'

Nishida's philosophy follows logic indefatigably but in the preface to a work from 1917 he admitted that 'after a long struggle with the Unknowable, my logic itself bade me surrender to the camp of mysticism.' Nishida practised Zen meditation in his early years and most of his work can be seen as an attempt to explore this experience. Ultimately, in Nishida's view, intellectualism will only take the thinker so far; logic, as Godel was to prove in 1925, shows the inadequacy of logic. Mysticism, or direct perception of the transcendent, has always been a part of Eastern thought, whether as meditation, yoga, *zazen*, Zen *koan* or *Bhakti* devotionalism.

One of the fundamental questions that is considered by Nishida is that of the relationship between subject and object. His solution to the polarities of mind-body, self-world, me-other is to posit an original ground of existence that goes beyond such distinctions. In his first work, *Zen No Kenkyo* (A Study of Good), he writes variously on this topic:

> *When one experiences directly one's conscious state there is as yet neither subject nor object, and knowledge and its object are completely united. This is the purest form of experience.*

> *Why is love the union of subject and object? To love something is to cast away the self and unite with that other.*

> *As emphasized in basic Buddhist thought, the self and the universe share the same foundation, or rather, they are the same thing.*

This is a traditional Eastern monism based on mystic experience. Language aside, these insights can be found not just in Buddhism but also in Advaita Vedanta, Sufism and Daoism. However, because of Nishida's awareness of Western philosophy, the concepts that underlie millennia of Eastern speculation and practice are allowed to play in a different context.

Nishida recognized that this scheme was problematic when applied to individual psychology. The appeal to mystical experience was unsatisfactory and Nishida worked with the ideas of the German philosopher Fichte next, an idealist and monist within the Western tradition. Nishida worked with Fichte's concept of self-consciousness as total free will but this, too, proved inadequate.

In the late twenties, Nishida proposed a new thesis: that of ultimate reality as *mu no basho*, the 'place of absolute nothingness'. 'Nothingness' here corresponds closely to **Nagarjuna's** concept of *shunyata* or emptiness. This 'nothingness' is not an absence of God or the self but an absence of quality, division or concept – of all of the things which we need in order to define the separate existence of the ego-self. Nishida also calls it the 'self without self'. By not being anything in particular, we are everything. Nishida eliminates the psychological terminology that had characterized his earlier work. By moving 'from the acting to the seeing self', we become an eternal, transcendental and undefinable witness.

> *As a Buddhist,*
> *the ultimate good for*
> *Nishida is the realization*
> *of the true self,*
> *the Buddha-nature.*

Again, the influence of the past is obvious, but Nishida's *basho* is a radically new concept. It seems to function as an antidote to Western philosophical preoccupation with the individual subjective self. By imagining the self as *basho* or 'place' rather than as a point, consciousness or presence, we move away from all ideas of individuality. Nishida sees in the extinguishing of the ego-self in the *basho* the birth of the 'self as *basho*'.

Another important influence on Nishida's philosophy of *basho* is Hegelian dialectic. The *basho* has the power to unify the contradictions which underlie all existence, to effect the 'continuity of the discontinuity'. In terms of Western logic, the *basho* violates the principles of contradiction (a thing cannot be both p and *not p*) and identity (a thing is itself and not something else). These selective violations prove extremely fertile for Nishida's later philosophy. Nishida claimed that the contradictions at the heart of everything were what caused the constant change and motion we observe in the universe. Only in the *mu no basho* are these dynamic oppositions reconciled.

Although Nishida led a quiet, academic life (and was castigated for this by Japanese nationalists before the Second World War), his philosophy demonstrates a strong ethical tendency. As a Buddhist, the ultimate good for Nishida is the realization of the true self, the Buddha-nature. As a Zen Buddhist, Nishida argues that this realization should take place in the active world. His concept of 'acting intuition' illustrates this – the physical world of actions is expressive of the inner creativity of the *basho*. Only by living fully as historical individuals will the power of the self as *basho* be made manifest. Nishida's thought is reminiscent here of the Zen of **Dogen,** who emphasized the need for full engagement in both the real world, which is also the social and ethical world, and meditation.

NOTES

1 This book uses BCE (Before the Common/Christian Era) and CE (Common/Christian Era) in preference to BC (Before Christ) and AD (*Anno Domini*, 'Year of Our Lord').

2 Brahmin is not grammatically correct, it should be Brahmana but is the usual Western spelling and helps to distinguish the priestly caste from Brahman, the Absolute, and Brahma, the Creator.

3 The *Chandogya* and *Mandukya* Upanishads are early and late examples of this argument.

4 Jaimini's view is not entirely upheld by the Vedas, which do depict others participating in sacrifices. Badari is also criticized for his willingness to let *shudras* participate, so the strict Mimamsaka teaching that developed from Jaimini was not inevitable. Later Mimamsakas also developed more reasonable doctrines.

5 According to some authorities, he is as early as fourth century BCE.

6 Translations of the *Gita* from Sargeant, Winthrop (trans.) *The Bhagavad Gita*, Albany: State University of New York, 1994.

7 Trans. by Jay L. Garfield.

8 For example, *Mundaka* Upanishad. I.i.4: 'there are two kinds of knowledge to be acquired – the higher and the lower'.

9 See also the Chinese philosophers Cheng-I and Cheng-Hao, in the chapter on Zhuxi.

10 The *Prajnaparamita*, on which Nagarjuna based his Madhyamika teachings.

11 The *Avatamsaka* (Garland) *Sutra* was greatly influential in Chinese Buddhism. See chapter on Fazang.

12 Idealism is used in the sense of a philosophy that believes in the primacy of the mind over matter, not in the more common sense of 'believing in ideals'.

13 See chapters on Badarayana, Gaudapada, Shankara, etc.

14 See chapters on al-Farabi and Avicenna.

15 See chapter on Fazang.

16 Quoted in Zaehner *Hindu & Muslim Mysticism*.

17 See the chapters on Rabi'ah, al-Hallaj, al-Ghazali and Rumi in the Islamic section.

18 *Mundaka* Upanishad, III i,6.

19 17:6

20 23:1

21 See chapters on Shankara *et al* elsewhere in this book.

22 The term 'fundamentalist' is not really appropriate as all Muslims regard themselves as fundamentalist. The Western sense of the word implies the extremist, unreflective and aggressive element in modern Islam.

23 Quoted in *Islam: A Short History* by Karen Armstrong, p. 9.

24 5:59

25 The kind of threat that hung over many Islamic philosophers, even if it did not always happen.

26 Ibrahim Madkour, *A History of Muslim Philosophy*, Sharif (ed.), p. 463.

27 For a discussion of this, see the chapter on Ramanuja.

28 MacDonald, *Development of Muslim Theology, Jurisprudence and Constitutional Theory*, pp. 200–201, quoted in Sharif (ed.), *A History of Muslim Philosophy*.

29 *Encyclopedia Britannica*

30 Quoted by Sharif, M.M. (ed.), *A History of Muslim Philosophy* (Wiesbaden: Harrassowitz, 1966), p 588.

31 The Islamic calendar has a different starting point dating from the *hijrah* or flight of the Prophet from Mecca. The dates do not correspond to solar years, being based on the lunar calendar instead. The Christian calendar is used throughout this book for simplicity.

32 See the chapter on al-Hallaj.

33 See al-Farabi and Avicenna.

34 Tahafut al-Tahafut, quoted in *A History of Muslim Philosophy*, Sharif (ed.), p. 559.

35 Quoted in Sharif, M.M. (ed.), *A History of Muslim Philosophy*, 2 vols (Wiesbaden: Harrassowitz), 1963–65.

36 All quotations are from the *Analects* (trans. D.C. Lau), Penguin, 1979.

37 Wing-Tsit Chan, *A Sourcebook in Chinese Philosophy*, Princeton, 1963, p. 218.

38 All translations of *Daode Jing* from Wing-Tsit Chan, *A Sourcebook in Chinese Philosophy*.

39 All *Zhuangzi* translations by Burton Watson unless otherwise indicated.

40 Translated by Harold Roth, '*Zhuangzi*', *The Stanford Encyclopedia of Philosophy*.

41 *Kena* Upanishad, I.5.

42 Translated by Lin Yutang.

43 A philosopher who apparently refused to sacrifice a hair of his head to benefit the state.

44 *Mencius* (trans. D.C. Lau), Penguin, 1970. IV.B.19.

45 Quotations unless otherwise stated are from Wing-Tsit Chan, *A Sourcebook in Chinese Philosophy*, Princeton, 1963, pp. 49–83.

46 *Mencius* (trans. by D.C. Lau), Penguin 1970. II.A.2.

47 All quotations from Xunzi are from Wing-Tsit Chan, *A Sourcebook in Chinese Philosophy*, Princeton, 1963, pp. 115–135.

48 Quotations from Wing-Tsit Chan, *A Sourcebook of Chinese Philosophy*, Princeton, 1963.

49 To make a chariot wheel.

50 Ibid., p 254.

51 Quoted in Cotterell, *China: A Concise Cultural History*, John Murray, 1988, p. 87.

52 Not to be confused with *li* meaning ritual or propriety, as discussed in the chapter on Confucius.

53 *On Contradiction*, from Mao Zedong *Selected Works of Mao Tse-Tung*, vol. I (Peking: Foreign Language Press 1967), pp. 311–346.

GLOSSARY

A

acharya
In Indian philosophy and religion, a teacher.

adrishta
In Indian Vaisheshika philosophy, 'unseen', a catch-all term for the power underlying phenomena that cannot be explained.

Advaita Vedanta
The non-dualistic interpretation of the Vedanta or Upanishads. Founded perhaps by Badarayana, developed by Gaudapada (who trained as a Mahayana Buddhist) and crystallized by Shankara in the eighth century CE, Advaita Vedanta became the most prominent of the Indian philosophies, a position still retained today. Its essential idea is that of the identity between the Brahman (universal spirit) and the Atman (self). It takes over Mahayanist logic, especially that of the Madhyamika thinkers, and applies it to the Upanishadic texts. Always highly intellectual, its later versions are however more populist and inclusive.

ahankara
In Indian philosophy, the 'self-sense' or egotism.

ahingsa
In Indian systems, especially Jainism, the principle of 'harmlessness'. Carried to extremes, it involves minimum harm to humans, animals, plants and the environment. Activities such as agriculture are seen as possessing an element of harm due to the killing of worms and other creatures when tilling the soil, and even breathing is regarded as harmful if small insects are inhaled. Some Jains wear a face mask to prevent this. An important principle of Gandhi's philosophy.

Ajivika
A now-defunct sect founded by Gosala, teacher of Vardhamana and founder of Jainism, at the same time as Buddhism. Gosala seems to have provoked ignominy and scorn by his outrageous behaviour in the belief that those who attacked him would accrue sin, while he gained spiritual merit. His thinking displays affinities with that of the Greek philosopher Diogenes.

Alvar Saints
A group of devotional mystic poets from the Hindu Vaishnavite sect who lived between the seventh and ninth century CE.

arhat
In Buddhism, especially within the Theravada tradition, a 'perfected one' who has overcome desire, hatred and ignorance.

Aryans
One theory suggests that the Aryans were a group of nomads from the Black Sea or a central Asian region who populated the northwest of India and Persia. They are thought to have spoken a language called Indo-European from which Sanskrit and Iranian are derived. *Arya* means 'noble'. The Aryan theory was used in the nineteenth and twentieth centuries to argue that the civilizations of India and Persia, and especially the advanced Vedic and Zoroastrian cultures, had not originated with non-white races. Although used as a pretext for racism, the theory has not been comprehensively discredited on this account.

astika
Sanskrit meaning 'orthodox'. The *astika* systems of philosophy are supposed to be those that hold the Veda to be revelatory, including Nyaya, Vaisheshika, Sankhya, Yoga, Mimamsa and Vedanta. However, this definition is not strictly true for them all. More important to their coherence is probably their acceptance of the traditional norms of Indian society, such as the caste system. Opposite of *nastika*.

atheism
In philosophy or religion, the belief that there is no God. In Indian philosophy, atheism can be restricted to non-belief in Ishvara, the Lord, a form of the Divine that is not necessarily fundamental. It is thus possible to be atheist but still believe in a divine spirit or consciousness.

Atman
In Indian philosophy, the self, sometimes signifying the spirit. The Buddha declared that there is no self, his 'an-Atman' doctrine.

atomism
The theory that matter is made up of fundamental particles known in Greek as atoms ('uncuttable'). Vaisheshika philosophy in India is also atomist.

Active Intellect
In the philosophy of al-Farabi and others, the idea, derived from Aristotle, that the world is presided over by a higher intellect. This is identified in Islamic thought with the Archangel Gabriel.

Angra Mainyu
Also known as Ahriman, the 'evil spirit' and opponent of Mazda Ahura, the 'wise Lord' of Zoroastrianism. At the end of the world, it said that a final conflict will result in the disappearance of Angra Mainyu. It is thought that the Judaic concept of Satan as the enemy of God developed from Zoroastrian influences, having previously been an agent of God sent to test mankind.

Asharism
Philosophy or theology based on the teachings of the tenth-century Muslim al-Ash'ari, who opposed the rationalism of the Mu'tazilah and instead argued that Allah was beyond the comprehension of human reason. Although seemingly anti-intellectual, the

Asharite system is highly innovative and thinkers such as Ibn Khaldun were adherents. A hugely influential system that was still active in the Ottoman Empire.

Avesta

The main scriptural writings of Zoroastrianism, of which the most important parts are the hymns or *gathas* attributed to Zoroaster. The Avestan language is a close relative of Sanskrit.

B

Bhagavad Gita

A philosophical poem in 18 chapters that forms the most important part of the Mahabharata epic. The *Bhagavad Gita* is a conversation between Arjuna, the leading warrior of the Pandava family, and Krishna, his charioteer, who turns out to be an incarnation of the Supreme Spirit and teaches Arjuna the numerous ways to liberation. Acclaimed as one of the greatest poems ever written, the *Bhagavad Gita* (Song of the Lord) is perhaps the most influential work in the Indian canon.

bhakti

In Indian philosophy, devotion to another, to God or the Supreme Spirit. *Bhakti Yoga* is 'the Way of Devotion', the means to liberation through devotion to a higher entity.

bodhisattva

A 'Buddha-to-be'. A *Bodhisattva* postpones his or her final enlightenment out of compassion for others. Concept in Mahayanist Buddhism.

Brahma

The least worshipped of the Hindu Trinity, of which the others are Vishnu and Shiva. Brahma is the Creator. Not to be confused with Brahman.

Brahman

The universal spirit of the Veda and the Upanishads, the Brahman signifies God or the Absolute Principle.

Brahmanism

Early religion or philosophy developed from the Vedic concept of Brahman, the universal spirit of all.

Brahmin

A member of the highest priestly caste who controlled the sacrificial rites in Vedic society and later.

Buddha, the

In Sanskrit, 'the Enlightened One'. Title applied to the historical Buddha, Siddhartha Gautama, living between 480 and 430 BCE.

buddhi

In Indian philosophy, the intellect.

Buddhism

Name for the religion and philosophies developed from the teachings attributed to the Buddha.

C

Chan Buddhism

Chan is derived from the Sanskrit *dhyana* (meditation) and gives its name to an original Chinese form of Buddhism that is centred on the search for enlightenment. There were two main schools, defined by their adherence to the 'gradual enlightenment' and the 'sudden enlightenment' (*satori*) methods. The gradual approach involved much study, meditation and reflection, while the sudden approach, which later became more popular, and which developed into Zen Buddhism in Japan, made use of a variety of methods including mind-defeating paradoxes and free meditation. The first historical advocate of *satori* Chan was Huineng (638–713 CE), although it may have evolved around 500 CE through Bodhidharma.

Chandala

One outside the Indian caste system. Sometimes used to indicate a person of mixed caste, as in the child of a Shudra (labourer) mother and Brahmin (priest) father; someone who has forfeited the right to belong to any caste. An outcast.

Charvaka

System of philosophy attributed to Charvaka, advocating materialism, the pursuit of self-interest and extreme scepticism. Also known as Lokayata, meaning '[the philosophy] of the people', because it was thought to correspond to the views of the unenlightened masses in society.

Confucianism

Philosophy founded by Confucius and developed after his death by his followers. It emphasizes civil society, propriety and leading by example, while avoiding metaphysics and the spiritual, although these matters became important in its later forms. The term Confucianism is not a Chinese one, as the universality of Confucian philosophy makes it almost synonymous with refined Chinese thought. Other important figures include Mencius and the Neo-Confucian Zhuxi, each of whom made modifications or refinements to Confucian thought, enabling it to remain central to Chinese culture until at least the twentieth century.

cosmological argument

The proof for the existence of God that argues that since things are in motion, each must have something that moves it. However, the series of movers cannot be infinite, meaning that there must be a prime mover, which is God.

cosmology
The study of the universe in its totality and of man's place within it.

D
Dao
The 'Way'. A key concept in Chinese philosophy, but above all in Daoism, in which *Dao* represents an order of things above and beyond nature, a meta-ethical reality to which we must conform ourselves. By contrast, the *Dao* is man-made in Confucian thought.

Daoism
Indigenous Chinese philosophy, the two most important founders being Laozi and Zhuangzi. Although all Chinese thought is concerned with the 'Way' or *Dao*, Daoism is distinguished by its particular emphasis on this meta-ethical concept of a higher natural order to which human beings and all things must conform. Daoism civilization and Confucian philosophy as two symptoms of its decline. Daoism has always been less overtly significant than Confucianism in Chinese culture but its influence has been felt in other ways. Chinese Buddhism from the first century CE onwards has always had a distinctive character due to the influence of Daoism leading to, for example, Chan or Zen Buddhism with its outward-directed mysticism. Neo-Confucian thought shows the influence of Daoism in its metaphysics.

darshana
In orthodox Indian thought, a 'view'. A school of philosophy, for example, is said to be a *darshana*.

De
In Chinese philosophy, the 'power' of the *Dao* or Way.

dependent origination
See *pratitya samutpada*.

dharma
Originally a word in Vedic Sanskrit signifying a 'prop' or 'support', it later comes to signify 'law', 'duty', 'reality'. In Buddhism, also the teaching of the Buddha.

dhyana
In Indian philosophy, 'meditation', especially on a *mantra*. In Chinese philosophy this becomes known as Chan, and in Japanese, as Zen, although often with very different meanings.

dialectic
In Greek philosophy, this signified discussion and debate about philosophical questions. Since Hegel, it normally refers to a specific process of development in which two opposed forces – thesis and antithesis – are finally resolved into a new synthesis. This was important to Marx and, in turn, Mao.

'drunken' Sufism
Islamic mystical strand in which the Sufi speaks directly from the revelations received in religious ecstasy or *fana'*. This has led to a conflict with the orthodox and at times to the religious persecution of the Sufis.

dualism
The philosophical belief that reality consists of two, often opposed, realities. See Sankhya philosophy in India and Mao's theory of 'contradiction' in China.

Dvaita Vedanta
In Indian philosophy, the dualistic interpretation of the Upanishads. Its best-known proponent was Madhva. Opposed to Advaita Vedanta.

E
emanationism
Theory founded in Islamic thought by al-Farabi based on Plotinus to explain how the immutable God may create without changing itself, and without positing another substance or entity that is not God. Instead, lower beings are emanated and then do the creating.

emptiness
see *shunyata*.

epistemology
In philosophy, the study of knowledge and how we can know anything. In Indian thought, see *pramanas*, certain sources of knowledge.

ether
The fifth element in Indian and Greek philosophy, known in Sanskrit as *akasha* or space. Said to be the element that corresponds to hearing and sound.

ethics
The branch of philosophy concerned with evaluation of human conduct.

F
fana'
In Sufism, a state of religious ecstasy.

falsafah
In Islam, 'philosophy', transliterated from the Greek.

fiqh
In Islam, the discipline of jurisprudence, law. One who studies the subject is a Faqih, and his pronouncements form part of the Shari`ah.

forming one body with all things
Important Neo-Confucian concept credited to Zhang Zai (1020–1077) which states that everything in the universe, including inanimate objects, is part of one body, and that it is thus possible and natural to feel compassion for all things.

G

gatha

The oldest and most sacred part of the Avesta, said to be composed by Zoroaster. The 17 chapters, or Ha's, of the *gathas* total about 6,000 words and are written in a language called Gathic or Old Avestan, which is close to Sanskrit. The *gathas* are addressed to Mazda Ahura, the deity of Zoroastrianism, as well as to an audience of the Prophet's followers, and there are hints at a coherent theology rather than a systematic exposition.

gentleman, the

See *zhunzi*.

Great Ultimate

The highest principle in Neo-Confucianism, especially that of Zhuxi. It represents a fundamental level of ideal moral reality that is above and beyond the perceptible.

Great Vehicle

See Mahayana Buddhism.

guru

In Indian philosophy or religion, a teacher.

H

Hadith

A story about the life of the Prophet Muhammad, his habits, his conversation and sometimes his physical appearance; a story about one of his companions.

haj

The pilgrimage to Mecca that every Muslim should ideally perform once in his or her life. One of the five pillars of Islam.

Heaven, Son of

A name in Chinese culture for the emperor of China. In Mohism, the Son of Heaven is the wisest person, chosen by others to be the arbiter of the Mandate of Heaven (the way things ought to be). For Mozi, this means that everyone has their material needs fulfilled.

Hinayana Buddhism

'Lesser Vehicle', a somewhat disparaging term, from the idea that the early form of Buddhism developed in India was capable of carrying only a few to enlightenment. Opposed to Mahayana 'Greater Vehicle' Buddhism, it is characterized by adherence to the Theravada, the original teaching of the Buddha and his followers. Formalized around 250 BCE into the *Tripitaka* (Three Baskets), it comprises doctrine, monastic disciple and philosophy. The philosophical *Pitaka* was a new addition considered to be ssential. South Asian and Southeast Asian Buddhism tends to be Theravadin.

Hindu

Originally a word signifying someone living beyond the Indus or Sind River, that is, in modern-day India, or perhaps northwest India. Also descriptive of followers of Indian philosophy or of the Hindu religion.

Huayen Buddhism

Chinese form of Buddhism based on the *Avatamsaka* (Garland) *Sutra*, a sixth-century text. Huayen means 'Flowery Garland' and has followers in Korea, where it is known as Kogen, and in Japan. A highly complex and intellectual form of Buddhism in which every part of the universe reflects every other part.

I

idealism

The philosophical belief that only the mind is real, and that physical objects possess reality only insofar as they exist in the perceptions of the mind. Berkeley is a famous Western idealist. Eastern idealists include Vasubandhu within the Buddhist tradition and Wang Yangming in the Chinese.

illusionism

See *vivarta*.

imam

An Islamic leader. Among the Shi'ites, the term refers specifically to divinely appointed rulers who followed Muhammad, beginning with Ali, his son-in-law. Generally the imam is the son of a previous imam.

inferior man, the

See *xiaoren*.

Ishvara

The Lord, or God, especially in more theistic forms of Indian thought and religion.

J

Jainism

Religion founded or revived by Mahavira, also known as Vardhamana, who was said to be a *jina* or 'conqueror'. Central to its practice is *ahingsa* 'harmlessness', applied not only to other human beings but also to animals and even plants. Its adherents undertake progressively more severe acts of austerity, combined with a lessening of harm to others and environmental impact, sometimes culminating in death by voluntary starvation.

jianai

In Mohism, the philosophy of Mozi, 'universal love', often opposed to Confucian 'graded' love which centres on appropriate relations between people. *Jianai* is a utilitarian concept, mainly manifested through ensuring that everyone has enough to eat, is free from disease, etc.

Jihad

From Arabic *Jahada*, 'to strive for a better way of life'. It does not signify a war to spread Islam but is more commonly a war to expand the territory of Islamic regimes. Often wrongly translated as 'Holy War', a Christian concept from the time of the Crusades. Conversion is not a strong aim in Islam, although in recent times, the concept has come to the fore in the hands of extremists. To the Sufis, the *Jihad* is a withdrawal from worldly life.

jina

In Jainism, a 'conqueror' or enlightened being.

jiva

In Indian philosophy, the individual spirit or soul or self (*jiva-Atman*).

jnana

In Indian philosophy, knowledge. *Jnana Yoga* is 'the Way of Knowledge', a means to liberation through right knowledge.

K
Ka'ba

From the Arabic word for 'cube', the roughly cube-shaped structure in Mecca that is the focal point of Muslim worship. According to the Quran, the Ka'ba was made by Abraham (Ibrahim) and his son, Ishmael. It includes as one of its cornerstones a black stone that may be the fragment of a meteorite.

kalam

Literally 'speech' or 'word', this term was originally used by Arabic scholars translating Greek philosophical works as an equivalent for *logos*. Accordingly it has a similar range of uses, including 'word [of God]', 'reason' and 'argument', and in the Islamic context comes to mean 'theology', specifically the discussion of the six articles of faith of Islam.

karika

In Sanskrit, 'verses'. Several important philosophical works, both in Buddhism and Hinduism, are in this form.

karma

Literally 'action'. In Buddhism, the law of *karma* illustrates how each action has a consequence: good actions will lead to good results for the perpetrator, whether in this life or in a later incarnations. In Hindu philosophy, *Karma Yoga* is 'the Way of Action', the means to liberation through doing one's duty with no attachment to the results.

kevala

In Jainism, 'isolation' or 'liberation', it signifies complete passivity and disengagement. The ultimate goal of Jain and Sankhya philosophy among others.

koan

Tradition, especially in Zen Buddhism, of mind-defeating paradoxes, intended to bring one to an understanding of the essential emptiness (*shunyata*) of all things.

Koran

See Quran.

Krishna

An incarnation of God or spirit, Krishna is the teacher of the *Bhagavad Gita*. Also said to be one of the periodic incarnations of Vishnu, the preserving principle in the Indian Trinity of gods, who takes physical form at difficult times for humanity.

L
Legalism

In Chinese philosophy, the name latterly given to a movement emphasizing absolute law and government. Based on assumptions about the innate evil of mankind, Legalism advocates perfect adherence to one's role. It is as bad, according to Legalist thought, to exceed one's brief as to fall short of it. The leading Legalist was Hanfeizi, advisor to the tyrannical Qin Emperor Shih-Huang-di who built the Great Wall and also burned all the books in China.

Lesser Vehicle

See Hinayana Buddhism.

li

Traditional ritual, propriety in Chinese culture. Includes one's relations and obligations to the family, ancestors and the state, as well as duties and religious observances. Important concept in Confucian thought, especially in the Neo-Confucianism of Zhuxi and others. Also in Mohism, *li* means doing good to others by supplying their material needs.

logic

The branch of philosophy concerned with defining correct and incorrect reasoning. Among the most developed logical systems in the East are those of the Hindu Nyaya philosophy and Mahayana Buddhism.

Lokayata

See Charvaka.

M
Madhyamika

The 'middle way' founded by Nagarjuna, based on the idea that the Buddha treads a middle path between total rejection and total affirmation. By doing so, he avoided the error of believing in the concepts of the mind. A key concept is *shunyata*, 'emptiness'.

Mahayana Buddhism

'Greater Vehicle', as opposed to Hinayana 'Lesser Vehicle', the Mahayana proposed to bring all beings to enlightenment. It was developed in the centuries either side of the beginning of the Christian Era and accepted as new teachings inspired by the Buddha. Mainly makes use of Sanskrit as opposed to the Pali of the Theravada. Extremely subtle and refined philosophies have developed within the Mahayanist tradition. Tibetan, Chinese, Korean and Japanese forms of Buddhism are mainly Mahayanist.

manas

In Indian philosophy, the 'mind'. Often specifically applied to the discursive 'mind' that translates sensory information to the higher functions of mind such as the *buddhi* or intellect.

mantra

A syllable, word or hymn, normally in Sanskrit, used to instill meditative concentration or to achieve some objective in ritual. Originated in the Vedic culture and adopted by Jain and Buddhist meditative traditions.

mappo

In Japanese Buddhist thought, *mappo* was the third and final age, the most degenerate of all, in which it would be almost impossible to practise Buddhism. Supposedly having begun in 1052, it stimulated the development of numerous 'easy' methods of Buddhism in Japan. It corresponds to the Hindu idea of the Kaliyuga.

materialism

The philosophical belief that all things and phenomena are composed of matter or are dependent on matter.

maya

Sankhya term for the illusion or play of *prakriti* (nature), which entertains and distracts the *purusha* or consciousness. Later adopted as a key concept in Advaita Vedanta.

Mazda Ahura

The 'wise Lord', god of the Zoroastrian religion and opponent of the evil Angra Mainyu. Also worshipped by the Assyrians in the pre-Christian era. As with Judaism and Islam, there is no image of Mazda Ahura.

meta-ethics

The branch of philosophy dealing with fundamental ethics, outside of any context, as opposed to the consideration of practical ethical dilemmas. See Daoism.

metaphysics

The branch of philosophy concerned with the search for ultimate reality, literally meaning 'that which is beyond physics'.

Mimamsa

A philosophy developed from Vedic religion based on activist principles. It teaches that the way to Heaven, or to any desirable objective, is through the performance of correct sacrificial ritual. Also known as Purva Mimamsa, 'the study of the earlier [part of the Veda]', it is the counterpart to Vedanta, or Uttara Mimamsa, the philosophy based on 'the study of the latter part of the Veda' (i.e. the Upanishads).

Mimamsa Vedanta

The twinned pair of philosophies, Mimamsa and Vedanta, each based on the study of different parts of the traditional literature of the Veda.

Mohism

The philosophy of Mozi, a thinker who rivalled Confucius in influence during the Warring States period (403–222 BCE). Its ethic of universal love is centred on the utilitarian provision of material goods and comforts to all.

moksha

Traditionally, 'liberation', the final step in spiritual progress in Indian philosophy.

monism

In philosophy or religion, the belief that reality is single. Often applied to Advaita Vedanta, although 'non-duality' is more strictly accurate.

Mu'tazilah

Arabic word for 'leave' or 'desert', the Mu'tazilah were a group of Islamic theologians who developed from the eighth century CE in Basra following a split from the mainstream. Their thinking was based on Aristotelian philosophy, and became influential from the ninth century, especially among the intellectual élite. Mu'tazilism had disappeared by the thirteenth century.

N

nafs

In Sufism, the ego or individual soul. Similar to the Atman in Indian philosophy and the *pneuma* in Greek. See also *qi* in Chinese philosophy.

nastika

Sanskrit for 'unorthodox', as opposed to *astika* or 'orthodox'. *Nastika* philosophies deny that the Vedas are revelatory. The principal *nastika* systems discussed in this book are Buddhism, Jainism and Charvaka.

Neoplatonism

Philosophy developed by Plotinus and others based on the metaphysical aspects of Plato's philosophy. This was very influential in the Arab world and subsequently in medieval Christianity.

Nirguna Brahman
The 'quality-less' Brahman, that stands above and beyond the universe, unmanifested. The opposite of Saguna Brahman, the Brahman 'in the universe'.

Nirvana
In Buddhism, literally 'blown out', as in a candle. *Nirvana* does not refer to extinction, but to the cessation of desire, hatred and delusion.

non-dualism
Similar to monism, the concept in Indian Vedanta philosophy that the Brahman or universal spirit is identical with the Atman or self.

Nyaya
In Indian philosophy, the tradition of logic, often twinned with Vaisheshika. One of the six *astika* or orthodox schools in India, Nyaya forms the logical basis for most of the philosophical systems, including many of the unorthodox.

Nyaya Vaisheshika
Twinned pair of philosophies Nyaya and Vaisheshika.

O
occasionalism
Philosophical system that denies causation, arguing that both the apparent cause and effect are themselves caused by a third force, normally God. In Western philosophy this was introduced by Malebranche and Geulincx, but it existed much earlier in the Islamic theology of al-Ash'ari.

P
Pali
The language of the Theravada or early teachings of Buddhism, derived from Sanskrit.

pinyin
Modern system of transliteration of Chinese into English, now largely preferred to the Wade-Giles system and used throughout this book.

Platonism
The philosophy of Plato, much of which purports to be the teaching of Socrates, who was Plato's teacher but who did not write anything down. Two important aspects of Platonic philosophy are its metaphysics, which argue that the material world is less real than the higher realms of Forms, Ideas and of the Good, and its ethics, which attempt to define various virtues, especially courage, justice, temperance and wisdom.

pluralism
The philosophical belief in a number of real things, for example, a multiplicity of eternal souls.

pratitya samutpada
'Dependent origination', the principle set out by the Buddha to show how the law of cause and effect does not necessarily suggest a first cause. All things have a reality that depends upon something else, which is itself dependent.

prakriti
In Indian philosophy, 'nature'. Thought to include not justs the physical but also most of the mental and emotional faculties. In Sankhya philosophy, *prakriti* with *purusha* equal two fundamental, absolute realities.

pramana
In Indian philosophy, the *pramanas* are a reliable means for acquiring knowledge, such as testimony, inference, analogy, inductive logic, deductive logic, sense perception, and so on. Different systems accept certain *pramanas* and reject others.

Puranas
Indian scriptures that form part of the *smriti* tradition, they deal with cosmology and the ancient history of the universe. Modern scholarship dates them between the fifth and eleven century CE.

Pure Land Buddhism
A form of Mahayanist Buddhism centred on the idea that it is possible to be reincarnated in a realm presided over by a Buddha, in which enlightenment is certain. It is important within Japanese Buddhism because it represents an 'easy' method that is appropriate to the degenerate age of *mappo*.

purusha
In Indian philosophy, the spirit or consciousness. Also a 'person' or 'self'. In Sankhya, opposed to *prakriti*.

Purva Mimamsa
See Mimamsa.

Q
qi
In Chinese philosophy, the concept derived from the ancient concept of *qi* (also known as *chi*), meaning 'energy' or 'life force'. In Neo-Confucianism, the manifest universe is seen as a meeting point between *qi* and *li* (Principle). Similar to concepts such as *prana* in India, *nafs* in Islam and *pneuma* or *spiritus* in Western philosophy, in that it associates breath with life force and with the spirit. Also the name of a Chinese state.

Quran
Holy book of Islam, literally 'the recitation'. Believed by Muslims to be the literal word of God, revealed to the Prophet Muhammad over 23 years through the Archangel Gabriel. It is regarded as being the culmination of the Judeo-Christian tradition rather than presenting a rival system. One of the very earliest texts in the Arabic language and script.

R

Ramadan

In Islam, the holy month, commemorating the month in which the Prophet Muhammad's revelations began.

rajas

One of the three *gunas* or fundamental qualities in Indian philosophy, especially in Sankhya. The active, creative principle.

Rectification of Names, the

A perennial concern of Confucian philosophy and also dealt with by most other thinkers. It is an attempt to correct any slippage that has taken place between a 'name' and its 'function'. Each part in life must correspond to its correct rank or title and authority should be exercised by the appropriate person and not by lesser figures.

ren

In Confucianism, the fundamental virtue, meaning loving-kindness, human-heartedness, humanity. Later Confucianist thought understood *ren* as universal love, encompassing the entire universe.

ru

Chinese word corresponding to the 'literati', the intellectual élite who were the Confucian philosophers.

S

Saguna Brahman

The universal spirit or Brahman 'with qualities' or 'with *gunas*'. The Saguna Brahman is the Brahman transformed into the universe. Opposed to the Nirguna or 'quality-less' Brahman that stands above and beyond the universe.

samadhi

In Indian philosophy, a state of elevated consciousness and unity with the Supreme. In Chinese philosophy, a state of inner calm.

Samhita

See Veda.

Samsara

The cycle of rebirth in Indian philosophy and religion, both Hindu and Buddhist. Generally opposed to an ideal of enlightenment: in Hinduism, *kevala*, *turiya* or *samadhi*; in Buddhism, *Nirvana*. Nevertheless, an important strand in Buddhism asserts that *samsara* and *Nirvana* are identical: even *Nirvana* must be seen to be empty, without essential being (*shunyata*), because it is just a concept and not the thing itself.

sangha

A term for the community of Buddhists.

Sankhya

A dualistic Indian philosophy that accepts two absolute realities: the spirit or consciousness (*purusha*) and nature (*prakriti*). Stimulated by the presence of *purusha*, *prakriti* develops into a further 24 categories or *tattvas*. The Sankhya philosophy is twinned with Yoga and was perhaps originally part of a single system: Sankhya being the intellectual method and Yoga the physical method. Sankhya is supposed to have been invented by the legendary Kapila, but classical Sankhya was formulated by Ishvarakrishna, who lived some time between the first and fourth century AD.

Sankhya Yoga

The twinned pair of philosophies, Sankhya and Yoga.

Sannyasin

In Indian tradition, a monk who lives as a solitary ascetic, surviving only by begging and teaching sacred knowledge. From about age 75 onwards, the final stage in the life of a Hindu.

Sanskrit

Literally, 'perfected' language, developed around the fifth century BCE in its classical form and formalized in the grammar by Panini and others. Also the language of the Veda, Upanishads and most of the philosophical and religious works of India, including much of the early Mahayanist Buddhist texts but not the Theravada of original Buddhism, which is mainly in Pali. Along with Iranian, Sanskrit is thought to be one of the earliest derivations from Indo-European, the source language for almost all languages from Western Europe to India.

sattva

One of the three *gunas* or fundamental qualities in Indian philosophy (Sankhya). The principle that conducts consciousness and corresponds to the spiritual.

satyagraha

Principle of 'holding fast to truth' in the teaching of Mohandas Gandhi. A key weapon in his political activism, it was originally known as 'passive resistance'. In practice, a declaration of opposition to an unjust law, breaking the law, and then suffering the consequences.

Scholasticism

Medieval European philosophy as practised in the universities by Christian thinkers such as St Thomas Aquinas. Often involved elaborate discussions about the interpretation of ancient authoritative texts.

shabda

In Sanskrit, 'sound'. In Indian philosophy, 'testimony'; one of the *pramanas*, the means for acquiring knowledge.

Shaivism
Hindu religious sect with some 220 million adherents, devoted to the worship of Shiva.

Shaktaism
In India, a sub-branch of Shaivism that involves worship of the Divine Mother as an intermediary for Shiva. Developed during the fourth to seventh century CE and associated with Vedanta and Sankhya philosophies.

Shankaracharya
A teacher (*acharya*) in the Advaita Vedanta tradition of Shankara. There are four *Shankaracharyas* to this day, based at seats in the north, south, east and west of India, supposedly founded by Shankara (*c*. eight century CE) and his original disciples.

Shankarism
The tradition of philosophy developed from the teachings of Shankara. Many of the works attributed to the original Shankara are thought to be composed by followers in his tradition, also known as Shankaracharyas.

Shari'ah
Islamic moral law derived from the Quran, the *Hadith* and the consensual opinion of the Muslim community. It is the counterpart of *fiqh*, specific laws that are derived from an 'understanding' of the Shari'ah.

Shi'ite
The second largest Islamic sect, though much smaller than the Sunni, began soon after the death of the Prophet Muhammad. While the Sunni accepted the power of the Caliphs, the Shi'a claimed that Ali, Muhammad's son-in-law, was his ordained successor.

Shiva
One of the three gods in the Hindu Trinity together with Vishnu and Brahma. Shiva is the Destroyer.

shruti
In Indian philosophy, revealed wisdom (literally, 'heard'). Distinct from *smriti*, 'remembered'. Can also suggest the verbatim utterances of the wise. An example would be the Upanishads.

shunyata
Literally 'emptiness'. An important concept in the Madhyamika Buddhism of Nagarjuna. It signifies a denial of the Hindu idea of *svabhava* or 'self-existence', the fundamental reality attributed by orthodox (*astika*) Indian philosophies to Brahman (the universal spirit), Atman (the self) or *prakriti* (nature). By contrast, the Madhyamika belief is that all things and concepts are *shunyata*, lacking fundamental reality.

Shunyavada
In Mahayanist Buddhism, the philosophy of emptiness (*shunyata*) developed from Nagarjuna and others.

sidq
In Islam, the virtue of sincerity or truthfulness.

smriti
In Indian philosophy, poetic or literary compositions thought to embody wisdom (literally 'remembered'). Distinct from *shruti*, 'heard'. An example would be the *Bhagavad Gita*.

'sober' Sufism
In Islamic mysticism, the tradition of reflection following religious ecstasy or *fana'* so that one's utterances conform with orthodoxy.

subjectivism
Belief in philosophy that we cannot know everything, or that we cannot know anything with any certainty.

Sufism
The esoteric, mystical branch of Islam. The word Sufi probably derives from the Tasawwuf, from *suf*, 'a wool cloak'. It is unclear whether the Sufis were originally an offshoot of Islam, or pre-existed and then joined with it. Most modern Sufi orders are part of Islam but there are some, popular in the West, that claim Sufism to be distinct. Sunni Muslims accept Tasawwuf as that aspect of Islam that deals with the heart, as opposed to Fiqh (law, the practical) and Aqidah (the intellectual).

Sunnah
The life of the Prophet Muhammad, similar to *Hadith*; a narration of his life or that of his companions.

Sunni
The most numerous sect of Islam, comprising eighty to ninety per cent of the Muslim population. The split with the next biggest sect, the Shi'a, came about over the question of the succession of power following the death of the Prophet. The Sunnis supported the Caliphs who ruled after him, while the Shi'as claimed that Ali, the Prophet's son-in-law, was the rightful leader.

superior man, the
See *zhunzi*.

sutra
In Hindu philosophy, a pithy aphorism. In Buddhism, a text spoken by or inspired by the Buddha. In Pali, *sutta*.

syadvada
'Maybe-ism', the name for the Jain philosophy that prefixes statements with a *syad* or 'maybe', expressive of the doubtful status of philosophical knowledge.

syllogism
A method of deductive reasoning in which a conclusion is deduced from two or more premises.

T
tamas
One of the three *gunas* or fundamental qualities in Indian philosophy, especially in Sankhya. *Tamas* holds the form of things.

Taoism
See Daoism.

Tasawwuf
See Sufi.

tattva
In Indian philosophy, a category of existence.

tawakkul
In Islam, the principle of total trust in God, even to the point of not providing for oneself, akin to Christ's injunction 'take no thought for the morrow'.

teleological argument
Also called the argument from design, the teleogical argument says that the order and purposefulness of the universe suggests a designer or maker, which is God.

theism
In philosophy or religion, belief that there is a God, especially a presiding deity watching over the world.

Theravada
'The teaching of the elders', that is, of the Buddha and his immediate followers, preserved in the Pali language. Theravada Buddhism was the form that developed in the centuries following the death of the Buddha, before the schism that led to the development of Mahayanist Buddhism. It was especially prominent in Sri Lanka and spread from there throughout South and Southeast Asia. Also known as Hinayana Buddhism.

Tian
In Chinese thought, 'Heaven' or 'Nature', corresponding to the way things are. In more religious contexts, the 'Way of *Tian*' or the 'Will of *Tian*' can suggest a deity.

tirthankara
In Jainism, 'ford-builder'. There are supposed to have been 24 Tirthankaras, of which Vardhamana, the founder and reviver of Jainism, is the most recent.

U
Ulama
Orthodox religious teachers and legal scholars who study the Shari'ah. Especially powerful among the Shi'a.

Uttara Mimamsa
See Vedanta.

V
Vaisheshika
In Indian philosophy, one of the six orthodox systems. Vaisheshika is usually twinned with Nyaya, and is the most scientific of the systems. It includes a theistic theory of atoms.

Vaishnavism
Hindu religious sect devoted to the worship of Vishnu, with some 580 million followers.

Vedanta
Literally, 'the latter part of the Veda' or 'the culmination of the Veda', Vedanta is the name given to the philosophy based upon the Upanishads. Along with Sankhya, Vedanta is the most advanced of the orthodox Indian systems. It was started by Badarayana, who wrote the *Vedanta Sutras* or *Brahma Sutras*, an exploration of the meaning of the Upanishads, especially the nature of the Brahman. Its most famous exponent was Shankara, who developed Advaita Vedanta, the non-dualistic Vedanta. Also known as Uttara Mimamsa.

Veda
Fundamental scriptures in the Hindu *shruti*. Veda means 'knowledge' or 'truth' and, as well as referring to specific documents (the Vedas), it can also mean pure intuitive knowledge that exists in an unmanifested state throughout the universe. There are four Vedas: the Rig Veda, Sama Veda, Yajur Veda and Atharva Veda, although the latter is considered much less important than the other three. The Vedas consist of hymns, poems, chants and instructions for sacrifice. The Rig Veda is thought to be the earliest section and dates as far back as the second millennium BCE. Each Veda is divided into four sections: *Samhita* (hymns), Brahmanas (ritual), Aranyakas (meditations) and Upanishads (philosophy). The different sections may have been composed at different times. The Upanishads, for example, are generally later than the *Samhita*, although the earliest Upanishads such as the *Brihadaranyaka* and *Chandogya* (sometimes called the Vedic Upanishads) were probably contemporary or even earlier than some of the *Samhita*. The Vedas were transmitted orally over a long period through an extraordinary system of cross-checked mnemonics, so that what we have today is an exact record of a 4,000-year-old culture.

Vijnanavada
In Mahayana Buddhism, the idealist philosophy of Consciousness-Only (*Vijnana*) based on the work of Vasubandhu and others.

Vishishta Advaita Vedanta

A refinement of the Advaita (non-dualist) Vedanta tradition of Shankara, Vishishta Advaita Vedanta is the school of 'qualified non-dualism' founded by Ramanuja. While Advaita claims that only the Brahman is real, though experienced in different ways, Vishishta Advaita argues for a qualified form of reality attributable to soul and matter. The soul is not real with respect to God or the Brahman but it has a dependent, though real, existence at its own level.

Vishnu

One of the three gods in the Hindu Trinity together with Shiva and Brahma, Vishnu is the Preserver. Incarnations of Vishnu include Krishna and Rama.

vivarta

'Illusionism'. Theory, especially in Advaita Vedantin philosophy, that the world as we perceive it is an illusion that obscures the reality, which is the identity (or non-duality) of the Brahman and the Atman.

W

Wade-Giles

Older system of transliteration of Chinese into English, now superseded by the newer pinyin method.

Wahabism

A 'fundamentalist' form of Islam, taking its name from its founder, Muhammad Ibn Abd al Wahhab (1703–1792), it is the form followed by Saudi Arabia. Puritanical and legalistic, Wahabism rejects aspects of Islam felt to be suspect, such as Sufism and Shi-ism. Its followers prefer the name al-Muwahhiddun, meaning 'the Monotheists'.

wuwei

The most important concept in Daoism other than *Dao* itself, *wuwei* means 'managing affairs without action', which does not mean inaction but going with the flow of *Dao*, achieving things through doing nothing that is contrary to nature. Also an important idea in Legalism, perhaps the polar opposite of Daoism, because in an extreme police state, all subjects act in accordance with law at all times. Because of the fear instilled in the populace, and the clarity and inflexibility of the instructions that are laid down, there should be no need to initiate action.

X

xiaoren

In Confucianism and Mohism, the 'inferior man', the common person. While in Confucian thought, the key figure is the *zhunzi* or 'superior man', the Mohists focused on helping the *xiaoren* through fulfilling the material needs of all.

xu

In Daoism, 'emptiness'. Unlike in Buddhism, 'emptiness' signifies not that things are essentially without real existence but a sense of the limitless and the potential of infinite space.

Y

yi

In Chinese philosophy, especially Confucian, morality or duty. Emphasized by Mencius as 'the path a man ought to follow' even unto death.

yin-yang

In Chinese thought, the ancient concept of two equal but opposing forces, *yin* and *yang*, that form the basis of reality. *Yang* corresponds to light, masculine, strong, extrovert and rational, while *yin* is dark, feminine, weak, introvert and intuitive. Laozi specifically identifies Daoism with *yin*.

Yoga

Founded by Patanjali, Yoga is the counterpart of Sankhya, a system of physical exercises based on Sankhya principles designed to bring about a separation or isolation (*kaivalya*) of the spirit (*purusha*) from nature (*prakriti*). The original Yoga may have been very different from its present form. The word Yoga is also used, notably in the *Bhagavad Gita*, to describe a 'way' towards liberation, as in *Jnana Yoga*, 'the Way of Knowledge' or *Dhyana Yoga*, 'the Way of Meditation'. Literally means 'yoked' or 'union'.

Yogachara

Mahayana Buddhist philosophy, especially that of Vasubandhu.

Z

Zen Buddhism

Japanese form of Chinese Chan Buddhism. Rinzai Zen, one of the best-known today, follows the 'sudden enlightenment' method, while Soto Zen is 'gradualist' in its approach. Rinzai Zen developed a tradition of practices that were connected to ordinary life, such as tea drinking, introduced from China by the Rinzai teacher Eisai, which has had an important influence on Japanese culture. Soto, on the other hand, emphasizes *zazen* (constant meditation).

zhunzi

In Confucianism, a 'gentleman', or 'superior man', a man capable of leading others because moral, serious, respectful, loyal, loving, benevolent and moderate. The exposition of the nature and duties of the *zhunzi* is perhaps the central concern of Confucian thought. What the *zhunzi* does, so others will do.

INDEX